Appliance Repair

Appliance Repair

Dennis Caprio

RESTON PUBLISHING COMPANY, INC.
 A Prentice-Hall Company
Reston, Virginia

Unless otherwise indicated,
all photographs were taken by the author

Library of Congress Cataloging in Publication Data
Caprio, Dennis.
  Appliance repair.
  Includes index.
  1. Household appliances, Electric—Maintenance and
repair—Amateurs' manuals. I. Title.
TK9901.C28 683'.83'028 79–13579
ISBN 0–8359–0244–7

© 1980 by Reston Publishing Company, Inc.
A Prentice-Hall Company
Reston, Virginia

3 5 7 9 10 8 6 4 2

PRINTED IN THE UNITED STATES OF AMERICA

Table of Contents

Preface

Everyone owns and uses appliances, from a simple electric toothbrush to a complicated refrigerator-freezer that makes ice automatically and provides a drink of cold water from a fountain in the door. In between are toasters, coffee makers, irons, dishwashers, dryers, air conditioners, and so on. If you inventoried the appliances that you depend on for comfort, food preparation, and housekeeping chores, you would probably find the list staggering.

Only when appliances break do we realize just how much we take them for granted. Depending on your patience, or lack of it, a broken appliance can either be a minor annoyance or a roaring frustration. A quick remedy is sometimes the only way to ease the pain of inconvenience, and in many cases the person most able to render the speedy treatment is yourself.

If you have ever found yourself muttering to the sick toaster "If only I had the right tools and a little knowledge, I could fix the damned toaster myself," perhaps you will appreciate the lessons contained in this book.

The reasons for repairing your own appliances may vary from a simple desire to save money, a wish to avoid the delay and/or hassles of dealing with a repairman, or the satisfaction received from having completed an intricate task.

Despite the knowledge gained from this book, you might from time to time leap into repair-land's deep water and find that a call to the pro is necessary. You needn't despair, however, because your newly discovered knowledge will allow you to deal more intelligently with the service representative. Instead of a look that says "You boob," you'll win respect and gratitude for making his or her life and job easier. Under no circumstances should you tinker with an appliance that is still under the manufacturer's warranty. Unauthorized tinkering will void the warranty, so learn to live with and respect your service representative.

You may never become an expert, and the information contained herein will not make one of you. But this book can, aided by a few simple tools, logical thinking, and a bit of patience guide you through many potentially costly repairs. It is not a substitute for workshop manuals, and it does not require an engineering degree. Dust off the old tool kit, puff up a little confidence, and tinker. You might even enjoy yourself.

DENNIS CAPRIO

Appliance Repair

Chapter 1

Safety

ELECTRICAL SAFETY

Repairing your household appliances can be entertaining as well as economical, but don't let your enthusiasm override caution. Losing a finger to a belt and pulley in your automatic washer or suffering a cardiac arrest from a shorted toaster are possibilities that you should not take lightly. Nor, on the other hand, should you fear electricity or the mechanical components of your appliances. Fear can present as great a safety hazard as an inflated ego and carelessness, because the tension and uncertainty it creates keep us from thinking clearly and working smoothly. Arm yourself with a large dose of careful thought, safe work habits, and a healthy respect for electrical and mechanical power. So equipped, you should be able to safely and easily make all of the repairs outlined in this book.

Electricity, because you cannot see it, poses the greatest threat to life and limb. The human body is a pretty good conductor, and its ability to withstand electric shock depends on its health and skin condition. Dry skin offers more resistance to the flow of electricity than wet skin or skin with an open cut. If you find that hard to believe, try this simple test. Take a multimeter—volt, ohm, milliampere—and turn the function dial to R×1000 or R×100. Plug in the leads. Take one lead between thumb and forefinger of your left hand and grasp the other lead in the same manner with your right hand. Read the meter. Now moisten the thumbs and forefingers and try again. The meter shows much less resistance. An appliance with a small electrical leak that gives you a mild tingle when your skin is dry might kill you when your skin is covered in perspiration.

In a 115-volt household power supply, which is able to carry 15 amperes, 0.0005 ampere to 0.002 ampere will give you a noticeable shock; 0.005 ampere to 0.025 ampere will give you a strong shock, often enough to cause you to lose control of your muscles and fail to escape. 0.05 ampere to 0.2 ampere can cause ventricular fibrilation, which is a heart muscle twitch that prevents normal rhythmic beating. From 200 milliamperes up, the shock interrupts the victim's breathing. The current needed to produce these reactions is less than one one hundredth of the current normally carried in household circuits. What follows are some do's and don'ts for safe operation and repair of your appliances.

- Make sure that all appliances requiring grounding are indeed grounded. Electricity, like water, takes the path offering the least resistance. When an ungrounded appliance develops a leak, the body or shell of the appliance generally offers the least-resistant path. When you touch the appliance, you share the grounding task and receive a shock. A proper ground would have left the body uncharged.
- The most common grounding system for 115-volt household circuits is the three-wire polarized receptacle and plug. It works very well when the receptacle is grounded. Later in the book, you will learn how to test the outlet for ground. Large 230-volt appliances are grounded directly to the neutral line of the main power supply through a third prong on the plug. Large 115-volt appliances can be grounded through a polarized three-wire plug, an 18-gauge ground wire from the frame to a cold-water pipe, or a combination of both.
- Locate and repair any defects that produce electric shocks.
- Never use or attempt to repair electrical equipment when your skin is wet or you are standing in water.
- Never use or attempt to repair an electrical appliance while it is touching another grounded object such as a cold-water pipe or another grounded appliance.
- Always turn appliances off before removing or replacing the plug.
- Before changing a light bulb, turn off the wall switch controlling the ceiling fixture and unplug the lamp cord.
- Never attempt to repair any piece of equipment without first disconnecting it from the power source.
- If you find it necessary to disassemble an appliance in order to make a diagnosis while it is running, disassemble it *before* reconnecting it to the power source.
- Be sure that your tools are in good condition. It doesn't make

much sense to solder a new connection with a soldering gun with a frayed cord, or to attempt to loosen a bolt with a wrench with worn out jaws.

- Use the correct tool for the job. You wouldn't use a straight-bladed screwdriver on a Phillips-head screw or pliers on a bolt head. Use insulated pliers and screwdrivers when working with electrical appliances. Grip them firmly, and be sure the handles are free from oil.
- When loosening a large nut or bolt that proves stubborn, position yourself in a way that allows you to pull the wrench toward your body with firm steady pressure. This method gives you more control, and if you slip you are less likely to jam your hand against a hard, immoveable part of the appliance.
- Make resistance tests (appliance unplugged) whenever possible. When a voltage test is the only way in which you can find the problem, make sure that the equipment is unplugged before you attach your VOM. It is also a good idea to use alligator-clip leads for voltage tests.
- When testing outlets for voltage, be sure to hold only the insulated part of the VOM (Volt-ohm-milliammeter) probes. A test light is even safer for this test.
- When using an appliance with a detachable power cord, always plug the cord into the appliance first and unplug it from the outlet first.

MECHANICAL SAFETY

- Keep hands and feet away from belts, pulleys, gears, fan blades, and other moving parts.
- Wear close-fitting clothing, remove neckties, tie back long hair, and roll up your sleeves when operating any appliance with exposed moving parts or when making running diagnosis.
- Avoid sharp edges, like a ragged weld bead on sheet metal parts. Avoid small holes and/or tight spots between moving parts and surrounding housings where your fingers can jam.
- Cover partially disassembled equipment if you have to leave it unattended for even a short time. Label it "Do Not Touch", and be sure you have disconnected the power source.
- Recheck your work before using the appliance.
- Lift with your legs and not your back. Be sure you are well balanced and have secure footing.
- Use safety goggles or glasses when you are using a grinder, drill, sander, or hammer and chisel.

- Keep your fingers away from moving tool parts.
- Keep your work area neat and clean. A cluttered work area breaks your concentration and increases the danger of tripping.
- Give the job at hand your undivided attention for your body's sake as well as that of the appliance.
- Never clean, adjust, lubricate, or otherwise tinker with any piece of equipment while it is running. Except for observation, the machine should be turned off and the power source disconnected.

If you follow these simple hints, proceed slowly and by logical steps, and above all *Think*, you can prevent accidents.

Chapter 2

Fundamentals

ELECTRICITY

Electron Theory: For many of you, electricity is that magical mystical force that provides light, heat, refrigeration, entertainment, hot food, clean clothes, big bills, and near helplessness when some calamity interrupts service. You know from reading Chapter One that electricity is invisible and can be dangerous. Well then, what is electricity?

Electron theory states that all electrical and electronic effects result from the movement of free electrons from one place to another, or because one body either lacks electrons (positive charge) or has too many electrons (negative charge).

In order to comprehend electricity, you have to understand matter in its simplest form, the *atom*. The atom is a submicroscopic particle composed of even smaller particles. The simplest atom, hydrogen, has a nucleus (proton and neutron) and one orbiting electron. The neutron is electrically neutral, and the proton is electrically positive. The negatively charged electron is bound to its orbit by the attracting force between itself and the proton. When left undisturbed, an atom contains equal numbers of positive and negative particles and is electrically neutral. Figure 2–1.

We know that electricity is the movement of electrons, but in order to understand what causes the movement, we have to examine an atom made up of many protons and electrons. Look at Figure 2–1 and imagine a large nucleus containing dozens of protons and neutrons, with electrons in orbit around it. All of those electrons cannot share the same orbit; therefore, they are arranged in many concentric orbits, at least when you picture an atom in two dimensions. The electrons

5

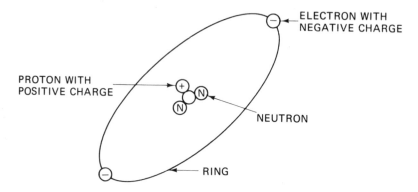

Figure 2-1 A typical atom. Simple atoms are very stable.

closest to the nucleus are held in orbit by a force greater than that pulling electrons in the outer orbits, and are called *bound* electrons. Electrons in the outer orbits are called *free* electrons and are generally more easily dislodged from their orbits.

You might remember from basic physics that molecules and atoms, even those that form solids, are in constant motion or agitation. During this random motion, free electrons are bumped out of orbit. An atom losing an electron becomes momentarily positive, a condition that attracts an electron from a neighboring atom. Atoms constantly exchange electrons in order to maintain an electrically neutral state. The electron exchange, however, is not electricity.

ELECTRICITY-INDUCING SOURCES

In order to produce electricity, a large number of electrons must be moved from one place to another, and some form of energy is necessary to get things moving. Friction, pressure, light, heat, magnetism, and chemical action are the six basic energy sources used to produce electricity.

Friction: Friction causes static electricity. Most of us have experienced this phenomenon at one time or another. It's winter; the furnace has been working overtime and the air is dry. You rise from your chair and walk across a room with a wool or nylon carpet. Your hard-soled shoes slip a little with each step. You reach for the refrigerator door handle, anticipating that apple you've been thinking about and ZAP! Your negatively charged body, having attained that state by collecting free electrons from the carpet, discharges itself through contact with the uncharged refrigerator. The result is a healthy shock, and if the kitchen had been dark you would have seen sparks.

Pressure: Quartz, tourmaline, and Rochelle salts, when subjected to pressure, generate modest electrical current. If you take a slice of quartz, place it between two metal plates, and apply pressure, multimeter leads attached to the plates will register a small amount of current. The amount of electricity produced depends on the amount of pressure applied. Pressure-induced electricity is used in crystal microphones, headphones, phonograph pick-ups, and sonar, all of which require only small amounts of current.

Heat: Take two wires, each one made from a different metal such as copper and aluminum and twist them together at one end. Set your multimeter function dial to the lowest milliampere scale and apply a flame to the twisted ends. You should see a small amount of current registered on the meter, the strength of which depends upon the difference in temperature between the heated and unheated ends. The union of twisted wires is called a *thermocouple* and is often used to operate a meter marked in degrees of temperature.

Light: If you own a camera with a built-in light meter, every time you take a picture you rely on electricity from light. The simple photo cell is a metallic sandwich of a translucent material, selenium alloy, and iron. Light shining through the translucent component strikes the selenium alloy and produces an electric charge between the alloy and the iron.

Chemical Action: When you light a flashlight, turn on your portable radio, or start your car, you are using electricity produced from chemical action. The dry cell that powers your flashlight, children's toys, and your portable radio is probably the most common chemical action power source. It is called a primary cell, and one needs two or more connected in series to make a battery, as shown in Figure 2–2.

The dry cell is constructed of a zinc case that also acts as the negative terminal. A tar-paper washer or disc is placed in the bottom of the case in order to insulate the positive plate from the negative container. Usually, a carbon rod inserted in the center of the container serves as the positive terminal or plate. Next, an ammonium chloride paste is packed around the carbon rod, filling the remaining space. The paste is called the *electrolyte*. The cell is sealed off at the top with a layer of sawdust, followed by a layer of sand and a layer of pitch.

Single Cell

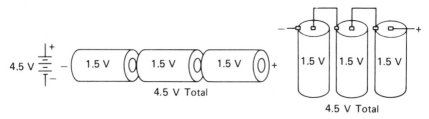

Three Cells Connected in Series

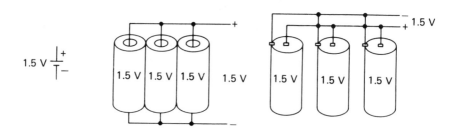

Three Cells Connected in Parallel

Figure 2-2 *Primary cells connected in series and in parallel. Current increases with the addition of each cell in a parallel circuit, but voltage remains the same.*

The electrolyte reacts chemically with the two plates. The chemical action takes electrons from one plate and forces them onto the other. The materials used to make the plates determine which one will lose electrons and become positive, and which one will receive electrons and become negative. As soon as the electrolyte is added to the cell, electron transfer begins. The process continues until the negative plate is full of electrons. The cell is now fully charged, and until something is attached to the cell to complete a circuit from negative to positive, electron transfer stops.

If you complete a circuit between the positive and negative plates simply by running a wire externally from one terminal to the other, electrons will flow from the negative to the positive terminal. You have completed a *direct current (dc) circuit.* As long as the circuit is complete, the electrolyte will continue shuttling electrons onto the negative plate. The chemical action eventually destroys the negative plate, at which time the cell is completely discharged. The cell is now dead and unable to produce electricity until we replace the negative plate with a new one. The destruction of the negative plate during discharge and its inability to accept recharging from a source other than plate replacement are the characteristics that distinguish this primary cell from the secondary cell.

Primary cells provide only small amounts of power for a relatively short time. Modern technology has added many hours to the primary cell's working life, but where one needs more power in short bursts over a long period of time, the secondary cell is used.

Secondary cells are commonly found in lead-acid storage batteries and in nickel-cadmium dry cells. You will find nickel-cadmium cells in rechargeable power tools, electric shavers, photographic equipment, and so on. Most of us are familiar with the rechargeable lead-acid storage batteries used to start our cars and trucks.

The lead-acid secondary cell is made up of a lead peroxide positive plate, a lead negative plate, and sulfuric acid electrolyte. The opposing plates are separated by a porous material such as wood. Two or more secondary cells connected permanently in series form a battery, with each cell rated at about 2 volts. The secondary cells depend on chemical action between their plates and the electrolyte to produce power in much the same manner as the primary cell. The materials used to make the secondary cell, however, allow it to accept a revitalizing charge from an outside source.

In order for a lead-acid storage battery of secondary cells to remain healthy for a long time, constant and gentle recharging is necessary. In your car, for example, the alternator supplies charging current through a rectifier that converts ac to dc. Just like the primary cell, the secondary cell can discharge completely, in which case both plates are converted chemically to lead sulphate.

Magnetism: The alternating current that lights our homes and powers our appliances is produced from magnetism. It is the only practical way to produce a continuous flow of sufficient voltage. One can generate electricity by moving wires through a magnet field, or by moving a magnet field through wires. In both cases, magnetic lines of force are broken and electrons set in motion.

Most generators are made from permanent magnets attached to the inside of a housing. An armature made from hundreds of wire wrappings rests in bearings in the center of the magnetic field. Power from an outside source such as a gasoline engine, flowing water, or steam turbine spins the armature, breaks the magnetic force lines, and generates electricity. The current's strength is usually regulated by the speed at which the armature rotates or the strength of the magnetic field. Adding or subtracting coils of wire in the armature will alter current strength as well, but it is impractical any time other than during manufacture.

We know how to produce current, but how, exactly, does it flow? We know from electron theory that free electrons move randomly from atom to atom. Normally, the movement is equal in all directions so that no part of the material has too many or too few electrons. Only when we create an electron movement from one place to another do we have electricity.

The particles with which we have been dealing radiate invisible force lines in all directions. If two protons (or two electrons) approach one another, they will repel because like lines of force or like charges do not attract. On the other hand, if a proton and an electron draw near, they attract. The strength of attraction between the nucleus' protons and the orbiting electrons determines the electrical characteristics of a material.

When the bond between electrons and protons is strong, it takes a powerful electric field to bump any electrons out of orbit. Glass, plastic, and wood are three materials whose atoms are tightly bound and thus are poor conductors and good insulators. Metals such as copper, aluminum, and silver have loosely bound atoms, and a small electrical force will bump electrons from orbit. These materials make poor insulators and excellent conductors.

You already know from our discussion of the primary dry cell that when you connect a wire across the terminals and complete a circuit, electrons flow. The negative charge of electrons cause them to repel one another, and when you attach a wire, they begin pushing free electrons in that conductor. Those electrons forced out of orbit encounter more free electrons in the next atom and push them out of orbit. In reality, all of the electrons begin moving at once and are eventually picked up by the positive charge of the cell's other terminal. As long as the wire is attached, the movement remains continuous. Electron theory maintains that for direct current, electrons travel from negative to positive.

ELECTRICAL TERMINOLOGY

You know that in order to have electricity, you have to have most of the electron movement in a given material going in one direction at a time. In order to start the electrons moving in that direction, you need an energy source that creates and maintains a difference in charge or a shortage of electrons in one place and an excess in another. Once the charge is created, it is changed to electrical energy, and the amount of electrical energy is exactly equal to that energy used to create it. The electrical energy used to set electrons moving in a given direction is called *electromotive force* or *emf*. It is this force that causes current flow.

Volt is the unit of measurement of emf. It measures electric pressure without regard to flow in the same way that a water-pressure gauge measures pressure in a pipe. One volt is the amount of electrical force that, when applied to a conductor with a resistance of one ohm, produces a current of one ampere.

Ohm is the unit measuring the resistance a conductor offers the flow of electrons. A conductor's resistance to electron flow is much like that a hollow pipe offers water flow. A short pipe of large diameter will carry more water than a long, small-diameter pipe. A short, large-diameter wire will carry more electrons than a long skinny one. It does not matter, for our purposes, whether water pipes are made of copper, iron, glass, or nylon. They will still carry the same amount of water for a given diameter and length. Wires, on the other hand, have to be made of a metal whose atoms possess a large number of free electrons.

Ampere is the unit of measurement of the actual flow of current through a conductor, much like the rate of flow in gallons per hour in a water system.

One *watt* is equal to 1/746 horsepower. Wattage is the amount of electric power required to do work.

Phase is the number of distinctly different voltage waves in a power source. Homes, offices, and most stores use single phase.

Alternating current is used throughout the United States for commercial power, because it is less expensive to generate and easier to transport over long distances. Unlike direct current, which simply flows from negative to positive, alternating current continuously peaks in one direction, reverses to zero, then peaks in the other direction. Picture a water system with a pump at twelve o'clock and a circular pipe line. First the pump drives the water clockwise, then very quickly reverses its pumping direction and sends the water counterclockwise. In electricity, the direction changes very rapidly and results in surges from the generator to the user and back to the generator at a rate of 60 cycles per second.

BASIC REPAIR CONCEPTS

Armed with a solid layman's knowledge of electricity, you are ready to begin thinking about basic diagnostic and repair concepts, tools you will need for the job, and tests that you can perform in order to determine what evil has befallen your machine.

Have you ever noticed while watching a professional service person work, just how easy he or she makes everything appear? Good, conscientious service men and women work with a kind of easy grace. They are able to diagnose quickly and accurately. Experience, of course, plays a large part in their ability, but they enjoy a sixth sense, if you will, that gives them an additional advantage. They have a sensitivity; a certain feel for the machinery.

You don't have to be a professional to acquire this sixth sense. A little careful thought, and a desire to do a good job and to understand the equipment should do the trick. The owner's manual that comes with each appliance is a good place to begin your search for the sixth sense. Some are more technical than others, but all of them will help you to understand how the appliance does its job.

Another extremely valuable publication is the manufacturer's parts manual. Many of these, aside from listing the part numbers, include line drawings that break the appliance down into components. Usually, the drawings are arranged in assembly sequence, and studying these will help you understand the working relationship among the components.

Once you have thoroughly read about the appliance, spend a little time watching it work. Listen to the clanks, whirs, thumps, and buzzes that accompany each cycle. When you have become accustomed to the sound of a healthy machine, you will find it much easier to recognize an unhealthy one.

When something does go wrong with one of your appliances, take a moment to think about all that you have read, seen, and heard, then proceed with simple preliminary checks.

1. Is the appliance plugged in? ... all the way? You would be surprised how often plugs get knocked loose during cleaning, and how often one leaps into a repair only to discover later that the plug wasn't making contact in the socket.
2. Is the fuse blown or the circuit breaker open? Large 230-volt appliances often have two 115-volt fuses. Check both.

3. Is your household suffering a community-wide voltage drop or brown-out? Such a voltage drop can keep motors from starting, or if the condition persists, damage motors that were running when it occurred.
4. Is your refrigerator broken or simply on the defrost cycle? Most refrigerators are set to defrost during the night. Perhaps a power failure has upset the timer.
5. That water leak from your dishwasher or clothes washer might be just a loose hose clamp.
6. Are all dials and/or buttons fully engaged and in the proper position? If they are, perhaps a switch has failed.
7. If the washer doesn't fill up, perhaps someone turned off the feed taps, or the city has interrupted service for repairs. Check other faucets.
8. Are the damp clothes in your dryer a result of a neglected lint filter?
9. Is your warm refrigerator suffering from dust-clogged vents or dust-covered condenser coils?

Use your eyes, ears, and mind . . . they are the best diagnostic tools available.

Before you attack a broken appliance it is wise to check the information panel attached to an inside panel, a door, or a base plate. You will find voltage, watt, and ampere information here. Keep manuals and other pertinent information about your appliances in a common place. It is a good idea to keep records of repairs made by yourself or a service person. Keep these stored along with the other information.

Disassembly Sense: Machinery of all types, including the simplest appliances, is assembled, part by part, in a particular order. When you have discovered that you must disassemble an appliance in order to find or repair a faulty component, you have to begin by removing the part that the maker installed last. Since we are not dealing with specific brands in these pages and can only suggest a variety of possible disassembly starting points, you will have to examine your broken appliance very carefully before attempting to take it apart.

In most cases, you will begin by removing covering panels, knobs, and other external paraphernalia. Often, you will find retaining screws hidden beneath logos, information panels, and other decorations. Sometimes screws will be deeply imbedded or countersunk in plastic or rubber feet. Once you have found all of the retaining screws, bolts, or tabs, remove the panels carefully. Many times internal components are attached to these exterior panels with clips that do not show on the outside.

As you disassemble an appliance, you may wish to make notes and drawings that will serve as references for reassembly. If your work area is safe from the curious hands of your children and other disturbing forces, you may simply wish to lay the parts out on the bench in order of disassembly. It is wise to number wires and terminals so that you will know which wire connects to which terminal.

It is also a good idea to make a preventive maintenance chart for each appliance and post it where it will remind you to oil a motor or adjust a belt. Remember that you don't have to be a professional to have a professional attitude toward your repair work.

TOOLS

Many of you have most of the tools that you need for basic appliance repair. They are common, relatively inexpensive, and easy to find. The following list is probably more complete than you think necessary, but I have included some of the items with an eye toward the future, when your experience and confidence lead you to more complex repairs.

1. Multimeter or VOM (See Figure 2–3.)
2. ¼-in. drive socket set with ratchet and breaker bar
3. 8-in. utility pliers
4. 10-in. arc joint pliers
5. Allen wrench set
6. ⅜-in. drive socket set with ratchet and breaker bar
7. Universal joint, 3-in. and 6-in. ratchet extensions
8. Slot screwdrivers from ⅛-in. pocket size to ⅜-in. blades
9. 5-in. ignition pliers
10. 4-in. and 6-in. needle-nose pliers
11. Nut driver set from 3⁄16 to ½ in.
12. Wire stripping and crimping tool
13. Combination wrench set from ¼ in. to ¾ in.
14. ⅜-in. electric drill and bit set from 3⁄16 to ⅜ in.
15. Soldering gun (See Figure 2–4.)
16. Pocket or utility knife
17. 6-in. diagonal cutters with insulated handles
18. Continuity test lamp

Tools are a lifetime investment, so choose them carefully and take good care of them. Keep them clean and dry and in good order.

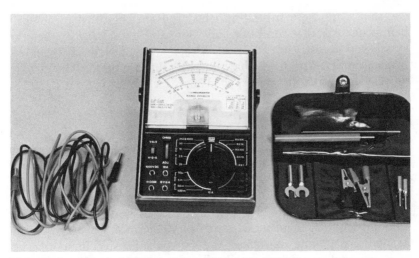

Figure 2-3 A typical VOM with test lead kit. VOM's range in price from about $20 to well over $100.

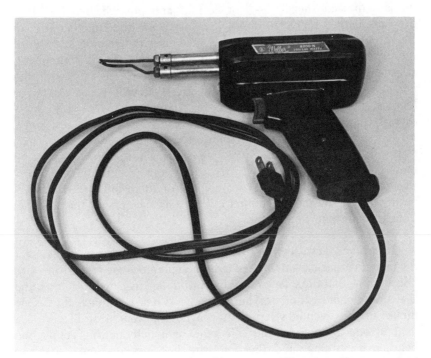

Figure 2-4 Trigger action electric soldering gun. The trigger lets you select low and high heat. A light just under the heating element helps you see in tight, poorly lit spots.

Few things are more frustrating when you are engrossed in a repair than to discover that you can't find your little screwdriver or that the wrench you need is covered in oil. Most tool manufacturers offer life-time warranties. You might have to pay a little more for these tools, but they are worth it. Besides, good tools feel better in your hand.

BASIC TESTS

Continuity Test: These tests are basic because they are common to most appliance and household wiring troubleshooting. The simple continuity test is probably the safest and most widely used. It's safe because you test for circuit continuity (making sure the circuit is not open) with the appliance or circuit disconnected from its power source. An uninterrupted circuit shows little or no resistance, whereas a broken circuit shows infinite resistance. We are not interested in specific fig-ures, expressed in ohms, but only the presence of a modest resistance normally associated with a complete circuit.

In order to test for continuity, plug the black VOM test lead into the jack marked "neg.," "—," or "com.," and plug the red lead into the jack marked for volts, ohms, and amps. Set the function dial to R×1, touch the probe ends together, and turn the zeroing knob until the meter shows 0 ohms. Touch your VOM leads to the component, as shown in Figure 2–5. Because we are concerned only with the presence of some resistance, the numerical value does not matter as long as it is small. Most continuity tests require the R×1 scale; how-ever, if your VOM indicates infinity or a large amount of resistance, try another scale before you pronounce the circuit open. In most cases, you will be dealing with circuits of unknown resistance. Although most home appliance circuits are made from low resistance wiring that requires a multiplication factor of 1 or 10 to indicate continuity on the meter, you may encounter a high resistance circuit that requires a higher multiplication factor.

Resistance Test: Testing for resistance is useful if you know what the manufacturer has established as an acceptable range for a given part. Let's assume that the solenoid coil has a working range of 3 to 5 ohms, and that the solenoid is not working properly. When you touch the VOM probes to the solenoid's terminals you note a reading of 10 ohms. A dent in one or more of the coil wires or a deteriorating connection between a terminal and the coil wire has increased the resistance beyond the manufacturer's recommended maximum. The solenoid should be replaced.

A resistance test can also establish if there is too much resistance

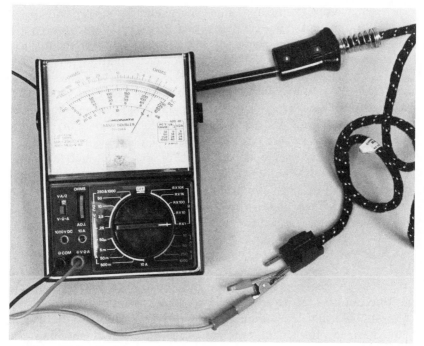

Figure 2-5 *Performing a continuity test on an appliance line cord.*

in a circuit for which you have no working figures, but for which experience has indicated 0 ohms as normal. If your continuity test shows a resistance of 50 ohms, you can assume that either the terminals are dirty or that the cord has a number of broken strands in its core.

Voltage Test: Voltage tests are rarely necessary, sometimes dangerous, and useless unless you have the manufacturer's voltage value for the part in question. However, you will occasionally find it necessary to test for the presence of voltage, regardless of the amount. It is a good idea to test an outlet for voltage by simply plugging a lamp into the socket that powered the malfunctioning appliance. This simple test will tell you if the outlet or the appliance is at fault.

When dealing with large, heavy-duty electric motors such as those found in large air conditioners, refrigerators, and clothes washers, you might wish to test an outlet for the correct voltage. Inadequate voltage at the outlet can cause permanent damage to large electric motors. If the motors are operated at more or less than 10 percent of the required voltage they will eventually fail.

Voltage drops from community-wide reductions in service may not be readily apparent. Your house lighting will usually appear as bright as always during power shortages, but the large electric motors will have a hard time starting. If the low-voltage condition persists, the motor windings will burn out.

If you want to test an outlet for correct voltage, turn your VOM to the lowest VAC range above the reading that you expect to get. Grasp the test leads by the plastic ends. *Never* under any circumstances should you touch any metal part of the test leads during a voltage test. Insert one probe into each of the outlet slots and take a reading. Because you are dealing with alternating current, it doesn't matter which lead goes into which hole. Your meter should register inside of the plus or minus 10 percent range of the appliance's voltage requirement.

A 7-Watt Test Lamp: The common 7-watt test lamp is a useful tool that you can make yourself. Take a pigtail socket and attach a test probe to each lead, as in Figure 2–6. It's a good idea to use probes to which you can easily attach alligator clips. (See Figure 2–7.) Screw a 7-watt bulb into the socket, and you're set. (Figure 2–8.) This test lamp is handy for testing switches, wall sockets, and anything else you might wish to test for voltage.

Let's assume that your waffle iron works only some of the time, and that the position of the cord has some bearing on the trouble. Test it with your test lamp. Find the cord terminals inside the appliance, and attach a test lead to each. When you plug the cord into the outlet, the lamp should light. (Figure 2–9.) Pick up the cord and move it around. If the lamp flickers, you have a wire that is about to break, a loose connection in the plug, or a broken wire that makes contact only in certain positions.

In order to test a switch, attach your test lamp lead to a power-cord terminal. Disconnect the lead from the load side of the switch. The load side is the terminal to which a heating element or motor lead is attached. Connect the other test lamp lead to the switch's load terminal. If you are working with a small appliance that draws between 35 and 40 watts (see owner's manual), put a 50-watt bulb in the test lamp. The bulb will draw as much current as the appliance and simulate its load. Plug the appliance in and turn the switch on and off several times and watch the lamp to see that it works every time.

You can test a wall outlet for voltage by inserting the test probes into the outlet. You can test for ground in a three-hole polarized outlet by substituting the 7-watt bulb with a 100-watt bulb. Insert one

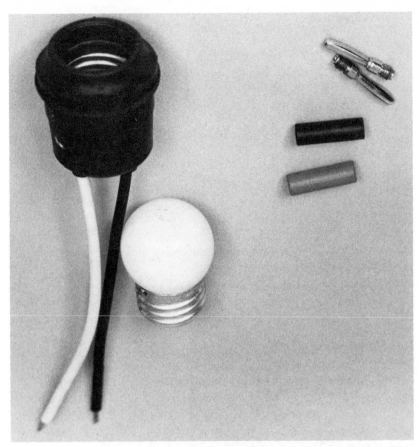

Figure 2-6 7-watt test lamp components.

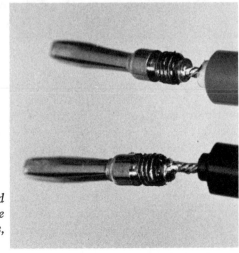

Figure 2-7 Solder the test lead tips, ones that allow you to use either alligator clips or probes, to the pigtail leads.

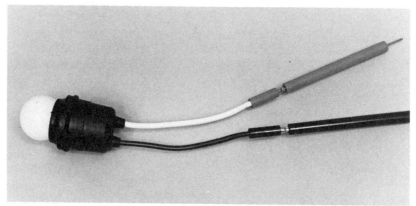

Figure 2-8   *The finished product with probes attached.*

Figure 2-9   *Using the 7-watt test lamp to test for voltage at a waffle iron line-cord terminals.*

probe into the ground side and the other into one hot side. If the lamp does not light, try the other hot side of the outlet. If it still does not light, the outlet is improperly grounded. A brightly glowing bulb indicates a healthy ground, and a dim glow means a deteriorating ground. Have an electrician inspect an ungrounded or poorly grounded circuit.

You may now consider yourself ready to tackle the nitty-gritty of appliance repair. Remember to think, work slowly and carefully, and to proceed in logical steps. You should be able to perform most appliance repairs.

Chapter 3

Wiring and Splicing

WIRING

Knowledge of proper wiring techniques is basic to all household electrical maintenance and repair. Wiring causes most of the problems arising in portable appliances such as irons, coffee makers, vacuum cleaners, and so on. And what about the extra outlet you need in the laundry room, or the lights you want to put up over the pool table? Have you asked an electrician recently what he or she charges per hour? Maybe you won't have to consult a professional because your working understanding of electricity plus the following wiring procedures will permit you to do the job yourself. However, before you attempt any household rewiring, check with state and local authorities regarding codes and ordinances and insurance requirements that regulate such installations and modifications. In many areas, only licensed electricians are permitted to install or modify household wiring.

Choosing Wire: Choosing the correct size and type of wire for the job is your first and probably most important step. Anything other than the correct material will ultimately lead to trouble. The factors that influence your selection are: application (Will you use it for house wiring, line cord, appliance internals?), the amount of current the wire has to carry, proximity to heat, exposure to weather, a rugged or an easy life. When you have to replace worn wiring, take a sample with you. If the wiring is old, the salesperson should be able to recommend an up-to-date replacement. If you are adding wiring to your home, be sure that it is compatible with existing wiring.

Stripping Common Wire: After you have selected the type and amount of wire needed you can begin your project. Before connecting a wire to any terminal, you have to strip away the insulation. The wire stripper-crimper tool shown in Figure 3–1 is a handy device. It should be large enough to accommodate 12- and 14-gauge wire.

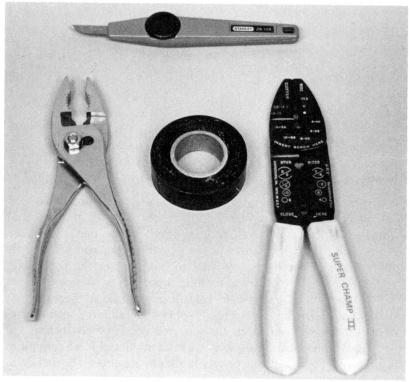

Figure 3-1   Tools that you will need for stripping and splicing wire.

Decide how much of the insulation you want to remove; find the appropriate size hole in the stripper jaws, then grasp the wire by the long end and clamp the tool around it, as in Figure 3–2. Rotate the stripper once around, making sure that you have cut through the insulation, then pull the wire out of the jaws.

Stripping Entrance Wire: Heavy-duty solid-core wire commonly found in 230-volt circuits or at service entrances requires several stripping steps in order to bare the core. Three separately insulated wires run through a thick plastic sheath. The wires share space with paper strands that provide additional insulation as well as protection against

Figure 3-2 *Stripping insulation from a length of wire*

damage from rough handling. This wire is extremely strong, weather-proof, and stiff.

In order to strip this wire, first take the end that you wish to bare and lay it against something solid such as the workbench surface. Holding a straight-bladed pocket knife or utility knife at about a 45° angle, slice through the plastic sheath by pulling the knife toward you. (See Figure 3–3.) Be sure that the blade is sharp, because a sharp blade requires less effort and reduces the risk of cutting yourself.

Peel back the plastic and paper strips and cut them off. Unless your stripping tool is large enough for this wire, don't use it. You might damage the core, which can cause early failure. You can, however, easily strip this type of wire with a knife. Carefully cut into the insulation at an angle and slice away from your body, as shown in Figure 3–4. With each slice remove a sliver of the plastic until you have exposed the core. Be careful not to slice a chunk out of the core. When you are stripping stranded-core wire, be careful not to cut through even a few strands of the copper core; that will weaken the wire enough to cause early failure.

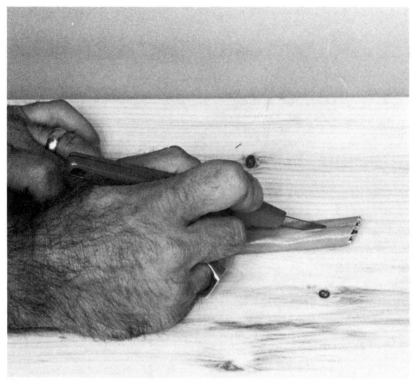

Figure 3-3 *The first step in stripping service entrance cable.*

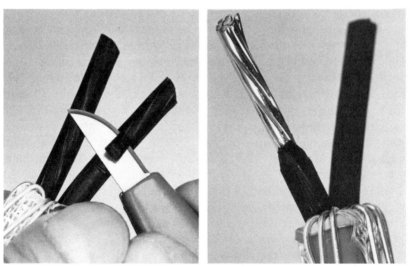

Figure 3-4 *Slicing the insulation from the aluminum core.*

Stripping Asbestos Heater Cord: Stripping asbestos heater cord is simple; however, if you are preparing it to accept an appliance plug you should be familiar with this safety tip. After you have sliced through the fabric of the outer covering, fold it back and cut it off. Then fold back the asbestos fibers to expose the wires. *Do Not*, however, cut these off. Just keep them out of your way until you have stripped the plastic insulation from the core. (Figure 3-5.)

Figure 3-5 *An asbestos heater cord prepared to accept terminal lugs for installation of a new plug.*

Attaching an Appliance Plug: To attach an appliance plug, place the coiled-wire cord protector over the cord. Remove the screws that hold the plug halves together and separate the halves. Now you are ready to finish preparing the cord for installation.

Slip an appropriate size terminal lug over each bare end. Make sure that you have inserted it far enough to make good contact. Pinch the terminal lug closed around the wire with your crimping tool, or solder it as Figure 3-6 shows. Wrap each wire with the asbestos insulation that you folded back and secure it with several turns of thread, as in Figure 3-7. Wrapping the individual wires in this manner provides additional insulation and protection from heat.

Female appliance plugs usually have strain relievers at the terminals. They prevent damage to the cord from repeated abuse, such as pulling the plug out of the appliance by the cord. To attach an appliance plug, remove the terminal screws and the top half of the strain reliever, then set the wires in place. Is everything clean? lugs, screws, and so on? A clean connection will carry its load at much lower temperatures than a dirty one.

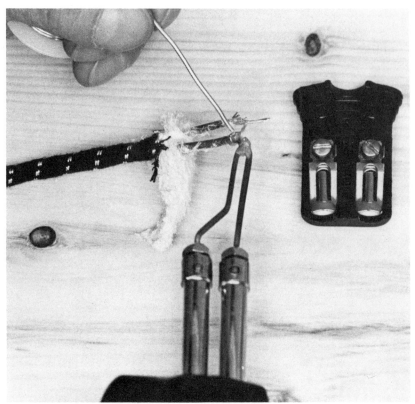

Figure 3-6 *Soldering the terminal onto the wire.*

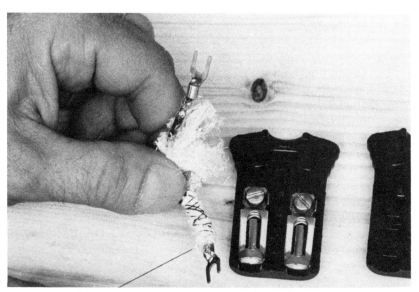

Figure 3-7 *Secure the asbestos insulation with several wrappings of thread.*

Be sure that the wires fit neatly into the bottom half of the strain reliever with no insulation bulges. (See Figure 3–8.) A sloppy installation will keep the plug halves from fitting together. Tighten the terminal screws and assemble the plug.

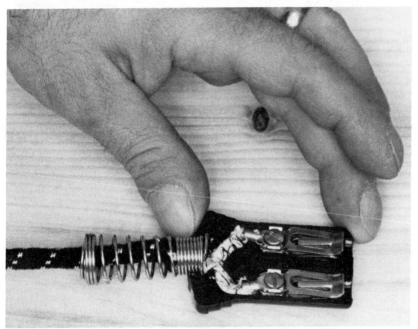

Figure 3-8 Make sure that everything fits neatly into one half of the plug

Soldering Techniques: Soldering techniques are essential to good wiring, so you will have to develop this useful skill. First, of course, you will need a soldering tool of some sort. I like the one shown in Figure 2–4. It feels comfortable in my hand and offers excellent control. The trigger allows me to cycle it on and off at will and to change the heat of the tip. It has a light at the base of the soldering head that is a great help in tight, poorly lit places, and it holds a variety of tips for soldering anything from the large and cumbersome to the delicate and difficult.

Before attempting to solder any joint, make sure that the metal is clean—free from oil and bits of insulation. Next, make a secure mechanical joint. If you are splicing two wires, be sure that you have twisted them into a solid, tight joint. Now, treat the metal with flux, a substance that helps make a permanent bond. Rosin flux is the only type that you should use for electrical connections. Common acid flux reacts with copper destroying its natural conductivity. Modern rosin-core solder has virtually eliminated the need for a separate flux treatment, but some experienced repair people insist that it is still a good idea.

The trick of good soldering is to get the wires as hot as possible and to do so quickly enough to keep from melting the insulation. The wires should be hot enough to melt the solder as soon as it touches them. (Figure 3–9 shows how to solder a spliced joint.) The solder will seep into the strands of both wires and give you a solid, permanent connection. When you are soldering a splice or a terminal connection that requires thick, heavy-gauge stranded wire, you might have to heat the joint with a propane torch.

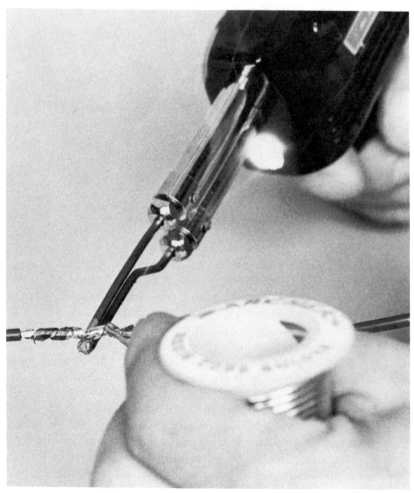

Figure 3-9 Soldering a spliced joint.

Attaching a Line-Cord Plug: Let's use our soldering skill to attach an ordinary line-cord plug. Slip the plug over the cord and pull about a foot of cord through, giving you plenty of working room. Make a slit in the groove that separates the two line sides and pull them apart until you have about 2 in. of separated cord. Tie an underwriter's knot. (Figure 3–10.) Strip about ½ in. of insulation from the wires and twist the strands together very tightly. Solder each bare end, as in Figure 3–11. Soldering makes a solid-core wire out of a stranded one.

Figure 3-10 The Underwriter's knot. It relieves strain on the cord terminals.

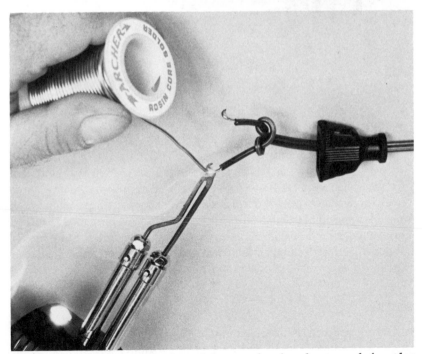

Figure 3-11 Soldering the looped bare ends of a lamp cord for plug installation.

With your needle-nose pliers, bend the end of each wire into a loop. When you attach the wires to the terminals, always place the open end of the loop facing clockwise. Tightening the terminal screws will tend to wrap the wire more tightly around the terminal and give you a more secure connection, as Figure 3–12 illustrates. If you place the loop's open end counterclockwise, tightening the terminal screw will force the wire away from the terminal.

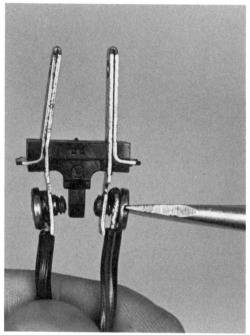

Figure 3-12 *Place the wire loop over the terminal with the open end facing the right or counterclockwise.*

Why solder the bare ends of a stranded wire? You will find that in tight spots, such as those found in plugs, simply tightening a terminal screw down on an unsoldered stranded wire forces strands out from the terminal where they can short out against one another. Unsoldered stranded wire connections sometimes suffer from broken strands during tightening, which weakens the connection. A solid core is easier to work with, stronger, and safer than loose strands.

SPLICING

Although splicing is not recommended in many applications, you should know how to do it and do it well. In some cases, splicing is the only quick repair, and is often perfectly satisfactory.

Pigtail Splice: Cross the stripped ends of the wire and twist them together as tightly as you can with your fingers, as in Figure 3–13. Finish the twist with a pliers, then cut off just a bit of the end to remove any sharp, ragged pieces. Figure 3–14 shows this technique. Solder the joint.

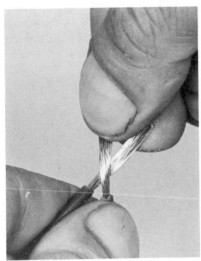
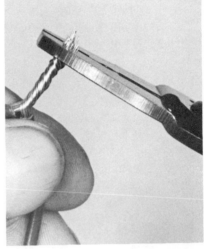

Figure 3-13   Start the pigtail splice by crossing the wires at a 45° angle.

Figure 3-14   Snip the ragged edges off.

Straight Splice: The straight splice requires a little more wire to work with, therefore, you should start with about 1½ in. of bare core. Cross the stripped portion of the ends at their centers, at an angle of less than 180° but greater than 90°, as in Figure 3–15. Wrap one free end around the intersecting wire, then the other. (Refer to Figure 3–16.)

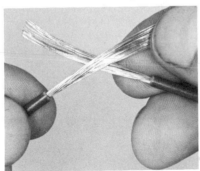
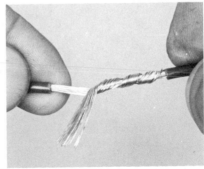

Figure 3-15   Crossing the wires for a straight splice.

Figure 3-16   Wrap the remaining end counterclockwise around the intersecting wire.

Tap Splice: To make a tap splice, make two cuts in the insulation of the wire you want to tap, 2 in. apart. You may use a knife or your stripping tool, as in Figure 3–17. Lay the wire against the bench and slice through the 2-in. section of insulation between the cuts. Remove that piece. Strip about 1 in. of insulation from the tapping wire and divide the stranded core into two equal parts. (See Figure 3–18.) Place it against the tapped wire with the insulation almost touching. Wrap the tapping wire toward you and around the tapped wire using as much of the available space as possible, as in Figure 3–19. Solder.

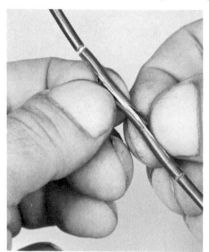

Figure 3-17 *Remove a 2-in. section of insulation from the tapped wire.*

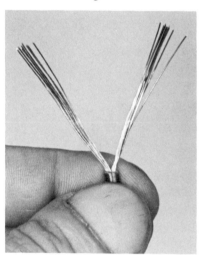

Figure 3-18 *Divide the core of the tapping wire into two equal sections.*

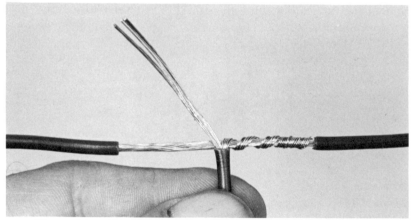

Figure 3-19 *Wrapping the tapping wire around the tapped wire.*

Wrapping Your Splice: Obviously, a spliced joint cannot be left bare. You must wrap it with insulating electrical tape. As with most other procedures, there's a trick to making a good insulating wrap.

Wrapping a pigtail splice: Start your tape about an inch above the splice and wrap once around to make sure that the tape is secure. Now, proceed at an angle toward the joint overlapping each wrap by half, as Figure 3–20 shows. Pull the tape with each wrap to stretch it. This makes the tape cling more tightly to the wire and provides a neat, well-insulated covering.

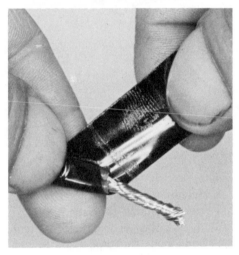

Figure 3-20 Be sure to overlap each wrap by half.

Once you have reached the end of the splice, continue wrapping for two more turns just as though you had more bare wire to cover. Pinch the tape together (Figure 3–21 shows you how), and fold it back along the splice. Now wrap the tape back toward the starting point. (Figure 3–22.) Continue in this manner until you have built up an insulating cover at least as thick as the original.

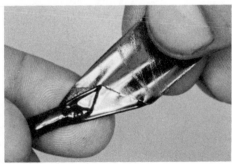

Figure 3-21 You will have close to an inch of extra tape to fold over.

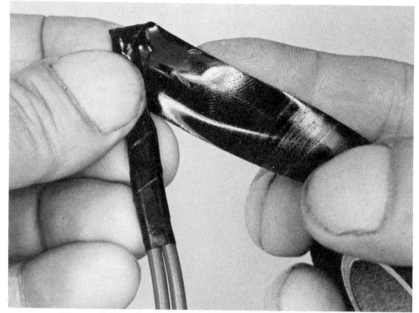

Figure 3-22 Wrapping back toward the starting point.

Wrapping a straight splice: A straight splice is wrapped by starting about an inch above the splice and wrapping the tape, pulling it
each time, around the splice, and overlapping by half, as in Figure
3–23. When you reach the other end, wrap the tape back to your
starting point. Once again, build up a good insulating cover.

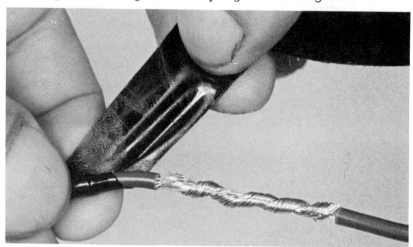

Figure 3-23 Wrapping a straight splice.

Wrapping a tap splice: This is the most difficult splice to wrap. Start at one end of the tapped wire and begin your wrapping as though you were doing a straight splice. Let's assume that you've started from the left and are wrapping clockwise. You have reached the tapping wire, and your next wrap will intersect that wire.

Bring the tape around on the right side of the tapping wire and go twice around, tight against the splice, as in Figure 3-24. The very next time you bring the tape around on the right of the tapping wire, angle the wrap through the 90° angle where the wires meet.

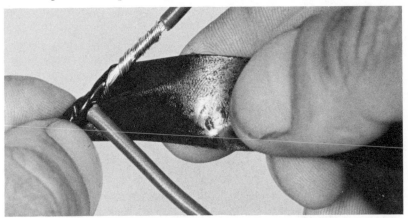

Figure 3-24 Wrapping the junction of a tap splice.

Continue over the tapped wire and around to the left side of the tapping wire and repeat the wrap through the 90° angle on that side. (Figure 3–25.) Wrap once more around the right side. Now, when you bring the tape up through the left side continue wrapping along the splice until you reach a point about an inch into the original insulation. Remember to stretch the tape as you go. Reverse your direction and return to the starting point.

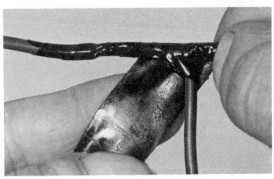

Figure 3-25 Wrapping through the left side of the tap splice joint.

Wire Nuts and Crimp Connectors: Wire nuts have a tapered, threaded bore. The two or more wires that you are splicing should fit comfortably into the widest part of that bore with very little room to spare. A good rule of thumb for selecting the correct size is to estimate the fit at the widest or open end of the bore. Wire nuts are graded by size, so when you buy them for a specific job keep in mind the wire size to be used and the number of wires to be spliced into a single joint. For example, a #18 wire nut will splice two #18 wires. But if you aren't sure, ask the salesperson at the electrical supply store for a recommendation. Wire nuts and crimp connectors make splicing easy. To make a wire-nut connection, hold the bare ends of two wires together so that they are parallel. You needn't twist them. Choose the correct size wire nut and simply screw it on. (See Figure 3–26.) Tug on the connection to make sure it is secure.

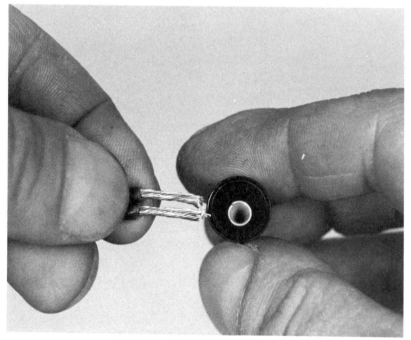

Figure 3-26 Wire nut connection.

To use a butt-type crimp connector, insert the bare ends of two wires, one on either side. Pinch it closed on each end with a crimping tool, as in Figure 3–27. Tug on it to check the connection. Crimp connectors are especially useful for splicing stranded wires that suffer a great deal of vibration.

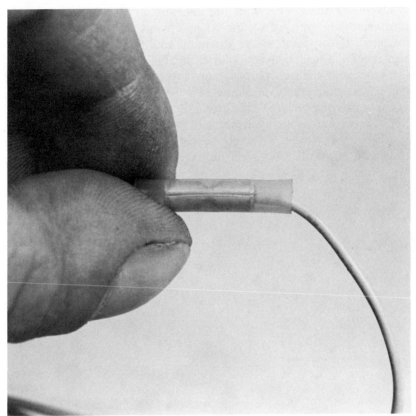

Figure 3-27 Butt-type crimp connector. Pinch the connector closed with a crimping tool at a point halfway between the dimple and the end of the metal connector.

Age and abuse are wire's worst enemies. Age breaks down the insulation, causing it to become brittle and cracked. Brittle insulation covering a wire that is forced to bend will chafe at the copper core strands and break them. Severe cracking causes electricity leaks. Except for emergency repairs, wires suffering from cracked and brittle insulation should be replaced.

Frayed insulation is most common on portable appliances such as irons and vacuum cleaners. Their use demands constant movement, and there is no way that you can avoid chaffing the insulation. If the offending section is close to the plug or the appliance, you can remove it and reattach the cord to the plug or appliance. If the fault occurs farther along the line, you should replace the cord with a new one.

Burned extension cords are not uncommon. All too frequently, zip cord extensions are used to carry more current than the manufacturer intended. If you must use an extension cord, select one that was designed for the load that you wish to impose on it.

Line cords used on portable appliances get bent, twisted, stepped on, pulled, and otherwise abused. Not only can the insulation give out, but the copper core can break. Because it will be hidden, you won't know until your appliance refuses to work.

Take care of your appliance wiring. Check the condition of the insulation frequently and avoid unnecessary abuse.

Chapter 4

Heating Elements and Thermostats

Wherever you find a heating element, you will probably find a thermostat. The thermostat functions as a temperature control and as a safety device, shutting the appliance off in case of overheating. Some hot plates and electric ranges use resistance elements to produce heat; the temperature is controlled by activating the high- and low-resistance loops of the element.

HEATING ELEMENTS

Heating elements come in a variety of sizes and shapes from heavy-duty, multiringed range surface elements to the tiny and delicate nichrome wire element found in hair styler/dryers. All of them use the natural resistance of the material from which they are made to convert electric current to useful heat. For safety and convenience, most of them control or protect themselves with a thermostat.

Most heating elements are made from a high-resistance alloy of nickel and chrome, known as nichrome. Engineers prefer quartz elements for some special applications. Most heating elements are either open ribbon, open coil, or enclosed coil. The length and diameter of the wire determine the resistance, and the resistance, along with current and voltage, determines the wattage.

Open-ribbon elements such as the ones found in toasters and hair dryers are made by wrapping a fine ribbon of nichrome wire around a sheet of mica insulation. This combination of materials and design allows engineers to pack high-output elements into small spaces. Many hair dryers contain 1200-watt heating elements in a space roughly 2 in.

in diameter and 3 in. in length. The secret? Many wrappings of very fine high-resistance wire.

Most of these elements cannot be repaired, and in some appliances, such as the average toaster, they cannot be replaced without replacing the entire chassis. Any element whose terminals are exposed, however, can be tested for continuity. Set your VOM to any one of four scales, beginning with R×1 and test across two terminals. Figure 4–1 illustrates the method. An infinity reading indicates an open (broken) element.

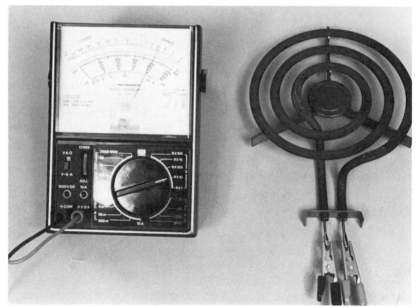

Figure 4-1 *Testing an electric range surface element for continuity.*

Open-coil elements are most often found in popcorn poppers, portable electric heaters, waffle irons, old-style hot plates, and electric clothes dryers. As the name implies, they are merely coils of nichrome anchored at each end to a terminal board and stretched over a series of ceramic supports. Oxidation and time are the open element's worst enemies.

Open-coil elements are suspended above the appliance's metal frame or chassis; as oxidation weakens the wire, it either sags or breaks from its own weight. In this case, you have a short to ground, and anyone attempting to use the appliance will receive a serious shock. It's a good idea to periodically inspect open-coil elements for sagging, especially in older appliances. A broken element that does not contact any metal surface will simply not heat.

Broken elements can be repaired, and sagging ones can be shored up. Since neither remedy is permanent nor particularly safe, you will have to learn those techniques elsewhere. Replacing an open coil, however, is only a little more difficult and very much safer.

Somewhere on the appliance in question you will find, either stamped into a panel or printed on a plate that is riveted to the body, voltage and wattage information. That information is essential for selecting the correct replacement element. You may buy a precut manufacturer's replacement part or a length of element from an electrical supply store. In either case, take the old element with you and ask the counter sales person to help you choose the correct element.

Installation: Taking things apart is almost always easier than putting them back together, and in some cases more fun. Remember, be patient and think. New heating element wire sold from bulk is very tightly coiled. Before you can install it, you have to stretch it to the correct length. First, remove the old element, twist it together at the break(s), and lay it out on the bench. As you remove the old element, take note of its path around the supports. It is a good idea to make a drawing.

Grip each end of the new coil with pliers and hold it against the bench parallel to the old element. Now, carefully stretch the new coil to a length about an inch or so shorter than the old coil. Leaving that inch allows for excessive stretch in the old element. Never attempt to stretch the new element a piece at a time, because it will come out uneven. The unevenly stretched element will develop sags and hot spots and fail early. Figure 4–2 shows how to stretch a new heating element.

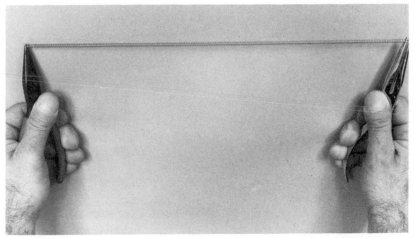

Figure 4-2 Stretching a new heating element to the correct length.

Make a little loop at each end of the new element and attach one end to the terminal board. Most appliances use small ceramic blocks to suspend and insulate the element. As you examine the blocks you will see that each one has a notch cut into the side. The element fits into these notches.

Starting with the block closest to the terminal to which you have attached the element, begin slipping the new coil into place. Use your drawing as a guide. (Refer to Figure 4-3.) In order to more easily attach the remaining free end to the terminal board, do not place the element over the last insulator block. Attach it to the terminal first, then gently stretch the element over the last insulator, as shown in Figure 4-4. Don't overstretch the element, because many appliances rely upon the coil's natural spring tension to hold the element and insulator blocks securely to the chassis.

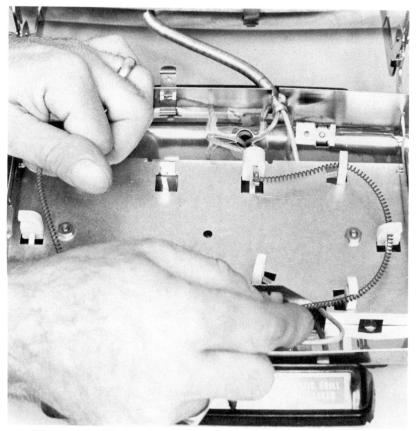

Figure 4-3 *Placing the new element over the insulating blocks.*

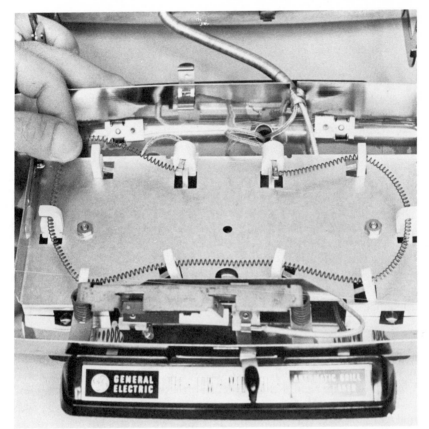

Figure 4-4 Attach your new element to the terminal before you place it over the last insulator.

Because heating elements are subjected to intense heat, their terminals suffer as well. They oxidize and corrode and make a high-resistance connection where a low-resistance one is desired. The heat generated at the terminal board eventually affects the connecting wiring. Loose terminal connections arc and corrode, resulting in a high-resistance connection. Whenever you have to replace a heating element, be sure to check the condition of the terminals and connecting wiring. Clean and polish the terminals and replace any heat discolored wiring.

An enclosed heating element is merely a nichrome coil covered by a metal sheath and insulated from the covering by manganese powder. You will find this type of element used as electric range surface elements, oven elements, modern hot plate burners, and dishwasher heating elements. In coffee makers, electric fry pans, steam irons, and food warmers, the heating element is enclosed in the casting that forms the appliance body.

Enclosed elements cannot be repaired, but you can test them for continuity. See Figure 4–1. Remember, when you have to replace an enclosed element, buy one of the same wattage as the original. Where the element is part of the appliance body, you will have to buy a new appliance.

THERMOSTATS

Bimetal Thermostat: Where would we be without the bimetal thermostat? One of the simplest and most dependable components in the modern appliance, it controls the temperature in stoves, toasters, electric fry pans, food warmers, steam irons, and so on. When combined with some other small components, it forms the basis for automatic and variable heat switches. Used alone with no adjustment provided, it serves as a safety device to prevent overheating in many small appliances.

Let's make a simple bimetal thermostat. Take two strips of metal with different expansion rates and weld them together. The molecular structure of metals allows them to expand when heated and to contract when cooled. Each metal has its own rate of expansion and contraction. The tighter the molecular structure, the slower its response to heat or cold. Aluminum expands more quickly than steel, so let's make our bimetal thermostat out of these two materials.

Drill a hole at one end of the bimetal strip. Bolt the strip to a mica block through which you have drilled a small hole. Insert the bolt from the underside of the mica, so that when you secure the bimetal strip with a nut you will have some threads left for a terminal.

Bond a silver contact point to the bimetal strip's free end. Bond another contact to a short copper strip and mount that to a mica insulator in the same manner used for the bimetal strip. Mount your thermostat parts to a base so that the contacts are directly opposite one another and touching, as in Figure 4–5. Connect the thermostat in series with a power source, and you have a basic bimetal thermostat.

As electric current flows through the bimetal thermostat, resistance to the flow produces heat. Both metals in the strip expand, but the aluminum one on the bottom expands faster and forces the upper half to curl up and away from the contact point. Eventually the strip curls enough to break contact, opening the circuit. As the strip cools it straightens and restores contact with the stationary point.

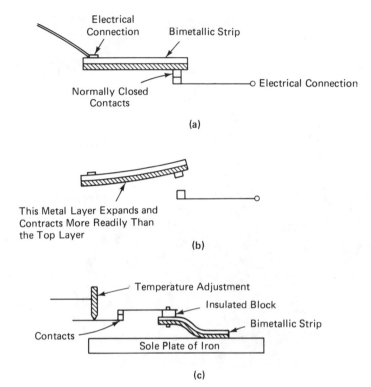

Figure 4-5 *A simple bimetal thermostat.*

Do you want to make it adjustable? Place an insulated-tip adjusting screw under the copper strip. (See Figure 4–6.) Screwing it in increases the tension on the points. Now it will require more heat and more curling to break the circuit.

Bimetal thermostats open and close slowly, and as a result are prone to arcing. Arcing corrodes the contacts, increases resistance through the points, and causes even more severe arcing. Eventually, the contacts will no longer allow current to flow. You can clean mildly pitted contacts with automotive contact point cleaner and Flex-Stone.

Generally, a good thermostat will show 0 ohms resistance, or at the most a few ohms. When a thermostat indicates high resistance or infinity, it should be replaced. Remember to isolate the thermostat from the circuit. If the thermostat has push-on terminals, simply pull one or both of the leads from the terminal. Some thermostats are connected to the circuit by open ended terminal lugs that are held to the thermostat's terminals with screws. Loosen one or both screws and

Figure 4-6 *An adjustable bimetal thermostat from a percolator. The bimetal is the blade with the white plastic tip. It bends up and the tip acts upon the upper switch contact blade to open the circuit. Turning the adjuster knob counterclockwise moves the switch contacts away from the bimetal.*

pull the lead free. Many modern small appliances use riveted thermostat terminal connections. The terminal lugs attached to the leads are similar to push-on and eye type lugs where they are attached to the wires. Usually, you will be able to find a good metal contact point on the terminal neck where the wire is crimped in place. Attach a jumper wire with an alligator clip on each end to each of the thermostat leads at the lug neck. This removes the thermostat from the appliance circuit. Touch your VOM leads to the thermostat terminal rivets.

High-heat Thermostat: Dual-heat appliances such as an electric percolator use a special high-heat thermostat to control the brewing cycle. It is made from a piece of semiconductor material (a ceramic magnet). When the thermostat is cold, the magnet attracts a small piece of iron to which the electrical contacts are attached. After the thermostat reaches a preset temperature, the semiconductor loses its magnetism, and the spring load on the iron piece breaks the circuit quickly and cleanly. The high-heat thermostat is sealed and cannot be repaired. Replace a defective one only with a manufacturer-made part.

Timing-Action Thermostat: Many pop-up toasters employ a timing-action thermostat to trigger the pop-up mechanism. It is a bimetal thermostat with no electricity flowing through it. Instead, it depends upon a small heating element that is wrapped around it and connected in series with the main heating element to cause the warping action. (See Figure 4–7.) The bimetal arm is connected to the pop-up linkage, and when the blade reaches a certain point it releases the bread rack. The temperature at which this occurs is preset at the factory and is not usually owner adjustable.

More sophisticated pop-up toasters and toaster ovens use an adjustable timing-action thermostat. It is adjustable through a knob or lever and allows the user to select lighter or darker toast. Instead of varying the distance between electrical contacts, it varies the distance or relationship between linkage parts.

When a timing-action thermostat fails, it is usually because the tiny heating element is open. Test it for continuity. Often, a bound releasing linkage will prevent the thermostat from functioning.

Capillary-Tube Thermostat: Capillary-tube thermostats are used to control temperatures in electric ovens, clothes dryers, large air conditioners, refrigerators, and freezers. These units are durable and extremely accurate. Figure 4–8 shows a capillary-tube thermostat from a refrigerator.

A long, small-diameter tube, the length of which depends upon the application, is connected to a spring-loaded, flexible metal bellows. A sensing bulb is formed at the other end of the tube, and the entire unit is filled with gas (usually Freon), and sealed at both ends. One electrical contact is fixed to the bellows, and the other is attached to the thermostat body. Some of these units work the contacts through a linkage. Figure 4–9 illustrates how a typical capillary-tube thermostat works.

When the gas is heated either from a refrigerator compartment's warming or from oven heat, the gas expands, putting pressure on the bellows. In refrigeration appliances, warming closes the circuit and starts the compressor. In heating appliances, the expanding bellows breaks the circuit, thus maintaining the desired heat.

Figure 4-7 A nichrome ribbon heating element is wrapped around the bimetal of this timing action thermostat. The terminals flank a phillips head screw near the center of the picture.

Expansion rate and thus temperature are adjustable through a knob that increases or decreases spring tension on the bellows. More tension requires more expansion to move the bellows. You cannot repair a broken capillary-tube thermostat, but you can test it for continuity at room temperature across its two terminals using the techniques described earlier.

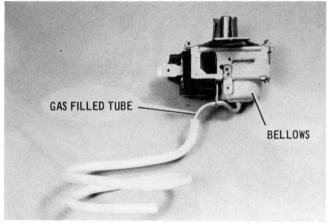

Figure 4-8 A capillary-tube thermostat from a refrigerator.

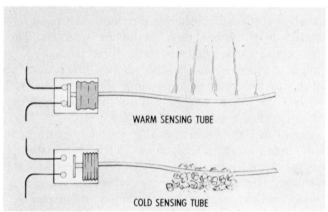

WARM SENSING TUBE

COLD SENSING TUBE

Figure 4-9 How a capillary tube thermostat works.

Chapter 5

Small Heating Appliances

Manufacturers produce small appliances as quickly and inexpensively as technology and reasonable quality control allow. Profit goals plus rising operating costs and continuing increases in demand have forced manufacturers to streamline their production methods. The innovations have proved to be good and bad. Some consumers, irate over broken appliances, curse the makers, whereas others rave about the excellent service they have enjoyed from those appliances. Mistakes are inevitable, but when weighed against the millions of appliances produced and sold, the record is outstanding.

In order to ease the frustration that mistakes create in the home and in the retail store, manufacturers offer immediate-replacement warranties on many of their small appliances. Others have established massive customer relation and service networks, that are a toll-free phone call away. Companies such as Presto have developed the *modular* appliance, the main components of which can be replaced at home by simply unplugging the malfunctioning part and plugging in a new one.

The reason for all of this effort? Manufacturers know that it is impossible for one service technician to disassemble, repair, and reassemble a small appliance for anything near the manufacturing cost. In many cases, repairs under warranty are just too expensive.

What then, you may ask yourself, am I doing with my nose in this book and why did this writer take the time to write it? We belong to the world's largest and most efficient throw-away society and, more often than not, the coffee maker that you tossed into the trash could have been restored to perfect working order with a ten-minute repair.

Not only is appliance repair fun, it frees the $25 or so that you would spend on a new coffee maker for something the family really needs or wants. Let's take a look at some of the common household appliances and see how easy it is to keep them working for you.

Despite the different tasks that each of the appliances discussed in this chapter was designed to perform, all of them share three common features—the conductor (plug, line cord, and connecting wiring), switch and/or bimetal thermostat, and the heating element. Generally, failure in any one or combination of these components produces the same symptom: the appliance will not work. Only when the switch or bimetal thermostat fails while closed (a less than common failure), do we discover a different symptom. In this case, the appliance will not shut off.

In the previous chapter, we learned how to diagnose and repair heating elements and thermostats. Before we investigate the individual appliances, let's look at line cord and on/off switch failures. Remember —*Never begin to test or repair any electrical appliance without first unplugging it.* You have no reason to make voltage tests on any of the equipment in this chapter. Simple continuity tests, appliance unplugged, will yield the needed diagnostic results.

The small appliance's portability is often its undoing. Think about the number of times you take an appliance out of the cupboard, plug it in, use it for awhile, wipe it off, and put it away. Now, think about the power cord. It gets twisted, bent, pulled, rolled, folded, and wrapped around the appliance so many times during its life span that it eventually just gives up.

First, a few strands in the copper conductor break and cause a higher resistance at that point. Then the remaining ones begin to grow tired of the extra heat and continued abuse and give up as well. Suddenly, one morning at breakfast when your first cup of coffee means so much, the percolator won't work.

Testing for continuity in cords that unplug from the appliance as well as the wall outlet is easy. Lay the line cord out on a counter. Touch your VOM probes to one prong of the outlet plug and to one side of the line at the appliance plug. Repeat the procedure for the other side of the line. You should read continuity on both sides.

If you want to test the cord because the appliance to which it had been attached worked intermittently, attach the VOM leads to the cord with alligator clips. Bend and twist the cord and watch the meter for signs of a broken circuit. If the failure occurs near either end, you can cut the offending section off and reattach the plug.

If your test revealed what appeared to be an open cord, disassemble the appliance plug and examine the terminals. Perhaps you have a broken connection in there. Refer to Chapter Three for plug details. We will deal with line cords whose terminals are located within appliances when we discuss the appropriate appliances.

POPCORN POPPER

The popcorn popper is perhaps the simplest heating appliance in your home. In its most basic form, the popper has a line cord and a heating element where resistance regulates the heat. Removing the liner pan will expose the heating element and its terminals. (See Figure 5–1.)

Figure 5-1   The simple corn popper. No switch, no thermostat. Simply plug it in and pop the corn. Note the sagging heating element.

Newer and more sophisticated popcorn poppers use an adjustable bimetal thermostat to cycle the popper on and off, maintaining a preset temperature. In order to expose the element, terminals, and thermostat on these models you have to remove a base secured to the popper body by three or four screws countersunk into the rubber or plastic feet.

Failure to heat or overheating are the only things that can go wrong with a popper. Failure to heat will be caused by an open line cord, open element, or open thermostat. Test each for continuity as shown in Figure 5–2. A short to ground usually results from a sagging element, a condition that you can see in Figure 5–1. Overheating in those popcorn poppers with thermostats is a result of thermostat contact points which have stuck together. A small electric arc occurs every time the points open or close. After years of use, these points can actually weld themselves together. Grease and other contaminants cause severe arcing and earlier failure. These simple bimetal thermostats are usually sealed against grease and dust but rough handling or a mistake in manufacture may have cracked the shell. These thermostats are not repairable and must be replaced when they malfunction.

Figure 5-2   *Testing the heating element for continuity.*

ELECTRIC FRY PAN, GRIDDLE, AND FOOD WARMER

Although these three appliances perform slightly different cooking functions, they operate on the same principle. All of them have their heating element cast into the base. All of them use a plug-in control thermostat. Only the food warmer operates at low temperatures where accuracy means little. Settings depend on the user's needs.

The long tubular probe on the end of the control unit contains the heat-sensing bimetal strip. A heat-resistant plastic button is attached to the end of the bimetal strip, and it acts upon a set of spring-loaded contacts within the switch. As the temperature of the appliance increases, the bimetal bends away from the switch blade and allows the contacts to snap open. Cooling straightens the bimetal and closes the contacts. If you are concerned about the accuracy of the thermostat, try this simple test.

Put about an inch of water in the fry pan and adjust the control knob until the pan maintains the water at a gentle but constant boil. At that point, the fry pan is very close to 212° F. If the knob points to 225° F or 180° F, make a note of the variation and adjust for it during cooking. Most of these controls are not adjustable for accuracy. You can test your griddle thermostat for accuracy by placing a shallow skillet containing an inch of water on the griddle's surface.

Let us assume that you want to test the thermostat of your fry pan because it cooks food more slowly than it should at the temperature selected. Perhaps you noticed the problem at breakfast. To get everyone seated and fed at the same time, you have the fry pan, percolator, and toaster on the same counter and plugged into the same outlet. If you live in an older house, the slow cooking probably results from a circuit overload. It's not enough to blow a fuse, but just enough to lower the voltage to each of the appliances on that line.

Any time that your fry pan, griddle, or food warmer refuses to heat, test its three components for continuity, beginning with the line cord. You will have to disassemble the control box in order to expose the line cord terminals and thermostat. Some control boxes secure the working components to the bottom half of the plastic box, in which case you will have to remove the knob first. Most, however, secure the controls to the upper half. (See Figure 5–3.)

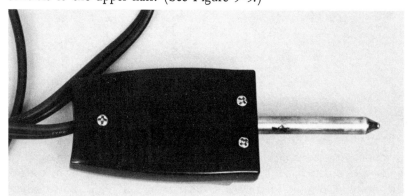

Figure 5-3 Remove three screws and lift the bottom half of the control box off.

Generally, you cannot disconnect the line cord from the terminals without wrecking the connectors. You can test one side of the line, as in Figure 5–4, without interference from the thermostat. In order to test the other side, you have to remove the thermostat from the circuit by attaching a jumper wire across the plug prongs. Examine the bimetal contacts and control-box-to-element terminals for corrosion.

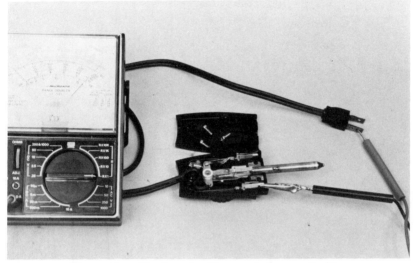

Figure 5-4   *Testing the line cord for continuity.*

To test the thermostat for continuity, attach a jumper wire across the line cord terminals and touch your VOM probes as indicated in Figure 5–5. Be sure that the control knob is on. If the fry pan suffers from overheating, heat the sensor probe with an open flame and watch the meter to see if the contacts open and break the circuit. An open circuit shows a resistance reading of infinity.

An open heating element will keep your fry pan, griddle, or food warmer from working. Test it for continuity, as shown in Figure 5–6. To test the element for ground, leave one test lead attached to the element terminal and touch the other lead to the appliance body. Make sure that the terminals and surrounding area are dry, because moisture will cause the meter to indicate ground where none exists. Test for ground at R×1 on your VOM.

Examine the element terminals for corrosion and discoloration caused by arcing. If they are rough and discolored, clean them with a piece of #600 sandpaper until shiny and spray with contact cleaner to remove any oily film. When you are ready to reassemble the control box, make sure all of the connections are clean and tight.

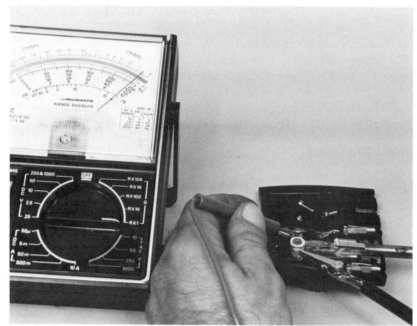

Figure 5-5 *Testing the thermostat for continuity.*

Figure 5-6 *Testing the heating element for continuity.*

56

SLOW COOKER

A fairly recent development, the slow cooker cooks at relatively low temperatures for long periods of time. The name "Crock Pot" was coined by Rival because of the ceramic inner pot that contains your meal until it's cooked. The pot doubles as a serving dish on units where it is removable. Slow cookers with removable liners locate the heating elements within the walls of the outer pot. Other models whose liners are not removable have fine nichrome elements plastered to the outside wall of the liner. (See Figure 5–7.) The location of the heating element working in concert with the liner provides even heat distribution.

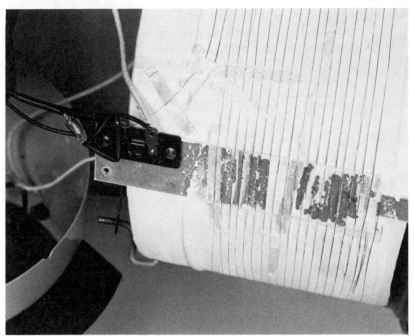

Figure 5-7 *The fine nichrome heating element plastered to the outside of a slow cooker's ceramic pot.*

Generally, a three-position switch controls the heat by selecting different combinations of heating elements in series or in parallel. "High" equals 115 volts applied to the entire unit in parallel. "Medium" equals only one energized element. "Low" equals 115 volts across both elements in series. The increase in resistance at the low setting lowers the wattage and produces less heat. Some models offer only a single temperature, and they may or may not include a thermostat to cycle the element on and off. The slow cooker unit in these illustrations has a line cord, switch, and heating element only.

An open line cord is the only failure that will keep a three-position switch slow cooker from heating at all. Let's examine the symptoms likely to surface and see which circuits are responsible. If the cooker will not heat on low but does heat on the other two settings, you know that both heating elements are good. The problem here must be in the switch. On low, both elements are energized by a single set of switch contacts. If the line cord shows continuity, the switch is open.

In order to service the switch, you will have to remove the base and probably the switch. Turn the cooker upside down and look for any screws that might secure the base to the pot, as shown in Figure 5–8. Remove the mounting screws and carefully pull the base away from the pot. Remove the knob. The switch may be held in place with a single large hex nut or a pair of screws on either side of the shaft.

Figure 5-8 *Remove 2 nuts from the mounting studs. Remove the large hex nut indicated by the screwdriver blade. Push the switch in and lift the base free of the body.*

Test the switch for continuity in the manner illustrated in Figure 5–9. Most switches are riveted together and not serviceable. If open, replace this kind of switch with a new one.

Figure 5-9 *Testing the switch for continuity across the common terminal, just behind the meter, and the element terminal.*

If the cooker refuses to heat on medium you will have to test the heating element as well as the switch. No heat in the single-temperature model means also testing the element. (See Figure 5–10.) If one element of the three-temperature model were open, the cooker would not perform to standard on the other settings because each of the other settings needs both elements.

Failure to heat on high will be caused by the switch. Inadequate heat on high can be caused by one open element.

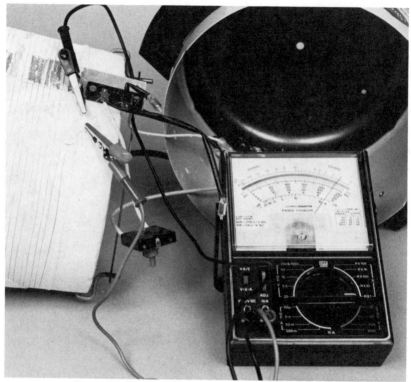

Figure 5-10   Testing the element for continuity.

DEEP FRYER

The deep fryer, a thermostat-controlled high-temperature appliance, works on the same principle as the electric fry pan. Many late-model fryers use immersible, sealed heating elements and plug-in control boxes just like the ones used in fry pans. For troubleshooting and repair, refer to the electric fry pan section.

Some late-model and most older deep fryers use a shielded, open-coil heating element. The element will be attached to the underside of the liner or mounted in the base. Liners in the second example lift out easily for cleaning.

Figure 5-11 shows a Hamilton Beach Fry All as it appears in the parts catalog. The liner (part 4) has the heating element attached to its underside. The thermostat (part 6) is attached to the liner and secured with a screw (part 13). To remove the liner, turn the fryer upside down and remove the screw (part 12) from the bottom cover (part 11). At this point, you will be able to see the two plug-pin terminals. One wire connects the heating element to the circuit, and the

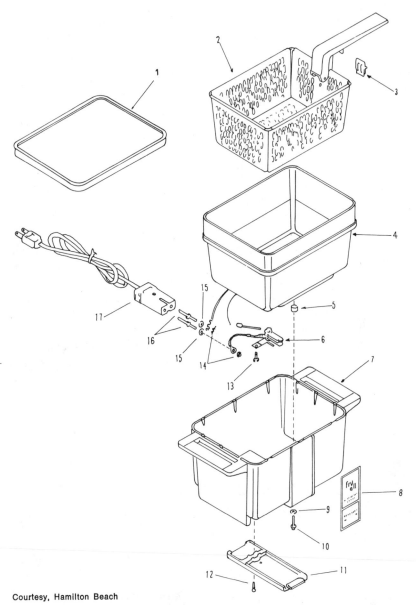

Courtesy, Hamilton Beach

Figure 5-11   A *typical deep fryer as it appears in a parts catalog.*

other wire connects the thermostat to the circuit. Disconnect the two wires.

The liner is held in place by two screws (part 10). Removing these will allow you to lift the liner out of the appliance body. You can test the heating element for continuity across its plug-pin terminal and its thermostat terminal.

HOT PLATE

Years ago, hot plates used open-coil heating elements set into a fire-brick-like base and a simple on/off switch to control the element. They were extremely dependable, and many of them are still in use. Later model hot plates enclosed the same element in a metal case. More deluxe late-model hot plates use single- and double-loop enclosed elements and infinite heat switches for control, or two-coil, multiloop elements controlled by three or five heat switch positions. You will find a detailed discussion of the switches in Chapter Seven.

When a single-coil, single- or double-loop element hot plate refuses to heat, it is suffering from an open element, an open switch, or an open line cord. The elements unplug and lift out in the same manner as those on your electric range. Even the open-coil, firebrick elements unplug from some hot plate models. Remove the element and test according to instructions given in Chapter Four.

To test the line cord and switches in most hot plates you will have to remove either the top panel or the single sheet metal panel that forms the back and bottom of the hot plate unit. Top panels usually fit over the edges of the hot plate body and are secured with a number of sheet-metal screws placed around the perimeter. Another method is illustrated in Figure 5–12.

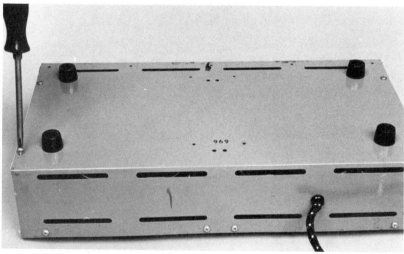

Figure 5-12 *Remove all of the Phillips head screws shown and lift the bottom and/or back from the chassis.*

In case of a "no heat" failure, begin by testing the line cord. In Figure 5-13 wire nuts form the line-cord terminals. Some hot plates may use a terminal board. Isolate the cord from the circuit before you test it. If the cord shows continuity, you might wish to test the connecting wiring before you go on to the switch.

Figure *5-13 Disconnect the two wire nut joints and test the line cord for continuity.*

If yours is a single-burner hot plate and the cord is good, wiring to the switch or the switch itself may be open. On a two-burner hot plate only an open line cord will keep the entire unit from working. It is unlikely that both switches and both heating elements would fail at the same time. Remove the switch by pulling the knob off and then removing its mounting screws. On/off toggle switches can be detached from the chassis by simply removing the mounting screws. Disconnect all of the wiring from the switch terminals and test for continuity. (See Figure 5-14.)

If you find any wiring from the line-cord-to-switch or switch-to-element open, replace the entire length. Splicing wires in high heat, high wattage appliances is not recommended.

Hot plates with infinite heat switches will sometimes overheat. This is caused by contacts in the switch arc welding themselves together. Arcing is usually accompanied by a crackling sound as the points contact one another. In this case, replace the control.

If at any time you receive a shock from your hot plate, disassemble it and check all of the circuitry for shorts to ground. As you reassemble the unit make sure that all connections are tight, clean, and free of interference from other wiring.

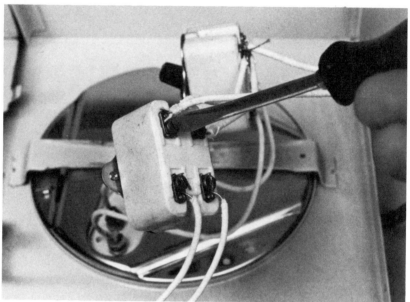

Figure 5-14   Disconnect the leads from four terminals and test across each pair in turn.

WAFFLE IRON

Waffle irons produce baking heat from an open-coil element in the base connected in parallel with a duplicate element in the lid. An adjustable bimetal thermostat controls the heat. Most waffle iron grids are removable for cleaning and reversible for grilling sandwiches. The grids are secured to the chassis with clips or screws. Removing both grids exposes most of the circuitry.

Refusal to heat is a symptom caused by an open line cord or an open thermostat. Many models use a removable cord; others attach the cord to terminals hidden behind a plastic cover between the rear feet. Figure 5–15 shows how to test the cord for continuity.

You will find the thermostat at the front in the bottom half of a waffle iron just under the baking grid. It will be a simple unadjustable one that merely cycles the elements on and off to maintain a preset 400° F temperature. Those thermostats adjustable for lighter and darker have an adjustment range of about 50° F. In case of no heat, test the thermostat for continuity, as in Figure 5–16.

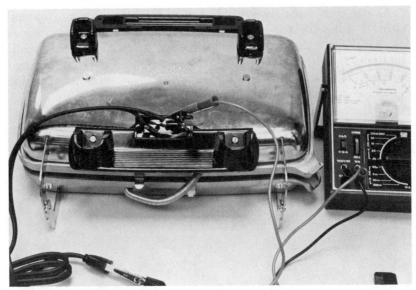

Figure 5-15 *Testing the line cord for continuity.*

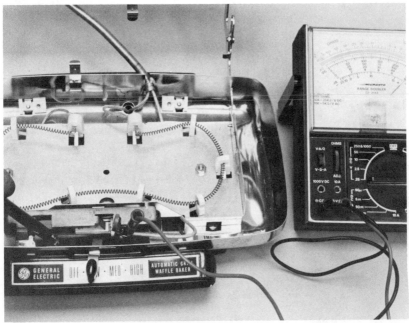

Figure 5-16 *Testing the thermostat for continuity. The terminals are hidden behind the appliance body.*

When your waffle iron hands you a half-baked waffle (top un-cooked), either the top heating element or the connecting wiring is open. Wiring to the top element is housed in a coiled metal sheath that protects it from chaffing, pinching, and nicking. However well protected these wires may be, constant flexing may break them. If the top element indicates continuity, test the wiring. (See Figure 5–17.)

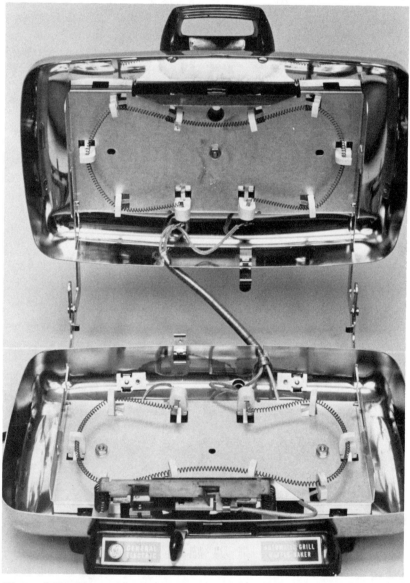

Figure 5-17 *Test each element from a point behind the terminals. Test the connecting wiring from their side of the terminals.*

Examine the heating elements occasionally for sagging. The condition indicates oxidation fatigue, and if you spot it replace the element before it breaks or shorts to ground.

Most waffle irons have indicator lamps built into the front control console to show that they are on. A faulty lamp shunt will keep the appliance from heating, and a burned-out lamp usually indicates a faulty shunt connection. If your waffle iron indicator lamp won't light, first check the lamp connections. The leads are very fine wire and easily broken. If you find a loose or broken connection, it's safe to assume that the lamp has burned out because of it. Replace the lamp. Some waffle irons provide a window that lets you see the glow from the heating element. No glow means no heat from the bottom element.

PERCOLATOR

The percolator is a dual-heat appliance; it has one element for brewing and another for warming. The thermostat is connected across the warming element and the pilot light. When the percolator begins its brew cycle, the thermostat contacts are closed and both the warming element and the pilot light are shunted out of the circuit. When the percolator completes its brew cycle, the thermostat contacts open, connecting the warming element, thermostat heater, and brewing element in series. Dividing the voltage like this reduces the current and the amount of heat.

The pilot lamp is connected in series with the other circuits after the brewing cycle is over, and the resultant voltage drop lights the lamp. The warming element keeps the coffee at a constant temperature and prevents the bimetal contacts from resetting and starting the brew cycle over again.

Mechanically, the percolator works by using the pressure of heated water in a confined space. The percolator pump has a valve at the bottom that sits on the top of the heater in the base. When the tube is placed in the pot, the water in it rises to the level of the water in the pot. As the water temperature increases, pressure in the tube increases. A check valve in the pump (See Figure 5–18.) keeps it from flowing back into the pot. The water flows up the tube, over the spreader, and into the coffee grounds in the brewing basket. Pressure loss from the evacuating water lifts the check valve and emits more water. The cycle continues until the thermostat opens the circuit.

An open line cord, thermostat, or heating element will keep your percolator from working. Since the cord is a separate component, testing it is quick and easy. When you test for continuity, make sure that the plug terminals are clean.

Figure 5-18 *The percolator pump check valve washer (at the screwdriver tip) must be free to move.*

In order to test the thermostat, you must remove the base of the percolator. It is held in place by a single nut and stud in the bottom center, by screws near or countersunk into the feet, or by a large hex nut threaded onto a tower extension of the heating element case, as in Figure 5–19. Knobs and other control levers will come off with the base.

Some manufacturers seal the thermostat in the heating element enclosure. It is a special high-heat unit, the operation of which was discussed in Chapter Four. In order to test one of these thermostats for continuity, simply connect your VOM leads across the two terminals as is done in Figure 5–20. If it is open, you will have to replace the heating element–thermostat assembly.

Figure 5-19 *Large hex nut holds the heating element/thermostat assembly to the pot. The plastic base is held to the element/thermostat by a single screw.*

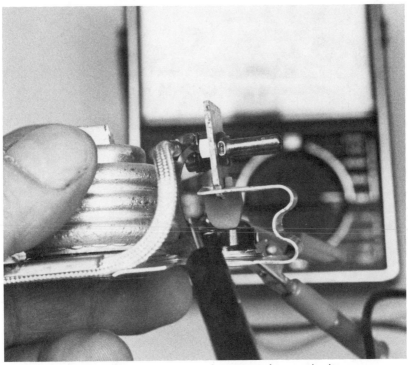

Figure 5-20 *Testing the thermostat for continuity.*

Other percolators have an ordinary bimetal thermostat enclosed in a metal case and cannot be serviced. You can test it for continuity in the usual manner. If it reads open or shows a large resistance, replace it. Other coffee makers may have a completely exposed bimetal thermostat that you can service.

When you suspect that an open heating element is keeping your percolator from heating, you can test it for continuity. (See Figure 5–21.) There are as many different heating elements as there are percolators, and all of them are secured to the pot or base by a slightly different method. Some clip onto the base, others are mounted to the base with a single center screw, and still others are secured to the pot by the large hex nut shown in Figure 5–19. In the case of the last mounting method, the price of the ½-in.-drive socket, ratchet, and extension required to remove this nut is larger than the price of some new coffee makers. If you don't already have the tools or can't borrow them, you might consider a new pot. Figure 5–22 shows how to remove the center screw and remove the heating element.

Figure 5-21 Test the main heating element across the two terminals attached with Phillips screws. Probes are attached to the warming element.

Figure 5-22 *After removing the giant hex nut from inside the pot, remove the screw from the center of the base and lift the heating element out.*

Some modular percolators seal the heating element in the base along with the thermostat and other circuitry. When the unit refuses to work, you can test the entire base unit for continuity across the appliance plug terminals. A reading of infinity indicates an open circuit somewhere in the base, but you will not be able to tell exactly where. Replace the entire base.

If the pilot lamp won't light and everything else works, the bulb is burned out. If, however, the pilot lamp is out and the percolator won't keep the coffee warm, the warming element is open. Test for continuity. Most warming elements are cast into the same metal case that contains the main heating element. When it fails, you have to replace the entire unit.

A corroded percolator pump valve will keep the unit from percolating after the water has reached the appropriate temperature. A good coffee maker cleaner such as Dip-It usually will cure this ill.

If the coffee is too strong or too weak, you may be using too much or too little coffee. Perhaps the brand of coffee is the cause. Be sure to follow the maker's instructions.

TOASTER

Automatic toasters use small ribbon heating elements wrapped around mica supports. A timing-action thermostat regulates how long the elements are energized. The up and down movement of the bread rack is controlled by a system of runners, levers, and springs. When you lower the bread racks a catch arm locks them in place while another part of the linkage closes a pair of switch contacts.

When the bread is ready, a bimetal thermostat opens the contacts and triggers the release mechanism: A friction damper controls the spring-loaded bread racks so that they rise slowly. Some toasters use a single-pole, double-throw thermostat for controlling heat and release. When this type of bimetal thermostat opens the circuit to the heating elements, it closes another circuit activating a solenoid that triggers the releasing mechanism. Refer to Chapter Four for thermostat details.

If your toaster either burns the bread or only provides enough heat to dry it out without really toasting it, you can suspect a faulty thermostat. Most modern toasters provide external adjustment for lighter and darker toast. When the adjuster fails, you will have to open the toaster and examine the adjusting linkage.

Toasters come apart in a variety of ways. Most have screws in the base section of the side panels that tie the whole assembly together. (See Figure 5–23.) Other models depend on tension between the outer shell and nubs on the underside of the frame. In order to remove the

Figure 5-23   Remove eight slotted screws from the base to expose the circuitry and releasing mechanism.

shell from these models, you have to push in on the shell sides with the palms of your hands while you pull out at the bottom. You'll wish you had four hands when you tackle this operation. *Do not turn this type toaster upside down.* When you release the shell tension the bread guards are free to fall out, and you won't enjoy replacing them.

Many toasters allow you to examine and test the circuitry and linkages by removing the bottom panel and plastic handles. Figure 5–24 depicts this. Remove the small panel adjacent to the handle first. Then slide the handle from the chassis as in Figure 5–25.

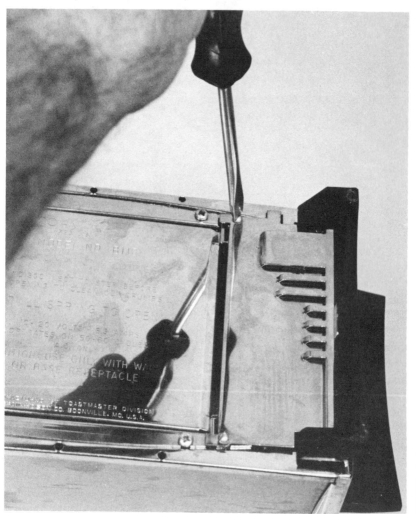

Figure 5-24   Removing the small bottom panel.

Figure 5-25 *Slide the handle from the chassis.*

A no heat failure that involves the entire toaster is usually caused by an open line cord or thermostat. You will usually find the line-cord terminals in the bottom section of the toaster on the side opposite the thermostat control knob. Test the cord after disconnecting it from its terminals. (See Figure 5–26.)

When a timing-action thermostat fails, it will be because the bi-metal heater, which is connected in series with the main heating elements, keeps the toaster from heating. You cannot isolate this tiny heater from the circuit because the terminals are riveted in place. You can shunt it out of the circuit by connecting a jumper wire across the terminals. Refer to Figure 5–27 and test for continuity. You will be able to see most of the bread rack linkage from this angle; push the racks down, then release them manually to see if they are working correctly.

Many manufacturers rivet the heating element structures and terminals to the chassis. When a heating element burns out, you have to replace the entire chassis. Generally, you can remove it by disconnecting the line cord and loosening the four screws that secure it to

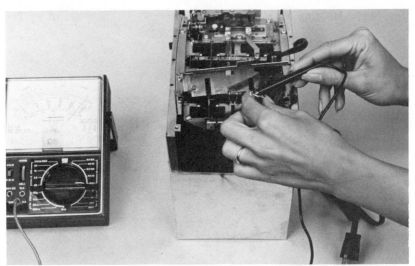

Figure 5-26   Disconnect the line cord from its spade terminals and test for continuity.

Figure 5-27   Attach a jumper wire to the two rivet terminals of the thermo-stat heating element and place your probes behind it to test for continuity.

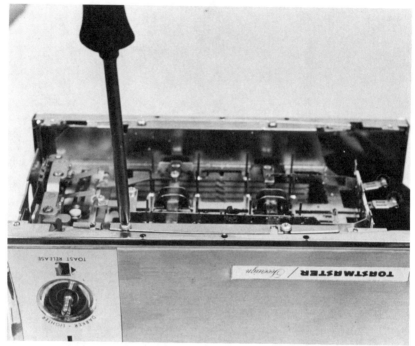

Figure 5-28 *Remove four screws from the chassis. Remove knobs, disconnect the wiring, and lift the chassis from the cabinet.*

the body. Figure 5–28 illustrates this sequence. The chassis is the heart of the appliance and is its most expensive part. Price the part and compare it to the price of a new toaster before you decide to replace the chassis.

Most older toasters allow you to remove the elements by disconnecting the terminals, removing the bread guards, and pulling the element out through the bread slot. Many makers discontinued supplying parts for equipment that is seven to ten years old. Check with your supplier before you disassemble your toaster.

An open releasing solenoid or a binding linkage will keep the toaster from popping the bread up. You will find the solenoid located near the thermostat. Most likely, the terminals will be solder or rivet joints. Test for continuity. A timing-action-thermostat-controlled releasing mechanism that is binding or dirty will keep the bread from popping up. You can test it by pushing it down and releasing it with the manual release button. Most often, cleaning, some judicious bending, and lubricating will repair binding linkages.

Bread will sometimes toast unevenly because of a difference in moisture content throughout the slice. Generally, the middle contains more moisture than the edges, thus causing the edges to brown more quickly. If only one side of the bread toasts, one element is open and should be replaced.

TOASTER OVEN

The toaster oven just might be the second most useful appliance in your house. It toasts, top browns, and bakes anything that you can squeeze into it. It's extremely dependable and almost impossible to repair without replacing assemblies. Most of the components are riveted or spot welded together.

Here's how it toasts. Pushing down on the start lever engages a double-arm, four-contact switch that completes a circuit to the power source. The heating element, the thermostat, a switch that eliminates the top element during bake, and a switch that eliminates the bottom element during "top brown only" are connected in series with the main switch. The bimetal thermostat hangs from a frame just under the right-hand bread rack and operates the thermostat contacts through a linkage rod. The solenoid activates the door's opening linkage and is connected to the main switch and the thermostat in parallel. Adjusting the thermostat control lever through a numbered scale from 1 to 9 increases the distance through which the thermostat linkage rod must work to open the contacts.

As the toaster heats, the bimetal thermostat bends toward the front and eventually engages a flange on the linkage rod that opens the thermostat contacts. When the circuit from the main switch to the thermostat is broken, the solenoid is activated. It acts through a linkage that opens the door and releases the start lever. When the start lever returns to its original position, it opens the main switch contacts.

Selecting "top brown only" opens a switch that disconnects the bottom element from the circuit. All other components remain active. Set in this mode, the toaster will not produce enough heat to activate the thermostat before whatever you are browning burns. This is a user-controlled setting.

Selecting any of the oven temperatures disengages a set of contacts that open the circuit to the top heating element and the solenoid. The bimetal thermostat operates the contacts through the same linkage described earlier. The linkage used to select the three modes, open and close contacts, and change the relationship between the thermostat linkage and contacts is extremely simple and almost indestructible.

The line cord, the start switch, and the thermostat are three components that will keep your toaster oven from working on any setting. You can test the line cord from the main switch terminals and gamble that the connecting wiring is good. If your test shows continuity, you have saved yourself the time needed to disassemble the entire appliance. In order to make this quick and easy test on the toaster oven shown in the illustrations, turn it upside down. You will see two hex-head bolts in each of the plastic side panel feet and two in the metal part of the chassis near the switch console.

Remove all six screws, pull the bottom of the side panels out, then lift the switch console cover off. You will have to remove the mode selector knob as well. The main switch is located at the extreme left side of the switch console. Figure 5–29 illustrates this procedure. Disconnect the wires from the two top left-hand terminals and test across each of the two wires and each of the plug prongs. If your test shows an open cord, you will have to open the appliance to expose the cord-connecting wiring terminals located in the left side panel.

Figure 5-29   *Test the line cord for continuity after disconnecting it from the two terminals at the left of the main switch.*

Remove two Phillips-head screws from the lower corners of the back and two hex bolts hiding behind the door in upper right and left corners. Free the outer shell from clips at the top of each side panel and remove it.

Remove the thin sheet-metal cover (one bolt) and the plastic strain reliever from the inside of the left side panel to expose the line-cord terminals. The connectors are crimped and soldered. Isolate the line cord with a jumper wire and test it again, as in Figure 5–30. Test the connecting wiring in the same manner. If you find either one open, replace it with the same type and quality material.

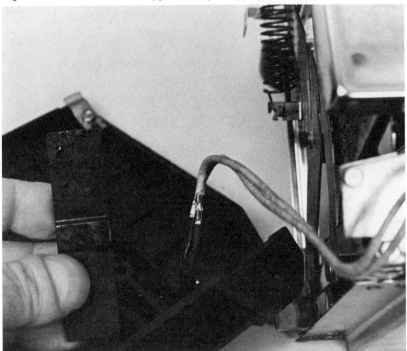

Figure 5-30 *Test the line cord for continuity across these two terminals to eliminate the connecting wiring.*

If you suspect that the switch might be preventing the toaster oven from heating, examine the points for corrosion. If you want to test the switch for continuity, disconnect the wiring from all four terminals. Refer to Figure 5–31 and test across each of the power and each of the load side terminals in turn. If the switch reads open, you will have to replace the entire switch assembly. In order to remove this assembly, disconnect all of the wiring, remove two bolts from the left side, one from the right side, then pull the assembly free of the chassis.

The switch will read open if the start lever fails to fully engage the contacts. You can check this by watching the action as you push the lever down into the locked position. A little bending here and there will probably solve the problem.

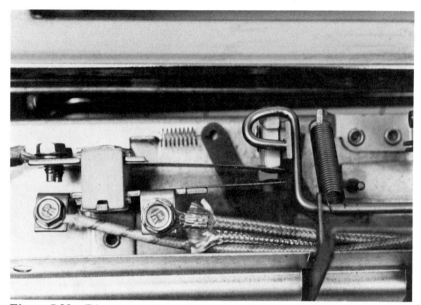

Figure 5-31 *Disconnect the wiring from these four terminals, push the start lever down and test the switch across each pair in turn.*

The thermostat contacts open and close slowly, and as a result are prone to arcing and corrosion. Over a long period of time, the points may become so pitted as to render them useless as conductors. As in Figure 5–32 you will find the thermostat contacts beneath the top element switch at the right-hand side of the switch assembly. A jumper wire across the thermostat's terminals will isolate it from the circuit so that you can test it for continuity. If it reads open, examine the points for heavy pitting. You may be able to restore conductivity with a Flex-Stone and contact cleaner.

If both elements refuse to heat, and you have determined that the thermostat is conducting sufficient current, you will have to examine the connecting wiring and test the elements for continuity. You can isolate the elements for your test by disconnecting their leads from the thermostat and top element switch terminal board. The elements and their leads are replaceable as units. The leads are spot welded to the elements, as in Figure 5–33.

When the top element won't heat on "toast" or "top brown only," either the element is open or the switch whose job it is to isolate the top element from the system during "bake" is open. Examine the contacts, then test for continuity. Figure 5–34.

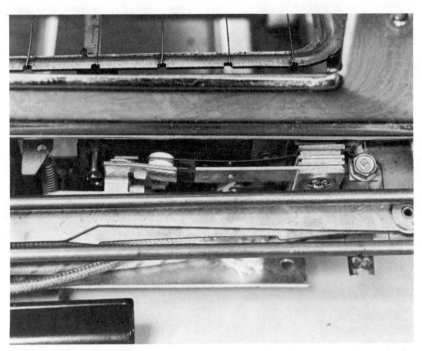

Figure 5-32 *The thermostat terminals are located beneath this top element switch.*

Figure 5-33 *Element leads are spot welded to the terminals.*

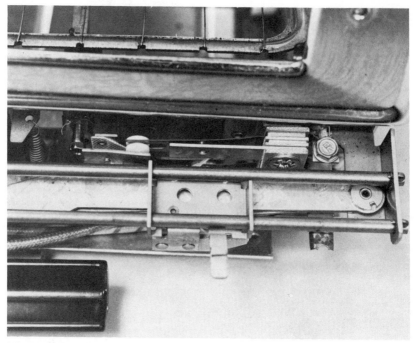

Figure 5-34 *Test this switch for continuity if the top element won't heat. The contacts are near the middle of the switch blades. Isolate by disconnecting the terminal at the right. Note the "top brown" switch arm sticking out from under the chassis at the extreme right.*

If the switch that removes the bottom element from the circuit during "top brown only" is open, the bottom element will not heat during "toast" or "bake." Examine the contacts and test them for continuity. You will find the switch arm at the extreme left-hand side of the switch assembly. It hangs beneath the assembly chassis and juts out toward the front of the unit. Refer to Figure 5–34.

If the toast burns or the oven overheats, the thermostat linkage may be binding or the contacts have stuck together from constant arcing. You can move the linkage rod manually to test for binding, and you can examine the contacts to see if they have stuck.

When the toaster oven door won't pop open, either the releasing linkage is binding or the releasing solenoid is open. You will find the solenoid hidden behind wiring and linkage arms on the base of the selector switch assembly chassis. The solenoid is shown in Figure 5–35. A fine, loosely covered wire connects the solenoid coil to the main switch and the thermostat. You can isolate it from the circuit for a continuity test by loosening the switch and thermostat terminal screws.

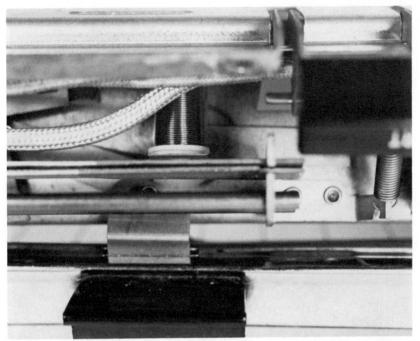

Figure 5-35 *Door release solenoid coil in the center of the picture.*

To check for binding linkage, close the door and work the linkage with a knife blade. As all of the mechanical linkage components work with ample clearance and appear to be well made, they should not be a problem. For better cooking results, keep the crumb tray clean and occasionally remove the outer shell and clean the inside reflective surfaces.

IRON

Electric irons have been with us for a long time. They have evolved from the simple one-temperature models to the complex models that not only iron but spray, steam, give an extra shot of steam, and provide the user with a host of temperatures. Despite their complexity, modern irons work on the same principles that governed the very first ones.

The steam iron works like this. When you set the selector lever to the desired temperature, you close a set of bimetal contacts that complete a circuit to the heating element. If you want steam, you depress a button located on the top of the handle, usually up front near the temperature selector lever. Depressing that button opens a needle valve. Gravity draws water from a tank above the sole plate. When the water strikes the sole plate, it turns immediately into steam.

Clogged steam vent ports cause more grief than all of the mechanical and electrical components combined. Distilled water or water softened with a chemical treatment kit eliminates the problem completely, but all of us get lazy or careless now and again. Clogs are caused by mineral deposits in the water. Average build-up can be removed with one of the many steam iron cleaners available. More stubborn deposits and complete blockage require some hand work before using the cleaner. You can free clogged steam vents with a machinist's scribe or a small nail.

The line cord is the second most common cause of trouble in irons. Although it is unmercifully tortured day in and day out, it copes remarkably well. The rubber strain reliever at the handle does a lot to preserve the cord's continuity. If one day your iron should fail to heat, test the line cord for continuity, as in Figure 5-36.

Figure 5-36 *Disconnect the line cord from its two terminals and test for continuity.*

You can expose the line cord terminals on most irons by removing a metal panel from the bottom just behind the sole plate. Other irons provide access through a panel on the handle near the strain reliever, and a few make you take the iron apart to reach the terminals. Refer to Figure 5-37.

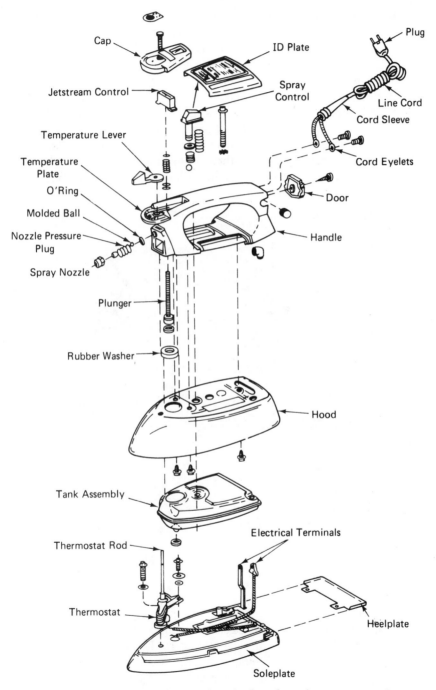

Figure 5-37 *A typical steam iron broken down into components.*

Irons ingest quite a lot of lint during their lifetimes. Even though they are well sealed, lint has a way of sneaking through the smallest openings. When enough lint accumulates on and around the thermostat, it insulates the contacts, and the iron will not heat. Generally, when this happens the lint will smoulder and give off an odor.

In order to investigate this possibility, you have to disassemble the iron. First, *Think.* The iron is built up in layers—sole plate, water tank, switches, and handle. (See Figure 5–38.) In many cases, you will have to remove the cord, because the connecting wiring will hold the handle in place after all other connections have been released. Look for mounting screws that might be hidden beneath identification plates, as in Figure 5–38.

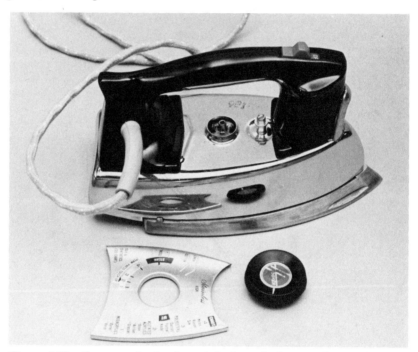

Figure 5-38 *Remove the knob, switch legend plate, and a single screw to expose the inside of this iron.*

With the handle and water tank out of your way, you will be able to service and test all of the electrical components. In case of a no heat failure, test the thermostat (Refer to Figure 5–39.), and the heating element (Figure 5–40), for continuity. Remember to either disconnect at least one lead or isolate the component with a jumper wire.

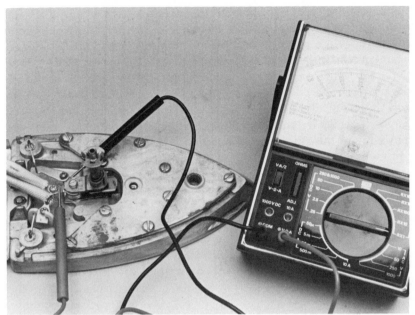

Figure 5-39 *Testing the thermostat for continuity.*

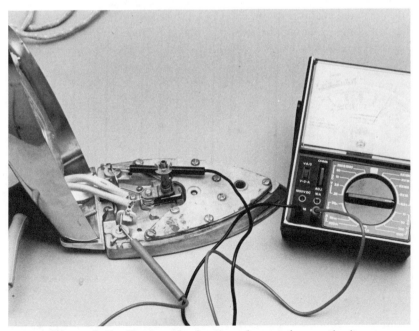

Figure 5-40 *Testing the heating element for continuity.*

If your iron heats up but will not steam, if the steam ports are clear, perhaps the needle valve is binding or the jet is clogged. Generally, the cause of both problems is mineral corrosion. Clean the steam system with the maker's recommended cleaner. If that doesn't work, you will have to disassemble the iron to discover the source of the problem.

Always use distilled or treated water in your steam iron. Always empty it while it is still hot; the heat will evaporate the moisture remaining in the passages and tank and help prevent rust and mineral corrosion.

HEATING PAD

The heating pad is made from material similar to that found in electric blankets. Generally, a three-position slide or push-button switch controls the heat, selecting a 20 watt, a 40 watt, or both elements. When the pad refuses to heat on any setting, you will probably find an open cord or switch. Rarely will both heating elements fail at the same time.

In order to test the cord for continuity, remove the screws from the control box. (Some boxes have two, three, or four retaining screws.) Figure 5–41 shows a unit with two screws. Separate the halves carefully to avoid disturbing the slide or push-button contacts. Most heating pad controls secure the switch contacts to the top half of the control box. Some rely on the bottom half to keep everything in place,

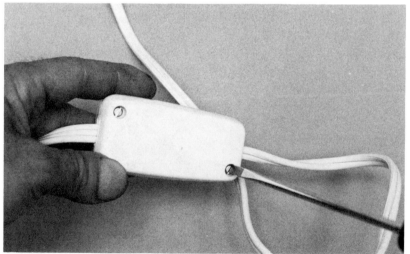

Figure 5-41   Remove these two retaining screws and separate the switch box halves.

and once you remove the bottom half the components are free to fall out.

Attach a jumper wire across the line cord terminals in the control box and test for continuity across the plug prongs. If the cord shows continuity, test the switch, as in Figure 5–42. If you want to remove the contacts for cleaning, be sure to make a note of their position. They must be installed exactly as you found them.

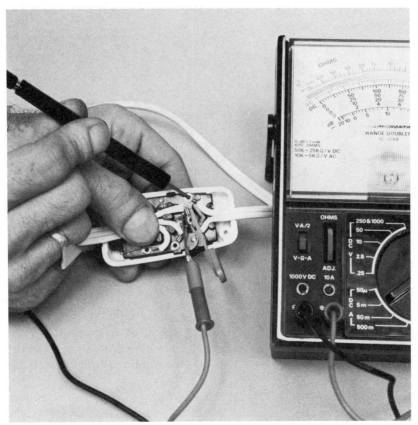

Figure 5-42 *Test the switch while holding the button in.*

An open heating element will keep the pad from heating on either low or medium, and it will prevent the pad from reaching full temperature on high. Test for continuity across the common lead and each of the other two in turn. (See Figure 5–43.) If either element reads open, you will have to replace the pad. Never attempt to repair a heating pad element. If the pad overheats, the safety thermostat in the pad has failed to open the circuit. Replace the pad.

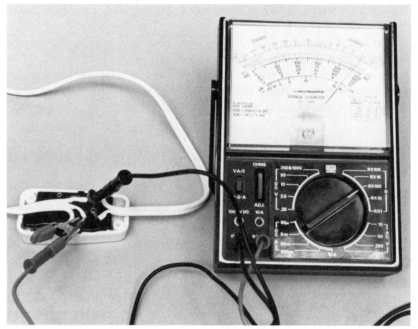

Figure 5-43 *Testing the heating element from the control box.*

ELECTRIC BLANKETS

Electric blankets have flexible heating elements woven into the fabric. Several safety thermostats connected in series with the elements prevent overheating. Most blankets use a room air temperature sensing thermostat in the control box; others place the sensors in the blanket. You can recognize the latter type by the four-prong connector at the blanket.

The control box thermostat employs a cup-shaped magnet contact on the bimetal arm. The magnet actually surrounds the contact and does not conduct electricity. The opposing contact is surrounded by a small iron washer. The magnetic attraction is small, but it is enough to allow a certain amount of spring tension to build up as the bimetal arm tries to warp away from the opposing contact. Finally, the spring tension overcomes the magnetic force and the contacts snap open. As the bimetal cools and returns to its closed position, the magnetic force snaps the contacts together. The snap action prevents the arcing associated with slow-acting bimetal thermostats.

A compensating heater is connected in series with the blanket heating elements and placed in the control box close to the bimetal arm.

When the element is energized, the compensator gives off a small amount of heat, the effect of which shortens the cycling time and smooths out the blanket's operation. Short cycling keeps the on and off periods from feeling too cool or too warm.

If your blanket will not heat, open the control box, disconnect at least one of the line cord terminals, and perform the continuity test on the cord as shown in Figure 5–44. If the cord shows continuity, test the thermostat. Also in Figure 5–44, you can see the tiny compensating heater attached to the thermostat bimetal arm. If it should become dislodged from its contact with the bimetal arm, it will interrupt the series circuit with the heating element and keep the blanket from heating.

Figure 5-44 *Test the line cord for continuity across the common terminal (top center) and the thermostat terminal at the left where the cord divides.*

Open heating elements will keep the blanket from heating. Test across the prong terminals, as in Figure 5–45. Some blankets will have three or four prongs. One of those is common and is set off a bit from the others. Test across the common prong and all of the others in turn.

Overheating can be caused by stuck thermostat contacts. Open the control box and examine them. Blankets that have temperature sensors sewn into the material have a bypass capacitor connected across the thermostat contacts. If the capacitor shorts out the blanket will not shut off. Defective safety thermostats will make the blanket overheat. Never place another blanket or bedspread over an electric blanket; that will cause the blanket to overheat. Never place a room-air-temperature-sensing control box near an open window or on a cold

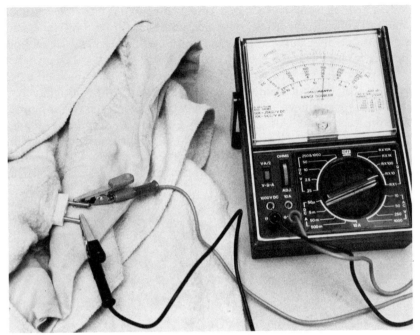

Figure 5-45 Test the blanket heating element across its plug terminals.

floor. That will make the blanket cycle on more frequently and provide you with more heat than you want.

When the pilot lamp doesn't light, it is probably because of a poor connection or a defective resistor. Disassemble the control box, examine the connections, and test the resistor. It should show a resistance of 30,000 to 50,000 ohms. Remember to follow the manufacturer's instructions for use and care.

HAIR SETTER

The hair setter's cast or stamped metal base receives heat from an element mounted to its underside. The metal base acts as a heat sink and transfers the heat to metal-lined curlers that fit over posts attached to the base. The curlers' metal lining helps them hold the heat long enough to set the curl. A simple unadjustable disc type thermostat controls the heat at a preset temperature. The hair setter's problems are no heat, overheating, and shocking.

To expose the electrical connections you have to remove the base. Loosen the screws or bend back metal tabs located in the top side of the base and lift it off, as Figure 5–46 shows. If your setter has a

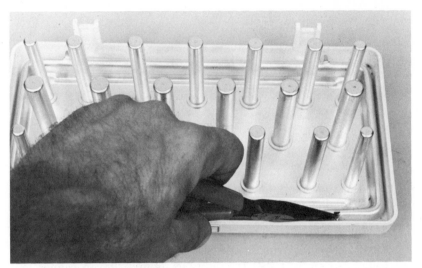

Figure 5-46 Bend tabs straight and lift the base from the chassis.

hinged lid, you will probably have to remove it before you can remove the base. The heating element is shielded on its underside and riveted to the base. In case of no heat, test the heating element for continuity. (See Figure 5–47.) You can test the thermostat for continuity from an inspection panel on the bottom of the hair setter's plastic shell. A faulty thermostat will cause overheating as well as no heat. Figure 5–48 shows how to disconnect the leads and test the thermostat. Most hair setters use detachable line cords. If yours does not, you will find the terminals under the base closest to the cord's point of entry.

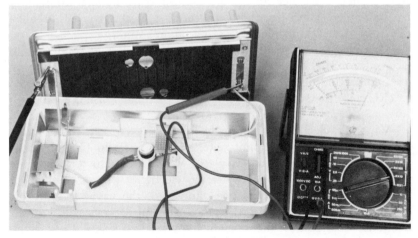

Figure 5-47 Testing the heating element for continuity.

Figure 5-48 Disconnect the thermostat leads from the spade terminals and test for continuity across them.

A hair setter that shocks you should be examined very carefully and have all circuitry tested for shorts to ground. If you cannot find the source of the short, replace the entire unit or have a professional fix it for you.

VAPORIZER

The vaporizer is unique because it uses water as the heating element. Remember the test in Chapter One where you tested your body's resistance to current flow by holding the VOM leads between your fingers? And do you remember the decrease in resistance when you wet your fingers? Water is a pretty good conductor and, like any conductor, offers resistance and produces heat. The mineral content of the water determines its ability to conduct electricity. If you filled your vaporizer with distilled water, it wouldn't work.

Two electrodes extend into the reservoir with one connected to each side of the line. They are placed close together and are kept from contacting one another by a plastic button, as in Figure 5–49. As electricity flows through the water, its natural resistance produces heat.

Vaporizer electrodes are usually housed in a plastic tube. Holes drilled through the tube admit water. As the water in the tube boils away, more enters to take its place. When the tank empties, the vaporizer shuts off. Without water, no electricity will flow.

Aside from an occasional open line cord, the vaporizer's heating element, water, is also its worst enemy. Mineral deposits will coat the electrodes and destroy their conductivity. Remove the electrode assembly from the plastic tube and clean it. First scrape away the heavy

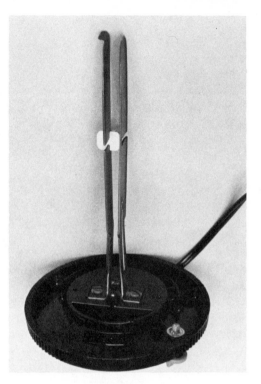

Figure 5-49 *Vaporizer electrodes. Note the white insulator button.*

deposits with a pocket knife, then polish the electrodes with #400 or #600 sandpaper. Be careful to maintain the gap between the electrodes. If the holes in the plastic tube become clogged, the vaporizer will not work.

You will find the electrode assembly either in the lid or in the base. Removing any visible screws will allow you to pull the assembly out for inspection and cleaning. (See Figure 5-50.) Be sure to keep track of any seals and washers associated with the electrode assembly.

If heavy mineral deposits will keep the vaporizer from heating at all, then a lighter coating of deposits will keep the appliance from reaching full temperature. The vaporizer will warm up, but it won't steam. Clean the electrodes.

An open line cord will keep the vaporizer from working. Test it for continuity, as shown in Figure 5-51. A vaporizer that blows fuses has either a shorted line cord or touching electrodes. One that spits water along with the steam is suffering from an overdose of water minerals. Try diluting your water with distilled water. Experiment with the proportions until the vaporizer stops spitting.

Figure 5-50 *Remove one screw from either side of the electrode case and remove the assembly from the tube.*

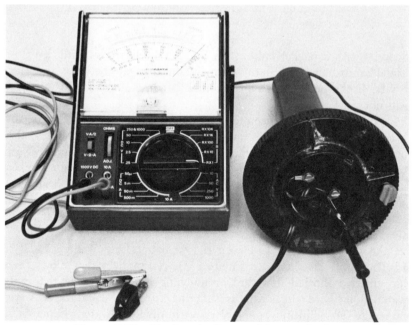

Figure 5-51 *Testing the line cord for continuity.*

Chapter 6

Electric Motors

Electric motors have been helping humans perform mundane tasks for years. They convert electricity to work that washes your clothes, cleans your house, prepares your food, and even grooms your body. Electric motors are mechanically simple and electrically complex. The complexity results from our need for self-starting and variable-speed motors.

BASIC INDUCTION MOTORS

The electric motor's most primitive form, the basic induction motor is quite simple. This motor contains at least two magnets on a stationary plate called the *stator* or *field*. Another magnet suspended in bearings so that it's free to spin is placed in the space between the field components. The spinning magnet is called the *rotor* or *armature*.

Without external assistance, the rotor of the motor will revolve to a point where unlike poles of the magnets align, and then stop. If, however, you could change the polarity of the field magnets just before the attraction of unlike poles stopped the motor, its momentum would carry it through another revolution. The rotor would continue spinning as long as the polarity alternated. This simple motor needs an outside power source to start it.

The field magnets in an electric motor are electromagnets, which are made by wrapping wire around laminated, stamped, soft iron pole pieces. Current passing through the windings magnetizes the pole pieces. Every motor has to have at least two of these, but, no matter how many it has, the number will always be even. The electromagnet's

97

polarity reverses when the current reverses. Remember alternating current? With 60-cycle alternating current the polarity reverses 120 times every second.

With the exception of universal motors, the ones that you will find in home appliances use a rotor that has no direct connection to the power supply. As the rotor cuts magnetic lines of force produced by the field coils, induction produces a current in the rotor. This current is exactly opposite to that in the field coils.

The speed at which the motor turns, measured in revolutions per minute (rpm), depends upon the number of poles in the field and the alternating current's frequency.

$$\text{Speed} = 120 \times \frac{\text{frequency}}{\text{no. of poles}}$$

or for a two-pole motor on house current:

$$120 \times \frac{60 \text{ cycles}}{2 \text{ poles}} = 3600 \text{ rpm}$$

A slip factor of 4–5 percent pegs the actual speed at around 3450 rpm. This simple motor will run with alternating current applied directly to the stator and an opposite current induced in the rotor if we start it with some outside force.

SPLIT-PHASE MOTORS

In order to make our simple motor a self-starting one, we need a supply of twisting force, called *torque*, built into the motor. The split-phase motor gets its starting torque from additional windings called starting windings. These windings have a higher resistance than those that keep the motor running. They are made from fewer turns of lighter wire and are usually wound on top of the running windings. The starting windings produce an electrical shift of 20° to 30°, which is enough to provide the starting torque.

Centrifugal Switch: When the motor reaches 75–80 percent of its top speed, or synchronous speed, the running windings produce as much torque as the start and running windings combined. At speeds beyond 80 percent of running speed, the starting windings become a drag on the motor reducing its torque and drawing too much current. Unless it is disconnected, the starting windings will damage the running windings. A centrifugal switch designed to open the starting circuit at 80 percent of top speed solves the problem. Figure 6–1 shows

Figure 6-1 *Centrifugal force acting upon the U-shaped weights on the rotor (left) pulls the flanged sleeve away from the switch arm (indicated by the technician's fingers) and opens the circuit to the start windings.*

a centrifugal switch. A mechanical governor attached to the rotor shaft opens the centrifugal switch at the prescribed speed.

Current Draw Relay: Some split-phase motors use a relay to disengage the starting windings from the circuit. The increase in current draw that the starting windings produce at 80 percent of top speed activates the relay. Figure 6–2 shows a typical start relay. The relay is matched to the motor's running requirements and cannot be interchanged between motors. Split-phase motors use overload protectors either built into the stator or attached to the housing that sense temperature and current draw and open the circuit if either exceeds design limits. Figure 6–3 shows an overload protector that uses a bimetal strip.

CAPACITOR START MOTORS

The capacitor start motor shares the starting winding idea with the split-phase motor but adds an extra punch. A capacitor is connected

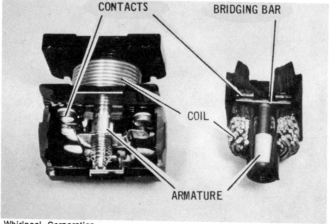

Figure 6-2 A typical start relay. When current draw reaches the prescribed level, the solenoid is de-energized, and the plunger opens the contacts to the start windings.

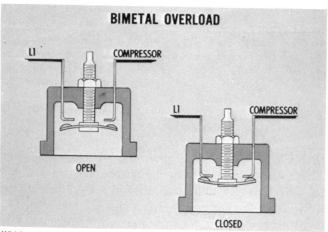

Figure 6-3 The bimetal will "oil can" buckle away from the contacts, and break the circuit to the motor when it is heated by high current draw or motor overheating.

in series with the starting windings and causes the current in those windings to lead the running-phase voltage. It creates a greater displacement angle between the start and run windings that produces as much as twice the starting torque while drawing about one-third the current. The secret lies in the capacitor's ability to store electricity. When this ability is correctly applied, it gives a boost to the circuit without drawing more current from the source.

SHADED-POLE MOTORS

The stator in shaded-pole motors has a slot cut into its face into which a coil of wire is looped to make a complete circuit. It is not connected directly to the line. The main field windings are wound around the remainder of the pole piece. When these coils are energized, a magnetic field is set up between the pole pieces and the rotor. A portion of the magnetic field is cut by the shading coil, the force lines of which are slightly out of phase with the remaining lines produced by the pole pieces. The slight shift is enough to start the motor, but torque is low. Shaded-pole motors are limited to use in small fans and other appliances needing little torque. The speed at which the shaded-pole motor runs varies according to the load and the voltage applied. Figure 6–4 shows a typical shaded-pole motor.

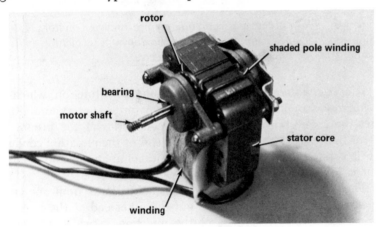

Figure 6-4 A typical shade-pole motor.

UNIVERSAL MOTORS

As the name might suggest, universal motors will run on either alternating or direct current. Two or more spring-loaded, carbon brushes ride against the armature (rotor in other motors) and connect the armature to the line and the field coils. (See Figure 6–5.) As the current alternates, the field winding arrangement changes the polarity from north to south and south to north. The alternating field polarity acts on the armature and starts it turning.

Figure 6-5 *The brushes and commutator in a universal motor. Note the cooling impeller and bearing bracket at the top of the picture. Note the armature coil—commutator connection notches.*

The *commutator*, an extension of the armature on which the brushes ride, supplies current to the armature. The commutator reverses the connection to the armature conductors at the instant that current in the conductors reverses. Each end of the armature conductor loop is connected to one segment of the commutator, and each segment is insulated from its neighbor.

The carbon brushes are set so that current flows from one end of the conductor into the brush and out the other end of the loop. This flow pattern occurs regardless of the direction in which the current flows. Current can flow through the brushes in only one direction; this is the characteristic that allows the universal motor to run on both ac and dc.

The universal motor's unloaded speed is relatively high (about 3500 rpm), and by adding a variable resistor in series with one motor lead you can vary the speed. The resistor controls magnetic flux in the motor, which in turn controls the speed. A *governor* opens and closes the circuit as the motor runs and can also control the speed.

Governor: A plate attached to the armature shaft serves as a base for the governor's components. A semicircular weight with a contact at one end is attached to the plate at a pivot point directly opposite and in line with the rotor shaft. It is spring loaded toward the center, its tension keeping it in touch with a stationary contact mounted on the plate. As the armature's centrifugal force increases with its speed, that force finally overcomes the spring load and opens the contacts. The slight speed decrease closes the circuit again, and the cycle repeats itself.

Momentum and quick action keep the motor at a constant speed. A stop mounted near the plate's circumference keeps the weight from flying off. The point at which the governor opens the circuit can be adjusted by a knob or slide lever.

Tapped Field Windings: Many small appliances use a tapped field winding speed control. Leads are tapped into the field windings at several points and each lead energizes a given number of coils. As the speed control contacts move from one to the other, beginning from low, more and more coils are energized, increasing the magnetic field strength and the speed. Only one of the taps will be energized at any given time, as the switch breaks the circuit to one as it engages another.

Although electric motors are generally very dependable, they can suffer failings of one sort or another. Listening to a malfunctioning motor will give you a clue to the cause. For example, if a motor hums when it is energized but will not run, it indicates seized bearings, open start windings, open start capacitor, or open start relay. You know that the motor is getting power, which eliminates the source and the line from probable cause. Try turning the shaft by hand. If it spins freely, the starting system is at fault. If it doesn't spin, one or both bearings have seized. Modern technology has virtually removed the seized bearing from electric motor failure with lubricant-impregnated materials. Many of these motors are sealed and are not serviceable at home. Older appliance motors do require lubrication and are not sealed.

MOTOR DISASSEMBLY

Electric motor disassembly is fairly easy. You will find the body with attached field windings, one bell housing at either end, and the rotor. Figure 6–6 shows a typical example. Generally, four long bolts extending the entire length of the motor secure the bell housings to the body. It is a good idea in many cases to mark the housings and body with corresponding punch marks, scribe lines, or magic marker lines. These serve as assembly reference points and allow you, by matching them, to reassemble the motor with body and housings in their original positions.

Figure 6-6   A typical high-performance, capacitor-start motor. Note the bell housing nuts at the right.

As you disassemble the motor, note the position of any washers or spacing shims on the rotor. These have to be replaced exactly as they came off. Lay the parts out on a bench in order of disassembly where they will not be disturbed. As an extra safety precaution, you may want to sketch the assembly.

Most large and some small electric motors use phosphor-bronze sleeve bearings with an oil groove cut into the inside surface in a spiral, as in Figure 6–7. Some are plain, but all of them are mounted in the bell housings and use felt wicks to supply oil to a small hole drilled through the bearing wall. The felt wick receives oil from a hole in the bell housing. Bearings in larger motors are press fit into the bell housing, and you should leave replacement to a qualified motor repair shop.

Many small appliance motors use a captive ball bearing to locate the rotor. It is a single brass ball with a hole drilled through the center for the rotor shaft. It is held in place by spring clips in the bell housing. (See Figure 6–8.) The ball is free to move slightly in all directions except back and forth along the rotor shaft, and it is self-aligning (within limits). Many of these receive lubricant from a felt wick, and others are lubricant impregnated.

Figure 6-7   *Phosphor-bronze sleeve bearing with an oil groove cut into the surface.*

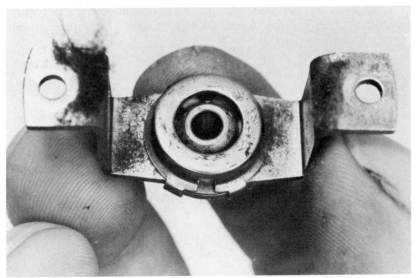

Figure 6-8   Captive ball bearing normally found in small motors.

Bearings cry out a warning when they need oil and are about to seize. They honk, groan, screech, and otherwise complain when they have been grossly neglected. If you pay attention to these warnings, you will be able to save the bearing from total disaster by applying a drop or two of oil. Run the motor a little between oilings so that it will distribute itself evenly. Apply the oil until the noise stops. You must avoid overoiling, because the oil eventually works its way into the windings where it attracts dust. Dust build-up reduces cooling and eventually causes the motor's windings to burn out.

Rattling noises accompany worn bearings. Most manufacturers recommend light oil for lubricating motor bearings, and its attendant film isn't strong enough to take up the slack caused by worn bearings. You have two testing options. Apply a few drops of SAE 40 or 50 motor oil to the bearings. If the noise stops, the bearings are worn enough to replace. Grasp the end of the rotor shaft and try to move it perpendicular to the bearing surface. Discernible play indicates badly worn bearings.

Testing Windings: Aside from testing the commutator on universal motors and centrifugal switches on some very heavy-duty motors, you can diagnose electrical troubles without disassembling the motor. In order to test the windings for continuity, you must disconnect the leads from the terminal board, as Figure 6–9 illustrates. Most if not all of the motors that you will encounter in home appliances will have clearly labeled terminals, "C" for common, "S" for start, "R" for run, or sometimes "M" for main, which is another label for the run windings. Some manufacturers provide a three-terminal plug connector that

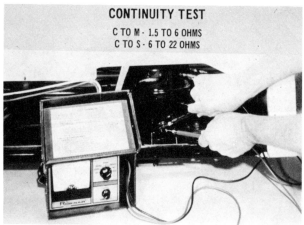

Courtesy, Whirlpool Corporation

Figure 6-9   Testing the motor windings for continuity.

prevents any wiring mistakes. In the absence of such a plug, be sure to mark each lead.

Windings should indicate continuity from C to R and C to S, but not R to S. If they show continuity through each other, they are shorted together. Most motor windings will show modest resistance when tested at R×1. You can test for a short to ground from each of the winding terminals or leads to the motor body. A reading of infinity indicates no short. Refer to Figure 6–10 for the procedure to test the motor windings.

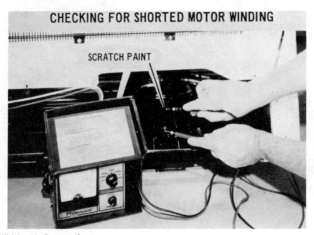

Figure 6-10 *Testing the motor windings for short to ground.*

Testing Capacitors: Some capacitor-start motors use running capacitors as well. The start capacitor is usually 3 to 5 in. long and 1 to 1½ in. in diameter and is housed in a dark Bakelite case. Figure 6–11 illustrates such a capacitor. Running capacitors are 6 to 18 in. long, 3 to 4 in. in diameter, and are housed in metal. A distorted or leaking capacitor case indicates failure.

Capacitors can, however, fail without showing any external signs. Before you test the capacitor, you have to discharge it with a 20,000-ohm resistor, as in Figure 6–12. After discharge, test across its two terminals at R×100. The meter should rise and then fall back as in Figure 6–13. Reversing the leads will produce the same results. If a resistor is connected across the capacitor leads, disconnect one of the resistor leads before you make the test. This isn't the best test for capacitors, but without buying a special tester it's the only one and certainly adequate.

Figure 6-11   Start capacitor.

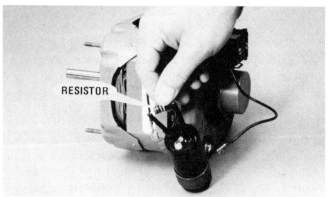

- CAPACITOR CHECKED WITH RESISTOR AND OHMMETER
- DISCONNECT LEADS AND DISCHARGE WITH 2 WATT 20,000 OHM RESISTOR
- ALWAYS DISCHARGE — CAPACITORS HOLD CHARGE FOR LONG TIME

Courtesy, Whirlpool Corporation

Figure 6-12   Discharging a start capacitor with a 20,000-ohm resistor.

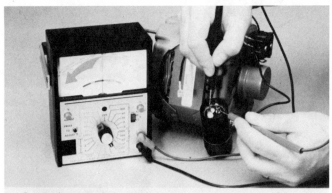

■ SET METER ON R X 100 SCALE AND TOUCH CAPACITOR
  TERMINALS
■ METER SHOULD DEFLECT TOWARDS 0 AND SLOWLY RETURN TO
  HIGH RESISTANCE
■ 0 OR LOW RESISTANCE INDICATES DEFECTIVE CAPACITOR
■ DISCHARGE OR REVERSE PROBES TO REPEAT CHECK

Courtesy, Whirlpool Corporation

Figure 6-13   Test the capacitor at R × 100 *across its two terminals.*

Universal Motor Brushes: Universal motors are subject to bearing and winding failure and should be tested in the same manner employed for other motors. The universal motor's brushes and commutators add a couple of new twists. The brushes are made from a carbon compound that provides excellent electrical contact with the commutator while creating little abrasion. Metal tubes insulated from the motor body guide the brushes, while a compressed spring attached to the brush rests against the terminal plate and applies pressure. The brush fits the tube in a manner that is neither too tight nor too loose. The brush should slide freely but show negligible side play. Figure 6–14 illustrates the brushes and holders. Too much side play causes the brush to chatter, resulting in excessive arcing and noise. A stranded and braided copper pigtail carries current to the brushes.

Removing the plate at the top of the brush holder will let you remove the brush for inspection. (See Figure 6–15.) Examine the pigtail. If it has a number of broken strands or is completely broken, replace the brush. An open pigtail forces the tension spring to carry the current, a task for which the spring was not designed. The heat of conductivity weakens the spring and allows the brush to bounce. A bouncing brush causes arcing between itself and the commutator, and eventually damages the commutator. There are, however, some universal motors with brush springs that are designed to carry current.

The condition of the brushes and the commutator affect one another a great deal. Whichever one fails first, it will take the other

Figure 6-14 Brushes and holders. Note the tension springs; they carry current to the brushes in this motor.

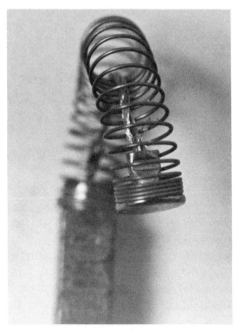

Figure 6-15 A brush with spring and pigtail. Note the brass contact button and broken pigtail strand.

with it. When the motor is running, you should be able to see a little sparking at the brush–commutator contact area. Too much sparking indicates badly worn brushes or trouble in the commutator. Remember to be very careful during running inspections.

Remove the brushes and have a look at them. Good ones will be concave, matching the shape of the commutator on the contact ends, and the rubbing surface will be smooth. (See Figure 6–16.) At their shortest, the brushes should be roughly half as long as the tube in which they ride. The pigtail should be intact, and the spring should have most of its resiliency. A spring that has carried current will appear pink and have almost no tension. Any shape on the contact end of the brush other than one that fits the contour of the commutator means that the brush should be replaced and the cause investigated. Misshapen brushes usually indicate trouble in the commutator.

Figure 6-16   *Note brush contour and smooth contact surface.*

Universal Motor Commutator: The commutator is made of copper bars mounted lengthwise on the armature shaft. Each bar is insulated from the shaft and its mates by mica sheets. On the inside ends toward the windings, a very small slot cut into the end of each bar holds the ends of the coil wires. These are soldered in place.

Brush–commutator contact eventually wears out both components. The softer carbon brushes wear out first and more frequently. At some point in its life, the commutator will develop a groove as wide as the brushes. This is normal and not a cause for concern unless it wears enough to expose the mica insulation. Mica insulation sticking up above the copper bars will cause the brushes to bounce, resulting in broken contact. You can eliminate the problem by undercutting the mica with a thin, fine-toothed hacksaw blade or a knife point. Be careful not to scratch the commutator bars. After undercutting, polish the commutator with a piece of #400 or #600 sandpaper as though you were buffing the toe of a shoe. Polish to a bright, smooth surface.

Universal Motor Field Coil: Field coil trouble often manifests itself in the commutator. If a coil is open or shorted, it will cause the brush to arc every time it passes over that particular bar. That bar will become either brighter than the others (rare) or darkened and pitted (most likely).

An important point to remember when testing universal motors is that the coils are wound lengthwise around the armature in the slots of the iron core and all of them are connected. Each bar on the commutator is connected to the start of one coil and the end of the next.

Occasionally, overheating universal motors will throw solder from the commutator bar ends and you will be able to see splashes of it on the armature and motor housing. It's important to discover the cause of the overload. Have you been using the appliance for work outside its design limits? Are the bearings worn or too dry? Are vent passages blocked? All of these contribute to overload.

Set your VOM to R×10 or 100 and test for continuity from the commutator bars to the core. It should read open. Any sign of continuity indicates a short to ground. Testing continuity between commutator bars reveals shorted or open armature coils. Determine a starting point by marking one of the bars with a magic marker. Call that bar number one. Touch your VOM leads to that bar and the one next to it on the clockwise side. Note the reading, then move the lead from bar one to bar number three and note that reading. Continue walking your leads around the commutator until you return to bar number one. You should get the same reading for each adjacent pair. An infinity reading or other drastic change in reading indicates a defective coil. Replace the armature with a new one or have the old one rebuilt at a qualified motor repair shop.

As you reassemble any electric motor, examine the rotor shaft for friction scoring, especially if you have just had new bearings installed. A worn shaft will ruin a new bearing very quickly. Be sure that all vent holes and air passages are clear. If you can't brush all of the dirt away, take the motor to your local service station and ask the attendant to blow it out with compressed air. Do not clean the motor with strong solvents, because they can cut through the lacquer on the windings and short the motor. Be sure to replace all spacers and shims in the correct position.

Despite the captive ball bearing's ability to align itself, you should take care assembling motors with this type of bearing. First, tighten the housing bolts just enough to hold everything together. Finger tight is usually good enough. Turn the armature by hand until it spins freely. Tap the motor frame smartly if it is a large motor, with a small plastic mallet or screwdriver handle on one side then on the other until the bearing aligns itself and the rotor spins freely. Tighten the bolts firmly.

Sometimes the electric motor's dependability record works against it. We tend to ignore things that perform well for long periods of time. If you would like your appliance motor to last, you can follow a few simple preventive maintenance procedures.

1. Keep the motor free of dust by vacuuming it at least once a year.
2. Lubricate the bearings where caps or oil holes are provided at least once a year; more often when the motor runs almost continuously. Use SAE 20 nondetergent oil or the maker's recommended type.
3. Be sure that motor pulleys are tight and that belts and driven pulleys line up.
4. Check and replace worn commutator brushes.
5. Follow the manufacturer's instructions for use and load. Overloads cause early failure.
6. Be aware of voltage drops in your neighborhood. Low voltage is hard on large capacitor-start, relay-start, and split-phase motors.

Chapter 7

Control Devices

SWITCHES

Without timers, switches, and solenoids, we would be chained to our appliances. These components combined with other systems add the "automatic" to the names of our modern appliances. You can load your clothes washer and retreat to another part of the house to do other chores while the automatic appliance cleans your clothes. Even the simple on/off switch makes life with our appliances easier.

A switch in the electric circuit allows us to interrupt the current flow at will and restore it just as easily. The most primitive switch has one movable and one stationary contact. The contacts can be made from sheet copper alone or sheet copper with a silver contact point attached to each half. Other metal conductors may be used to hold the contact points as well.

Toggle Switch: Toggle switches are probably the most common switches. They are spring loaded, and snap the contacts open and closed. Toggle switches that you will encounter in the home are merely components in a more complex system and are not serviceable. They generally fail to open because of broken contact point linkages or corroded points. Toggle switches are used as on/off switches on vacuum cleaners and hair dryers. These are single throw and can be tested for continuity from the power or the line cord terminal to the load side terminal.

Basic switches used in conjunction with other components form the variety of control devices found in your home appliances. Thermostats, timers, relays, and motor governors contain switches.

114

Variable Heat Switch: The variable heat or seven-position switch such as that found controlling many electric range surface elements selects inner, outer, or both elements and applies either 115 or 230 volts to them to arrive at the different temperatures. This is how it works.

High = both elements connected in parallel to 230 volts.
Medium High = 230 volts to the inner coil only.
Medium = 230 volts to the outer coil only.
Medium Low = both elements connected to 115 volts in parallel.
Low = inner coil connected to 115 volts.
Very Low = outer coil connected to 115 volts.
Simmer = 115 volts connected in series to both elements.

The switch is wired so that it can select either all or just half of the 230-volt line.

Bimetal Infinite Heat Switch: These switches are found controlling the surface elements of most modern electric ranges and many hot plates. The knobs are calibrated with low at one extreme, high at the other, and either numbers or a variety of mediums in between. A tiny nichrome ribbon heating element connected in series with the two output terminals and the surface element heat the bimetal. (Figure 7–1 illustrates a bimetal infinite heat switch.)

Figure 7-1 Bimetal infinite heat switch. Second set of contacts is at the upper right. Magnet is at lower left behind contact. The bimetal spring load is parallel to the switch lobe follower at right.

A disc, the thickness of which varies on an incline from low to high as it rotates counterclockwise, is attached to the base of the control knob shaft. Just beyond the high point, a sharp ramp descends to the off position. This ramp allows the user to turn the switch directly from off to high. The disc varies the distance between the bimetal and stationary contact points. A tiny magnet mounted to the stationary contact bracket snaps the contacts closed. A spring load attached to the bimetal snaps the contacts open. The quick action prevents arcing. The knob controls a second set of contacts as well, which when closed allows the surface element to be energized when the switch is turned to any position from off.

In the high position, the inclined disc has placed the arm on which the spring load must act to open the contacts so far away that it cannot work. Refer to Figure 7–1. The bimetal cannot warp enough to make the spring load touch the arm and the element stays on all the time. In any position below high, the bimetal opens and closes in cycles as short as once every few seconds to as infrequently as once in 60 seconds.

The condition of the contact points influences the switch's performance. Do they meet squarely? Are they pitted? Electrical corrosion will cause nonconductivity. Test for continuity across the terminals marked L1 and H1 and across L2 and H2 in Figure 7–2. Test the pilot lamp circuit across P and H1. A good switch will show few to 0 ohms

Figure 7-2   Testing the switch for continuity.

resistance. The most common failure associated with these switches is an open bimetal heating element. You can test it for continuity across terminals H1 and H2 at the attachment point.

You can open a bimetal infinite heat switch by prying the metal tabs away from the sides, removing the cover piece, then removing a plastic cover. You can clean the contacts and lubricate the shaft. Professional repair persons, however, do not recommend such service because cleaning pitted points is only a temporary repair. They feel that replacing the switch is best.

TIMER

The heart of the timers found in most appliances is the synchronous motor. It has a rotor in which the poles are slotted to accept a small bar of copper or brass. (Figure 7-3 shows a typical synchronous motor.) Unlike large synchronous motors that have to be started by an external dc power source, these little ones start easily on alternating current. They are normally very dependable but are not immune to failure. You can test the windings for continuity at R×100 across the only leads going into the motor.

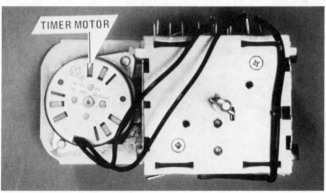

Courtesy, Whirlpool Corporation

Figure 7-3 *The motor is usually the only serviceable part of a timer. It is secured to the timer with two screws.*

You can free a sticking motor shaft with one drop of very light machine oil, applied as in Figure 7-4. These motors are inexpensive to buy and easy to replace. Maytag and some other manufacturers have made the timer so that you can simply unplug a malfunctioning motor and plug in a new one.

Add a series of cams, gears, and switches to the synchronous motor and you have a sophisticated timer. Figure 7-5 illustrates timer cam

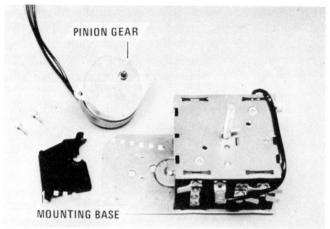

Figure 7-4 *Apply one drop of oil to the pinion gear shaft on sticking motors.*

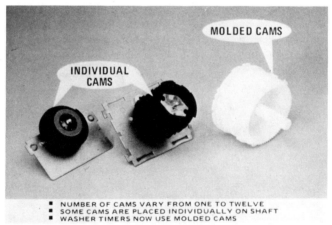

- NUMBER OF CAMS VARY FROM ONE TO TWELVE
- SOME CAMS ARE PLACED INDIVIDUALLY ON SHAFT
- WASHER TIMERS NOW USE MOLDED CAMS

Figure 7-5 *Timer cam wheels.*

wheels. Here's how it works. The motor drives a pinion gear that meshes with a larger gear in the switch assembly. The timer switch assembly activates contact arms through inclined projections or cutouts along the circumference of one or more cam wheels, as shown in Figure 7–6. The duration of each cam lobe or cutout, as well as its position on the disc with respect to other discs on the same shaft and other cams in the system, is carefully planned so that they cycle properly.

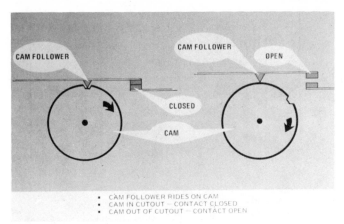

Courtesy, Whirlpool Corporation

Figure 7-6   *Timer cam wheels and switch contacts.*

The timer seems very complicated at first glance, but proves quite simple when you break it down into component parts. When a timer fails to advance, you can suspect open motor windings or binding gears. Test the windings. Remove the motor from the timer assembly and turn the pinion shaft by hand. A tiny screwdriver placed on the teeth of the switch assembly gear will allow you to determine whether or not that segment is binding.

If the timer stops the machine at the beginning of a particular segment, isolate the circuits involved with help from the wiring diagram, and test the timer switch contacts for continuity. Generally, testing across two terminals will show if the contacts for that segment are open. When you discover open contacts, you should replace the timer switch assembly. Think through your diagnosis and take it a step at a time.

SOLENOIDS

Solenoids are electrical components that convert electricity to work. Any conductor with current flowing through it creates a magnetic field around it. If you coil the conductor many times, you concentrate the magnetic force in one small area and produce an electromagnet. Add a movable bar, and you have a solenoid. Figure 7–7 shows a typical solenoid.

Depending on the size of the conductor and the number of windings and levers involved, you can make a solenoid do any number of different jobs. It can change gears in your washing machine, hand you

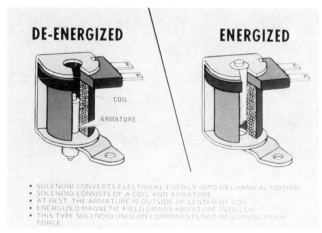

Figure 7-7   Typical solenoid and how it works.

your morning toast, and dump ice into a tray in your freezer. Unlike a switch that merely breaks or completes a circuit, the solenoid consumes electricity and converts it to work. It is a load component.

A broken winding, or a bent, binding, or broken linkage are the only failures that you will encounter with solenoids. Linkage problems will almost always be visible during a running inspection. You can test the coil for continuity across its two terminals as shown in Figure 7–8. A solenoid plunger that is exposed to water mineral corrosion such as those in your washer's inlet valve can fail because of binding plunger bars. Generally, a good cleaning will restore them to working order. You might be able to straighten a bent linkage or free up a binding one, but an open coil means that you will have to replace the solenoid.

Figure 7-8   Solenoid from an automatic washer inlet valve. Test across the two terminals.

Chapter 8

Small Appliances with Motors

Hardly a single day goes by that one of the appliances discussed here hasn't helped you in some way. Despite this fact, all of us are guilty of neglecting them. How many hours did your window fan run during the summer? When did you last oil the bearings? How many hours of comfortable climate did your humidifier provide without so much as a glance of appreciation and a water tank refill? The fact that these appliances can operate for so long with so little attention is a modern engineering miracle. However, their motors are complex and demand more maintenance.

ELECTRIC FAN

Fans are probably the simplest motor-driven appliances in your home, and you can keep them in excellent condition for years with just a few drops of oil and a good cleaning every twelve months. Most household fans use a shaded-pole motor that is controlled by a one, two, or three-speed switch. A three- or four-bladed prop measuring anywhere from 8 to 21 in. in diameter moves the air. The prop is secured to the motor shaft by an Allen-head set screw in the side of the hub or a single bolt through the hub center. Some blade assemblies are keyed to the shaft by matching flattened areas. The speed control lets the user select field windings that produce the desired revolutions per minute.

A fan that has received a reasonable amount of care will almost never fail completely. When it does, you can begin your troubleshooting with those components that never ask for attention, the line cord and the switch. Unplug the fan and remove the protective grillwork from the body. Most are held in place by four or more screws placed around the perimeter. Others merely clip into place. Generally, you will find the line cord terminals at or near the switch box. One side of the line will be connected to the white lead from the motor, and the other side will be connected to a terminal on the switch housing opposite the three speed terminals. Many fans use spade connectors, whereas others use double-lug and wire-nut connectors. Disconnect at least one of the line cord terminals before you test for continuity.

An open switch will keep your fan from running. Two- and three-speed switches usually fail on only one of the speeds unless the line connection fails. Isolate the switch from the circuit if you can and test from the common lead to each of the motor leads, as in Figure 8-1.

Figure 8-1 Testing a three-speed fan switch for continuity.

If the fan motor hums when you turn it on but doesn't run, it is probably suffering from gummy or seized bearings. Gummy bearings are caused by disuse or from dust that works its way into the bearing oil. Seized bearings result from a lack of oil. A bearing that is about to seize will make a loud groaning or honking noise. Humming in split-phase motor fans may indicate open start windings. Refer to Chapter Six for details.

Rattling fans are annoying and, fortunately for those whose nerves they assault, easy to repair. The first thing to do is check the fan body and grill for loose screws or broken clips. Despite the engineer's effort to balance the blade assembly, all fans vibrate a little. A fan that sits on an uneven surface will rattle and shake enough to make noise. Older fans whose bearings have worn a bit are especially prone to noise induced by loose fittings and uneven placement. The play in the bearings causes excess vibration.

A fan with a blade assembly that has worked loose on the motor shaft will be very noisy. Not only will it make more noise than you can bear, it will vibrate so badly that you will be able to see it shaking. Unplug the fan, remove the grill, and try rocking the blade assembly to and fro on the shaft. Tighten it as Figure 8-2 shows. If you don't have the proper Allen wrench, take a flat-bladed screwdriver that is small enough to span the hex from corner to corner and tighten carefully. You will not succeed in tightening it enough to last for very long, but it will do until you can get the proper Allen wrench.

Figure 8-2 *Tightening a loose fan blade assembly.*

If the hub is tight on the shaft, check the individual blades for loose rivets. You might be able to tighten the loose rivets enough to stop the vibration. Remove the blade assembly and place the rivet against a very solid backing such as a vice head or a thick piece of steel. Make sure that the blades are not contacting anywhere but at the rivet, then tap lightly with a small ball-peen hammer. If this doesn't work, take the blade assembly to a sheet-metal shop and have them install new rivets.

You have to be careful when handling the blade assembly. Do not bend any of the blades. To check them for alignment before reassembly, place the prop on a perfectly flat surface. A heavy glass table top is ideal, but the top of a dryer or a refrigerator will do. All of the blades should touch the surface. (See Figure 8–3.) Next, measure the height of each blade from the surface. They should measure to within a hair's breadth of one another. Reassemble your fan.

Figure 8-3 *Checking to see that none of the fan blades are bent or twisted out of alignment.*

ELECTRIC HEATER

Most portable electric heaters are merely fans with a heating element and reflector built into the cabinet. Figure 8–4 shows a typical electric space heater. Most space heaters use shaded-pole motors because the fan blades are small and the heater is not required to move large amounts of air. Refer to Chapter Six for motor details.

The least expensive heaters use a simple on/off switch to energize the motor and heating element. More deluxe heaters use an adjustable thermostat to control the heat range. These are rarely calibrated in degrees, because warmth is relative. Whatever feels comfortable is good enough. Knob markings from high to low serve as reference points.

Other heaters use a switch that selects a variety of wattages ranging from 1000 to 1600. The temperature selector is marked low, medium, and high. One or more elements receives current depending on the switch position. Usually, these elements are connected in parallel. Some heaters use a voltage-dropping resistor connected in series with the heating element to change the heat output. The resistor is a small section of nichrome wire mounted near the main element. It is suspended in ceramic insulators much like those used to secure the main heating element. If the resistor should fail, the heater will not heat.

Many modern space heaters have a tip switch safety device that breaks the circuit to the element and fan when the heater is knocked

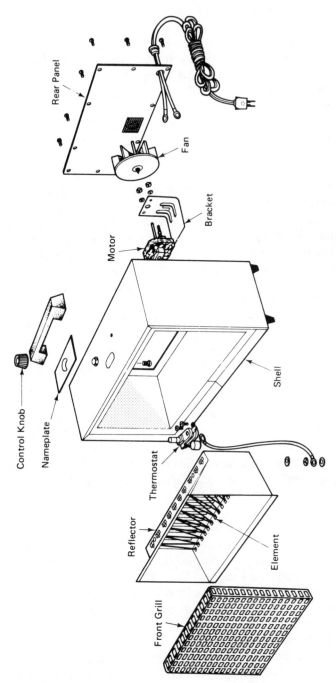

Figure 8-4 A typical electric space heater broken down into components.

over. One type is mounted on the bottom of the heater and consists of a spring-loaded plunger that protrudes through the heater body. As long as the heater remains upright, its weight keeps the plunger depressed and the contacts closed. As soon as the heater is lifted or knocked over, the spring load opens the contacts. The weighted tip switch keeps the contacts closed as long as the weight is centered. Tipping the heater in either direction opens the contacts. An open tip switch will keep the heater from working at all.

Space heaters use open-coil nichrome ribbon and quartz rod heating elements. Thermostats are the simple bimetal type found in many home heating appliances. If you suspect the element or thermostat when trouble arises, follow the guidelines for diagnosis and repair discussed in Chapter Five.

Generally, you can expose the element for testing by removing the heater grill or the back panel. Look for screws or spring clips around the perimeter. Switch–thermostat assemblies are accessible either through a control panel, the grill, or back panel. Most heaters allow you to remove the switch after loosening a pair of mounting screws often hidden beneath the control knob.

Total failure is caused by an open line cord, open switch or thermostat, open tip switch, or open motor windings. You will find the line cord terminals at the switch or at a terminal board near the point at which the cord enters the cabinet. Isolate the line cord and test it for continuity.

A simple on/off switch works through three terminals. One is common, one energizes the heating element, and the other energizes the motor. Test from the common to the other two in turn. A bimetal switch will have a similar terminal arrangement. You will find the plunger tip switch located at the bottom of the cabinet, and the weighted tip switch located higher in the cabinet. It will be wired in series with the heating element and motor.

Many modern portable heaters wire the motor and heating element in series so that one will not work without the other. It is a safety feature designed to prevent overheating if the motor fails. Single-speed motors will have two leads. Test the windings across these two leads or terminals. Two- and three-speed motors will have one common lead and two or three tapped field winding leads. Test from the common to each of the others in turn. Three-speed motors will be controlled from a separate switch.

If the motor runs but the element won't heat, test the element for continuity. You will find its leads attached to the switch terminal board. If the element heats but the motor won't run, test the windings for continuity.

Shaded-pole motors have very little starting torque, and it doesn't take much in the way of gummy or dry bearings to keep them from running. Find the oiling holes and apply a drop or two of light machine oil. Wait a few minutes to allow the oil to coat the bearing surface, then turn the heater on. Try starting the motor by hand. If it starts slowly then runs normally, the oil has freed the bearings. Oil may or may not free a seized bearing.

A motor whose windings show no continuity must be replaced. To remove the motor for replacement or repair, remove the grill or back panel first. Unbolt the motor from its mounting frame, disconnect the wiring, and remove the motor. Test the shaded-pole coil at R×100.

A noisy heater may be caused by a loose grill or other part of the body. Perhaps the fan blade or squirrel-cage blower is loose on the shaft. Keep the heater motor free from dust, and vacuum the grill, outlet vents, and reflector frequently.

HAIR DRYER

Hair dryers are compact heater–fan units. Many hand-held dryers are constructed in a way that makes them impossible to repair. These units are enclosed in heat-sealed plastic cases and cannot be opened without destroying the case. Immediate replacement warranties are common with this type of dryer.

Despite the wide variety of hair dryers available these days, all of them function on the same principles, and all of them share three main components—motor with fan, heating element, and selector switch. Figure 8–5 shows a typical dryer. Most include a safety thermostat to prevent overheating.

Any line cord attached to a hand-held dryer suffers unmercifully. It gets twisted, pulled, bent, and wrapped around the appliance more times than anyone would care to count. Therefore, when your dryer refuses to work, suspect the line cord before all other components. The cord enters most hand-held dryers through the handle. Some models provide a swivel contact to help eliminate the cord tangling associated with most dryers. If you want to test the line cord for continuity, you have to separate the case halves and locate the terminals.

Most dryer cases will be held together by a number of small Phillips-head screws countersunk into the plastic. Removing all the screws will allow you to separate the case halves. Generally, the working components will be secured to the case half into which the screws thread, as in Figure 8–6. You will find the line cord terminals on the back side of the switch. Most are soldered in place and require a jumper wire for the continuity test. (See Figure 8–7.) Line cord

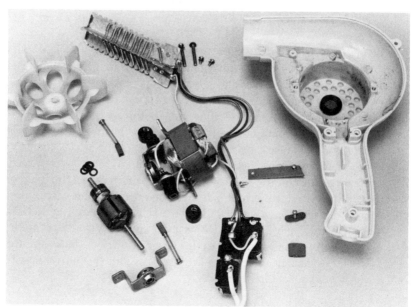

Figure 8-5   *A typical styler/dryer reduced to components.*

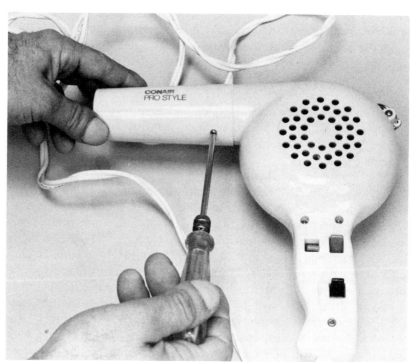

Figure 8-6   *Remove the heating element cover (one screw); remove three screws from the handle and one from the ring bracket (upper right). Separate the case halves carefully.*

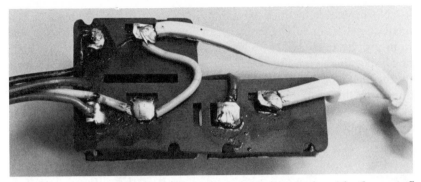

Figure 8-7 *Test the line cord across its two terminals with the on/off switch off.*

failure on swivel cord models usually occurs at the swivel contact. Arcing and dust corrosion are the swivel cord's worst enemies.

Switch failure will keep the dryer from working. Most dryers combine an on/off switch that controls a single-speed, high-rpm universal motor with one or two additional switches that select one low wattage, one high wattage, or both elements in parallel. The switches allow the user to turn both elements off while the blower circulates room-temperature air. The switches provide very hot, hot, warm, and cold drying temperatures.

The on/off switch is wired in series with the element switches. The elements will not heat nor will the motor run if the on/off switch fails open. Attach a jumper wire across its two terminals and test the switch for continuity, as in Figure 8–8.

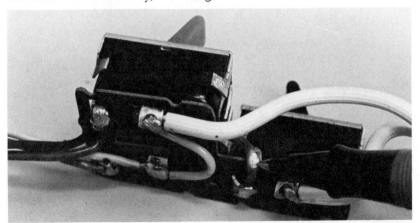

Figure 8-8 *Test the on/off switch for continuity from the line cord terminal (left of pen tip) to the switch terminal. Note the bare wire. Careless assembly chaffed the insulation away.*

No heat accompanied by a running motor results from open element switches, open elements, or an open safety thermostat. No heat from a dryer that uses two elements and two switches is unlikely, but not impossible. Test the switches from the common or line cord lead to the element lead. Test the elements for continuity. Figure 8–9 illustrates the procedure. The safety thermostat is connected to both elements in series. If it fails open, neither element will heat. Test it for continuity, as in Figure 8–10.

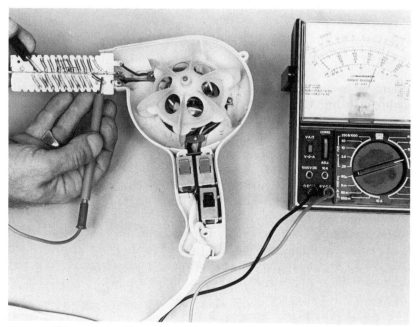

Figure 8-9   Testing the heating element for continuity.

Figure 8-10   Safety thermostat. Test for continuity across its terminals.

Open motor windings or open brush contacts will let the dryer heat up until the safety thermostat intervenes and opens the circuit to the elements. You can inspect the brushes in some dryer motors by removing a large plastic slotted screw cap from either side of the case. (See Figure 8-11.) The brushes should be at least a quarter of an inch long. Refer to the section on universal motors in Chapter Six for more details on checking brushes.

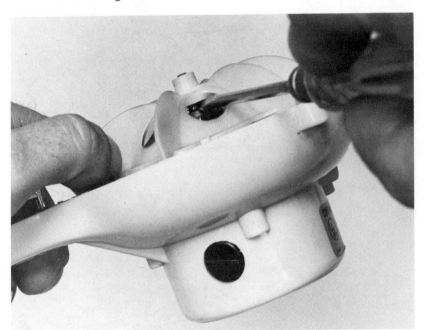

Figure 8-11   Black plastic slotted screws (one on either side) hold the brushes in place. In order to expose the motor, gently pry the impeller off of the motor shaft.

If you want to remove the motor for further investigation, separate the case halves, then pry the fan blade assembly from the motor shaft. Refer to Figure 8-11. Remove two screws from the motor bracket then remove the fiberboard wiring harness retainers. (See Figure 8-12.) Now you can lift the motor out of the case. You can test the motor's field windings across the brush holder and winding terminals. Refer to Figure 8-13. Test the commutator bars for shorts to ground and test the armature windings as discussed in Chapter Six.

If the dryer runs normally for a while and then blows cold air, it is probably suffering from inadequate air circulation caused by a slow turning motor. Dust and hair pulled in through the intake vents can

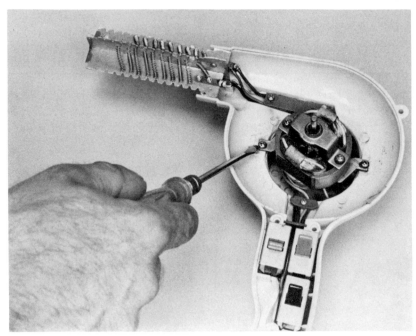

Figure 8-12 *Remove two Phillips screws from the motor bracket and lift the motor out of the case.*

Figure 8-13 *Test the motor field windings for continuity across the brush terminals.*

work their way into the bearings, slow down the motor, and cause overheating. Figure 8–14 shows an example of such buildup. Remove two screws from the bell housing on the inlet side of the motor and lift it free of the shaft. The bearing is lubricant impregnated and requires no oil. Wipe it clean with a dry cloth. (See Figure 8–15.) If the safety thermostat had not opened the circuit to the heating elements the overheating caused by the buildup would have melted the plastic case.

Figure 8-14   *Note the accumulation of hairs around the motor shaft.*

Figure 8-15   *Clean dust and hair from the bearing.*

HUMIDIFIER

These appliances are found in a variety of shapes, sizes, and outputs, from a simple, relatively inexpensive portable unit to a sophisticated one connected to your central heating–air conditioning system. Although the central unit works on the same principles that govern the portable humidifiers, they are only part of a more complex system, and any problems encountered with them should be left to the experts.

Humidifiers add moisture to the air and are especially useful during the winter months when heated air reduces the relative humidity in your home to as little as 6 percent. Air that dry causes skin to flake, saps the moisture from furniture, and creates enough static electricity to light the entire house, and has less humidity than the air in the Mojave desert. Maintaining a decent humidity level reduces the heating bill, because a person should feel more comfortable in a 70° F room at 40 percent humidity than in the same room at 10 percent humidity.

Humidifiers are classified as either evaporative or atomizing. Most portable units fall under the first classification. A wide continuous media belt made from an absorbent, porous material is stretched over a driver and an idler drum. The idler drum is immersed in the water tank. A small motor drives the opposing drum through a gear train that reduces the motor's speed and increases its torque. A separate motor, usually shaded-pole, powers the air-circulating fan that blows air through the moisture-laden belt and into the room. Some humidifiers wrap the media belt around the circumference of a large-diameter drum that is closed on one end. The fan draws room air from vents in the back of the unit and blows it into the closed drum. The air escapes into the room through the wet media belt.

A moisture-sensing device called a *humidistat* controls the appliance. It is calibrated from low to high. Generally, a three-speed switch controls the fan motor. It is connected in series with the humidistat and will not energize the fan unless the circuit is complete through the humidistat.

Some humidifiers contain a heating element just behind the air outlet grill on the down side of the flow. It heats the air to room temperature. Some larger console portable units dispense up to 18 gallons of water in 24 hours and can service up to 2500 square feet of floor space. Many of these humidifiers use a float connected to a switch that shuts the unit off when the water level drops near zero.

Console humidifiers are usually very dependable. If you clean the media belt once or twice a year, depending on the mineral content of your water, and oil the motors once a year, you should have no trouble. It helps to remove and clean the holding tank once every two to three weeks, because corrosion there will settle into the media belt. Because bacteria grow in standing water, you might want to treat the water with antibacterial and antiliming chemicals. You can find these additives at your dealer's store.

Although the humidifier is fairly complicated, it is merely a collection of simple components. It has a fan motor and a media belt-drive motor, of which the latter will probably be universal. It has a line cord, a humidistat, a fan-speed selector switch, perhaps a heating element, and a float-valve shut-off switch. Some units include an on/off switch that completes a circuit to the humidistat.

The humidistat works on a principle similar to that normally associated with bimetal thermostats. Instead of a bimetal heat-sensing switch, it has a nylon ribbon or human hair ribbon that stretches and shrinks with changes in moisture levels. The ribbon is anchored at one end of the unit and attached to a movable, spring-loaded switch arm at the other end.

Dry air causes the ribbon to tighten, which pulls the spring-loaded switch arm into contact with a stationary point. The circuit is completed, and the humidifier runs. As the room air absorbs more and more moisture, the ribbon begins to stretch under the influence of the spring load. Eventually, the spring load overcomes the ribbon tension and breaks the circuit. The adjusting knob applies more or less tension to the sensing ribbon.

The humidistat switch controls current to all other components in the appliance. Only the water-level switch can override the humidistat. If the humidistat fails, the entire appliance will shut down. Broken sensing strands is the most common failure. Test for continuity across the humidistat's two terminals with the knob set to low. (See Figure 8-16.) Most humidistats are sealed and not serviceable. Those with exposed sensing ribbons cannot be repaired because the manufacturer offers only complete humidistat assemblies as replacement parts.

Figure 8-16 *An humidistat. Spiral ramp varies the tension on the sensing strands. Test across the two terminals.*

Other components associated with complete shut-down include the line cord and the water-level switch. You can test both of these through the rear inspection panel. Removing screws from the panel's perimeter will allow you to remove it from the cabinet. Some humidifiers have detachable line cords; other models allow you to make all of your tests from the control panel. Remove two screws from the back of the control panel, remove the knobs, and lift the panel free of the cabinet, as in Figure 8–17.

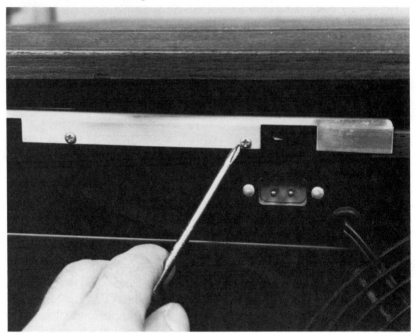

Figure 8-17   *Removing the control panel. You can test system continuity across the two plug prongs.*

Models with a separate on/off switch will not run if that switch fails open. Test it for continuity, as in Figure 8–18. Most humidifiers connect everything in series with the humidistat. The female end of the spade connectors will have a number of spade terminals branching out from it. Simply unplug these to isolate the humidistat from the system for testing. (See Figure 8–19.)

An open fan motor will let the media belt drive motor run, but the humidifier will not perform its moisturizing job. Test the fan motor windings for continuity, as in Figure 8–20, to isolate this problem. If the fan runs, but the media belt doesn't, the humidifier will not shut off and the air will remain dry. Test the media belt drive

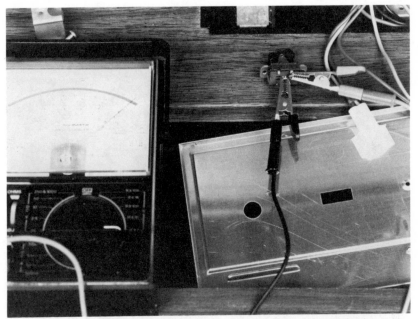

Figure 8-18 Testing the on/off rocker switch for continuity.

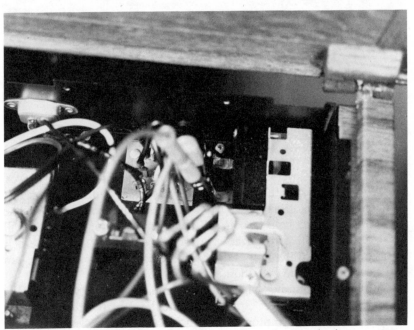

Figure 8-19 Testing the humidistat for continuity.

Figure *8-20   Testing the fan motor windings for continuity across its two terminal leads.*

motor from its humidistat terminals. Some models mount the belt drive motor within the media belt drum support structure. These units have a multipronged connector that plugs into the appliance wiring harness. (See Figure 8–21.) Test the motor windings across two of those prongs.

Have you encountered the following problem? You turn your humidifier on and everything seems to be working normally. However, it won't shut off and the air feels as dry as ever. When did you last clean the media belt? It might be clogged with mineral deposits. The belt will be wet enough, but air will not circulate through it. You will be able to see light through a clean media belt. If not, wash the belt in a solution of water and humidifier descaling chemical. You can find descaling products at most humidifier dealers.

A normally running humidifier accompanied by dry air can be caused by an empty water tank and a water-level switch that has stuck closed. Usually this symptom is caused by a corroded or rusty linkage. Remove the rear inspection panel and examine the linkage. Clean

Figure 8-21 *Testing the media-belt-drive motor windings for continuity.*

and lubricate a sticking linkage. Check to see that the media belt is actually moving, because the drive gears may not be engaging.

DEHUMIDIFIER

The dehumidifier is a refrigeration appliance. It uses a compressor to pump refrigerant through the evaporator coils, a condenser to change the refrigerant gas back to a liquid, and a motor with a fan to circulate the air. Here's how it works.

When you turn the unit on, the fan draws room air through a grill in the front of the cabinet. It spills over the compressor, the evaporator coils, and the condenser coils before it exits through a rear grill into the room. Meanwhile, the compressor pumps vaporized refrigerant through the condenser under high pressure, where cool air flowing from the evaporator changes it to a liquid. The liquid enters a capillary tube under high pressure, the diameter and length of which serve to reduce the pressure. Warm air flowing over the evaporator coils once again changes the liquid to a gas, and the cooling effect collects moisture from the air. The vapor, now hot, flows back into the compressor where the cycle continues. Moisture collected on the evaporator drips into a condensate pan located on the bottom of the chassis.

When the temperature is low, about 65° F, and the humidity high, the evaporator will ice over during the first twenty to thirty minutes of operation. Generally, the frost will melt away during the next ten minutes. Severe icing occurs at room temperatures below 65° F or when air flow is restricted by a blocked intake or dirty evaporator fins.

Many dehumidifiers use a deicer bimetal thermostat clamped tightly to the line that carries the refrigerant back to the compressor. When icing becomes heavy enough to reach the deicer control, which is located at the extreme end of the evaporator coils and is normally warm, the bimetal closes a circuit that bypasses the compressor. The compressor shuts off, but the fan continues to run. Relatively warm air circulating over the evaporator defrosts it. The deicer opens and restores the circuit to normal.

Dehumidifiers are generally dependable. Most poor performance complaints result from using a unit too small for the job, or subjecting the unit to excessive amounts of outdoor air. A dehumidifier located in a garage where the door is open a great deal of the time is a good example of the latter abuse.

When you purchase a dehumidifier, be sure to get one that is capable of dealing with your moisture problems. Shop around and solicit more than one opinion and be sure to present an accurate assessment of your dampness problems.

Insufficient air flow is another cause of poor performance. Keep your dehumidifier a respectable distance from walls, furniture, and draperies. Consult the owner's manual for distance figures. Vacuum dust and lint from the evaporator and condenser coils frequently and remember to oil the fan motor at least once a year. The compressor is sealed and needs no attention.

A low refrigerant level will keep your unit from dehumidifying as it should. If you suspect that this is the case, have a qualified refrigeration technician check it for you. One way to tell whether or not your dehumidifier is suffering from a low refrigeration level is to feel the evaporator coils. They should be uniformly cold. You can expose the evaporator by removing the sheet-metal cabinet. Look for screws along the base of the appliance. Removing these should allow you to lift the cabinet from the chassis.

When your dehumidifier won't run, begin your diagnosis with the line cord. You will find one side of the line attached to a terminal on the humidistat. The humidistat will be secured to the top, front, underside of the cabinet. In order to remove the cabinet, you will have to disconnect the two humidistat leads. (See Figure 8–22.) The other side of the line is attached to a relay terminal marked L1. Test the cord for continuity.

Figure 8-22 *You will find the humidistat behind the control knob at the top of the cabinet.*

An open overflow prevention switch will shut the appliance off in the event you forget to empty the condensate pan. You will find this switch just above the drain pan. A short to ground or a stuck actuating linkage may be keeping it open if you are having an overflow problem. If the linkage works easily, test the switch for continuity while working the linkage by hand. With your VOM leads still attached, fill the pan with water and see if the switch works normally.

To test for an open humidistat, turn the adjustment knob to its lowest setting and read across the two switch terminals, as in Figure 8–23. If you have any doubts about the relative humidity in the work area, remove the humidistat and take it to an area that you know is dry. The humidistat should read 0 or near 0 ohms at R×1. Humidistats are not field serviceable and should be replaced when they fail.

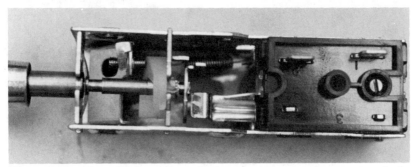

Figure 8-23   *Test the humidistat for continuity across its two terminals.*

Look for loose connectors along the internal wiring harness and test connecting wiring for continuity. A break or a short along the harness can keep the appliance from working at all. Look for any wire that might have been crimped during assembly, or one whose insulation might have been chaffed away by the compressor's vibration.

If the fan runs, but the compressor does not, first check for evaporator icing. The deicer bimetal switch may have turned the compressor off. If the coils are clear, test the deicer for continuity. A reading of 0 to a few ohms usually indicates a healthy switch.

An open compressor overload switch will keep the compressor from working while the fan runs. First try to determine the cause of the overload. Poor air circulation from a dust-covered evaporator? Not enough clearance around the appliance? Perhaps the start relay is defective? Once you are satisfied that the dehumidifier is getting sufficient air circulation, test the relay, as in Figure 8–24.

You will find the start relay located within a metal box on the side of the compressor. Test across the terminals marked "L" or "C," both of which stand for common lead, and "R" or "M," both of which stand for running windings. A good relay will indicate 0 ohms at R×100. If it reads open replace it with a manufacturer-made part. To test the starting contacts of this relay, first test across the terminals marked "L" and "S" with the relay in its correct position. Be sure

Figure 8-24 *The start relay is located to the right of the cylindrical overload protector. Refer to text for test procedure.*

that the word "top" or an arrow indicating top is indeed facing up. Your VOM should read infinity at R×100. Turn the relay upside down and test again. It should read 0 ohms. If the relay tests out, go on to the overload switch.

The overload protector switch opens the circuit to the compressor in the event of an increase in current flow that exceeds design limits, or if the temperature reaches an unsafe level. The overload switch prevents compressor winding failure that might be caused by a failure in another component, such as the start relay. When the overload switch fails it is usually open, and the compressor will not run. The switch is located on the top of the compressor case or in the metal box along with the start relay. Test across its two terminals.

Open compressor motor windings will keep the compressor from running. Test the windings for continuity from C to R and from C to S. If they read open, refer the problem to an expert. Compressors are sealed and beyond home repair. If the blower fan runs and the compressor buzzes, call an expert.

When the refrigeration system functions normally but the fan won't run, the evaporator will ice up first. If your dehumidifier ices up regularly under conditions where it operated normally before, check the fan motor. Gummy or dry bearings may be causing it to spin too slowly, thus circulating inadequate amounts of air. If the fan won't run at all, you will have to test the windings for continuity. Check for binding bearings by spinning the fan by hand. The blade should coast a while before it stops. Try oiling the bearings. In many cases that is all the motor needs. If you have to remove the fan motor for replacement, disconnect the wiring then unbolt the motor bracket from the chassis. Figure 8–25 shows how this should be done.

Figure 8-25 *In order to remove the fan motor, unbolt the motor bracket from the chassis, then remove the motor mount nuts.*

FOOD MIXER

Food mixers use a universal motor that drives the beaters through a gear train. A worm gear is cut into one end of the armature shaft. It drives two pinion gears, one on either side, in opposite directions. The gear ratio between worm and pinions is low enough to develop substantial torque relative to the motor's size and horsepower.

The armature spins in two captive ball bearings held in place by small metal clamps. An impeller fan attached to the armature shaft just behind the drive-side bearing circulates cooling air over the motor. Motor and gears fit into the molded lower half of the mixer body, and when the top half is in place the unit is sealed against any lubricant leaks.

The beater shafts are keyed at the end so that you cannot install them incorrectly. They rotate in opposite directions and have to mesh just like a pair of gears. In some mixers, the beater drive gears are held in place by retaining rings at the bottom or beater end, whereas others use the top half of the case to locate and secure the gears.

Most small portable mixers use a three-speed, motor field winding tap speed control. The different positions on the selector switch engage more or less of the field windings to vary the speed. Refer to Chapter Six for more details. The continuously variable speed control used since the mixer's commercial introduction changes speed by varying the brush position on the commutator relative to the field windings.

The brushes are mounted in insulated holders on a slotted, movable disc. The speed control handle or knob is attached to this disc. The electrical theory behind this speed control is much too complicated for our purposes. If anything goes wrong with this or one of the newer solid-state speed controls, consult an expert.

In order to service your food mixer, you will have to separate the case halves. On the underside of the mixer you will find three or more screws recessed into the case. These hold the case halves together; they may be slotted or Phillips head. (See Figure 8–26.) After removing

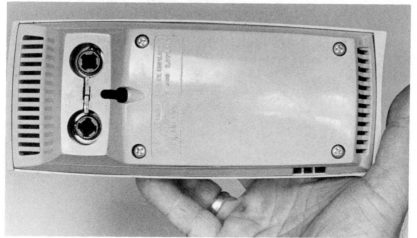

Figure 8-26 Remove four screws from the underside of the body, then separate the case halves.

these screws, carefully lift the top half of the case assembly up while gently prying along the seam with a thin-bladed screwdriver. Mixers with metal bodies usually provide a pry point along the seam. Once the top half of the case assembly is free, you will be able to see and test all electric circuits and service all of the mechanical components.

When the motor refuses to run, test the line cord for continuity. Most have removable cords. Check for terminal corrosion.

A broken brush holder or sticking brush can cause the motor to stop or to run intermittently. Remove the brush retainer and slide the brush in its holder by hand, as in Figure 8–27. It should slide freely. Often, carbon dust buildup in the holder causes the brush to stick, and the commutator wears the brush away, eventually breaking the circuit. A motor that hums but won't run is telling you that the armature is binding or that the brushes aren't making good contact.

Figure 8-27   Removing the brushes.

Inspect the brushes for wear and check the pigtails for breaks. Clean dirty or gummy bearings and apply one drop of light machine oil. (See Figure 8–28.) Open motor windings will keep the motor from running at all. Test the windings for continuity. Refer to Figure 8–29.

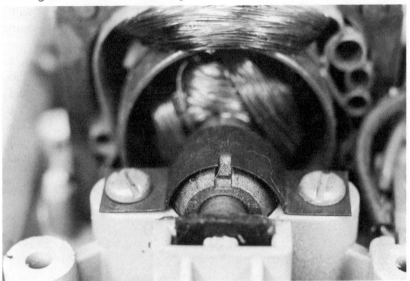

Figure 8-28   *Clean and lubricate the bearings.*

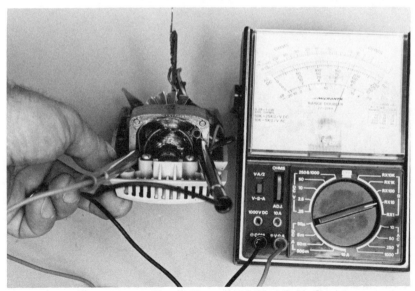

Figure 8-29   *Testing for open field coil windings.*

If a three-speed mixer runs irregularly or intermittently, dirty switch contacts as well as brush problems could be the cause. Figure 8–30 illustrates how to clean the switch contacts and check for any loose wiring. An open switch will keep the mixer from running on one or all of the speeds depending on the location of the break. Test the switch for continuity from the common lead to all others in turn, as in Figure 8–31.

Figure 8-30   *Clean dirty switch contacts.*

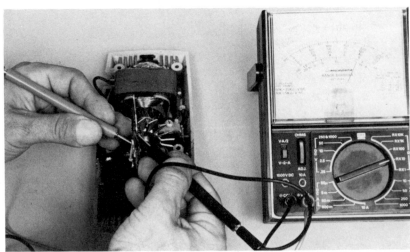

Figure 8-31   *Testing the switch for continuity.*

A food mixer gearbox problem is easy to spot and easy to repair. If the motor runs, but the beaters don't rotate, you can count on a power transmission problem. The worm gear cut into the steel armature shaft will outlast both pinion gears. In the interest of quiet running and a small degree of self-lubrication, pinion gears are made from nylon, plastic, or brass. Figure 8–32 illustrates a mixer's drive gears. In order for an all-steel gear set to run quietly and effectively, it would have to work in an oil bath. A mere oil film will not do. In order to eliminate oil-sealing problems and the extra bulk imposed by an oil sump, the makers chose the materials best suited to the application. Because the worm gear is part of the motor, the engineers wisely decided to make it the most durable component in the drive-gear assembly. A rattling noise from the mixer usually indicates worn pinion gears.

Figure 8-32 Mixer's beater drive gears. Note the timing mark at 3 o'clock on the left-hand gear.

In the early stages of wear, the pinion gear teeth become pointed and almost knife-edged; then they weaken and begin to break off. When the beaters are under load, the worm gear will slip at the point where teeth have broken off of the pinion gears. Most often, one beater will stop, and the noise generated by the other as it pushes the dead one along will tell you it's time to investigate the cause.

Removing the top half of the mixer's case assembly will let you examine the gears. Most mixers use circlips or C rings to hold the gears in place. (See Figure 8–33.) You will need a pair of circlip pliers to remove these. Figure 8–34 shows typical circlip pliers. You can purchase a simple, inexpensive pair at almost any automotive supply store. Insert the plier tips into the circlip ears, squeeze the handles together to expand the circlip, and lift it off of the shaft. Lift the pinion gear out from the top. Most gears are marked with a dot or an arrow that indicates its relationship with its neighbor. Be sure to make a note of that relationship before you remove the gear(s). The gears are not interchangeable left to right, so be sure to purchase the correct gear and to install it correctly.

Many of these gears have spiral grooves cut into their shafts to keep the lubricant that works into the bearing area returning to the gears above. Interchanging these gears left to right will change the disposition of the spiral grooves and force the lubricant out through the bottom of the shaft and onto the beaters. During disassembly, note the position of any shims or seals and be sure to replace them in their correct position, as shown in Figure 8–35. Before installing new gears, clean the area and lubricate the new gears with the maker's recommended grease.

You can maintain a mixer in excellent condition for years with a little cleaning and a drop of oil on each bearing once a year.

Figure 8-33 *Gear retaining circlip. Insert the circlip plier tips into the tiny holes in the ears.*

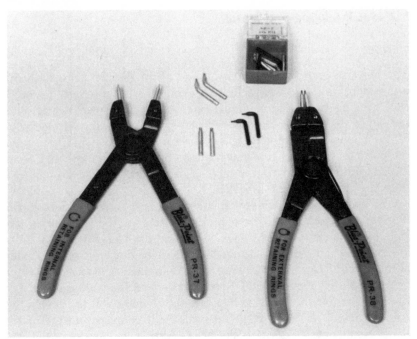

Figure 8-34   *Circlip plier set for outside and inside circlips.*

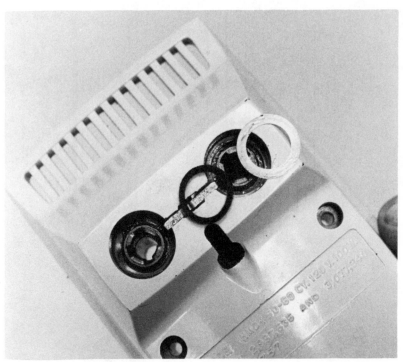

Figure 8-35   *Felt sealing washer fits under the metal thrust washer.*

BLENDER

The universal motor, speed control, and all of the blender's electrical connections are in its base. The speed control is a push-button tapped field winding type. The coupling, often made of rubber, screws onto the motor shaft with a left-hand thread. You have to turn it clockwise to unscrew it. The coupler engages the blade unit, which screws onto the bottom of the jar. This design allows the user to remove and clean the jar without disturbing the motor. The cutter unit can be removed from the jar for cleaning as well.

To diagnose and repair your blender, you have to remove a base pan or remove the outer shell from the base. Remove the jar, unplug the blender, and turn it upside down. Examine the base for screws, bolts or hex nuts. Many manufacturers hide the screws or bolts in the center of the rubber feet whereas hex nuts will be in plain sight on the bottom of the base. (See Figure 8–36.) Remove these and you will be able to lift the base pan off the blender. Blenders that require you to remove the outer shell will also require the removal of the coupler from the motor shaft. Remember to turn it clockwise. After you have removed the base screws, bolts or nuts lift the outer shell off the base.

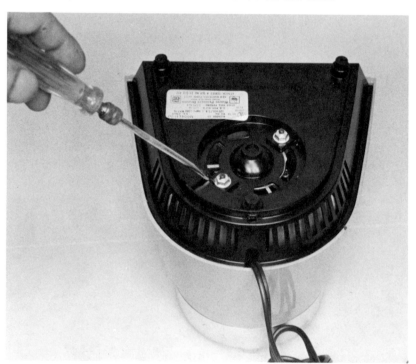

Figure 8-36 *Remove these two hex nuts and lift the base from the blender.*

When your blender refuses to run, first test the line cord. Trace the cord from its entry to its terminals. Disconnect at least one of the spade terminals before you test the cord. Figure 8–37 shows how to test the line cord for continuity.

Figure 8-37 *Testing the line cord for continuity.*

Have the brushes lost contact with the commutator? Remove the bell housing. (See Figure 8–38.) Inspect the brushes. Are they worn out? Are they sticking in the holders? Are the pigtails intact? Perhaps the commutator is open or shorted. Test it as shown in Figure 8–39.

Are the motor's field windings shorted to ground? Test them. (See Figure 8–40.) Are the field windings open? Test them. (Refer to Figure 8–41.) Does the motor hum but refuse to run? Poor brush contact will cause this symptom. Most modern motor-driven appliances have permanently lubricated motor bearings. These should never present a problem. A binding cutter blade assembly will stall the motor and make it hum. Remove the jar and run the blender. If it runs normally, the trouble is in the blades. Clean them. Look for a bent blade.

Unless the common lead fails to make contact at the switch terminal it's not likely that a multispeed push-button switch assembly will fail to operate the blender on at least one of its speeds. If the

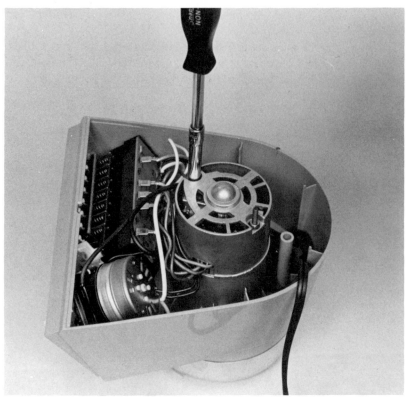
Figure 8-38   *Removing the motor bell housing.*

Figure 8-39   *Testing the armature windings through the commutator bars.*

154

Figure 8-40 Testing the field windings for short to ground.

Figure 8-41 Testing for open field windings at the brush terminals.

blender refuses to work on one or more speeds, test the switch assembly for continuity. A wiring diagram is a must for quick diagnosis here. Without one, you have to test across combinations of terminals until you find the open pair. Test from the common and all of the others in turn until you find the open switch, as in Figure 8–42. One open set means that you will have to replace the entire unit.

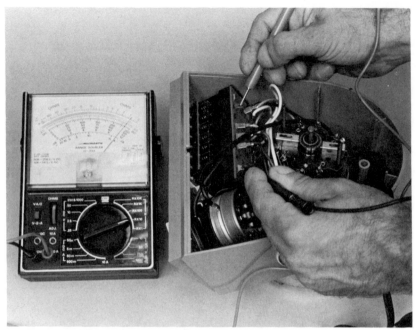

Figure 8-42   *Testing the switch for continuity.*

When your blender loses power and cannot cope with those jobs it normally performed easily, check the blade assembly for sticky buildup. If you keep the blade assembly clean, then perhaps the brushes are worn or the commutator is dirty. Unusual noises from the blender are usually caused by loose or bent cutter blades.

You can repair a leaking blender jar with new gaskets. Remember to keep the cutter assembly and the coupler clean.

ELECTRIC KNIFE

A universal motor with a worm gear, similar to that found in the food mixer, machined into the armature shaft turns a single pinion gear. Studs molded into the nylon pinion one on either side engage holes in the knife blade sockets. The disposition of the studs converts the motor's rotation into a back and forth motion of one blade against the other and results in the cutting action. (See Figure 8–43.) A rivet joins the two blades at their leading edges. The blades are matched and rippled for neat, efficient cutting.

Many cord type as well as cordless rechargeable knives use a tiny dc universal motor. A diode that acts as an electrical check valve by

Figure 8-43 *Off center spindles convert clockwise motor rotation to forth and back blade motion.*

permitting current to flow in only one direction converts ac to dc in the plug-in models. The control switch is a simple spring-loaded on/off push-button or slide that needs constant pressure to keep the circuit closed. It's a safety switch that shuts the knife off if you drop it during use. The motor bearings are made from oil-impregnated sintered metal and never need lubricating.

You can disassemble your electric knife for inspection and testing by removing three or more screws from the body. The top half of the body will lift off easily. Figure 8–44 shows how to remove the top of the case. Drive gears are usually housed in a metal case held together with two screws or a single spring clip. With the exception of cordless knives and the diode in cord models, electrical testing for the motor, cord, and related components is exactly the same as that discussed in the food-mixer section. Refer to universal motors in Chapter Six for more details.

The diode is a small black box connected in series with the line cord and motor. In order to test the diode, set your VOM at R×100 and read across the terminals. Reverse the leads and read again. If you failed to get a reading in either direction, the diode is open. If you get a reading in both directions, the diode is shorted internally. Either

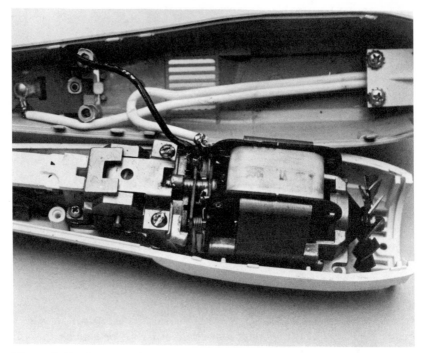

Figure 8-44 *Remove the top case half to expose the motor and drive gear assembly.*

fault means replacement. A healthy diode should read low in one direction and high in the other.

The knife's on/off switch is the simplest type available. A movable contact made either from copper with a silver point or a sheet of copper alone is attached to the push button. A stationary contact is attached to the switch body. When you push the button, the contacts engage with a wiping action that helps keep them clean. If your knife won't run, test the switch for continuity, as shown in Figure 8–45. Dirty contacts or bent contact blades can keep the switch from closing the circuit. Clean and straighten.

In the gearbox, the pinion gear that rides in support notches cut into the gear case sits atop the worm gear. A light, all purpose grease lubricates the gears. A worn-out pinion gear will keep the blades from reciprocating. A binding pinion gear shaft will keep the blades from working. A loose gear-to-shaft joint will keep the blades from working. Remove the gear cover and examine the system. Severe binding in the gear train or between the blades will overload the motor and eventually burn out the windings. If the blades won't stay locked

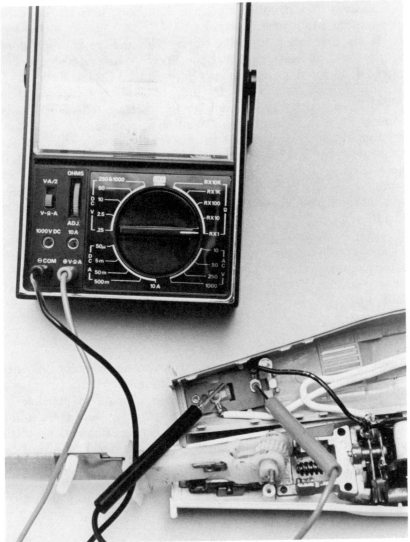

Figure 8-45 Testing the on/off switch for continuity.

into the sockets, they are probably worn out. You will have to replace the pinion-gear–blade-socket assembly.

Cordless knives suffer the same problems as cord types. They do not have a diode, because a battery of nickel-cadmium dry cells supplies direct current. When you are making an electrical test with power on, note that the positive wiring is red and the negative wiring is black. You have to connect your VOM accordingly, because direct current flows from negative to positive. Continuity tests can be made without regard to current direction.

If you have just charged the battery pack and the knife performs poorly, check to make sure that the dry cells have accepted a full charge. Find the charging terminals on the back of the knife housing. The dry cells are connected across these terminals. Set your VOM to 10VDC and attach the test leads to the charging terminals. Always connect negative to negative and positive to positive.

Run the knife and take a voltage reading. You should get 5.7 volts. If it drops below 4, charge the battery pack overnight. If it doesn't come up to full capacity after the overnight charge, one or more of the dry cells is dead, or nearly so. When this happens, you should replace the entire pack, especially if it is three or more months old.

Take good care of the knife blades. Do not drop the knife on the blades or try to use them for any purpose other than the one for which they were designed. Bent blades are a constant source of grief, and an unnecessary one. Keep the knife clean, and keep the gear drive assembly lubricated.

CAN OPENER

Electric can openers are powered by small shaded-pole motors. A series of gears multiplies the motor's limited starting torque and power to a usable amount. The opening mechanism is identical in principle to that found on manual can openers. The switch is located under the locking handle and is engaged by a cast-in handle extension or a small plastic button attached to the handle. Cutting tension is regulated by a spring-loaded screw located to the right of the cutting assembly. It is usually marked "keep screw tight." If it comes loose, the can will rotate without being cut. The cutting assembly on most can openers can be removed for cleaning by removing the aforementioned screw and its mate on the left.

The cutter–drive gear assembly is riveted in place. If anything goes wrong with it, you will have to replace the can opener or send it back to the manufacturer for repairs. In cases where parts are not easily removed, the maker does not offer them as spare parts for replacement.

An open line cord, switch, or motor windings will keep the can opener from working at all. You can expose the cord terminals and switch by removing four screws from the bottom panel (Figure 8–46), one screw from the top rear (Figure 8–47), and two screws from inside the base (Figure 8–48). Remove the front panel, and the motor will come with it (Figure 8–49).

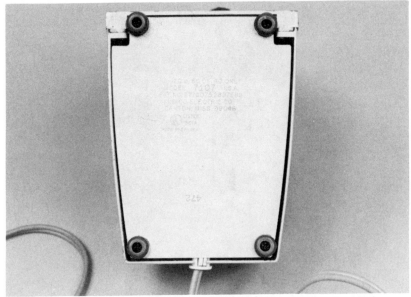

Figure 8-46 *Remove the screws from the bottom panel.*

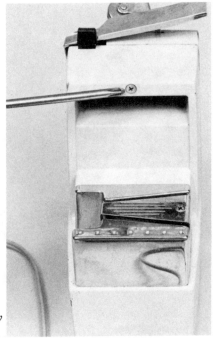

Figure 8-47 *Remove one screw from the back.*

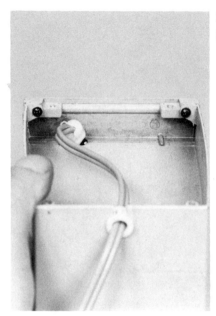

Figure 8-48 *Remove two screws from the front inside bottom.*

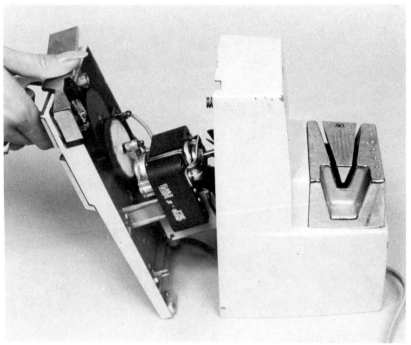

Figure 8-49 *Removing the working part of the can opener.*

You will find the line cord terminals near the motor. One side is attached to the switch and the other side is attached to one of the motor leads. Test the cord for continuity, as in Figure 8–50. Disconnect the motor and line cord leads from the switch and test them for continuity across those two terminals. Be sure to push the switch button in. (Refer to Figure 8–51.) Test the motor windings across its two leads, as in Figure 8–52. If you find the motor windings open, you might want to compare the price of a new motor with the price of a new can opener before you commit yourself to repairing your old can opener.

If you discover any gear problems with a can opener that is out of warranty, buy a new one. The drive gear assembly is not home serviceable. Keep the motor bearings and the cutting assembly clean. When the cutting assembly wears out, you can replace the individual components by removing the screws from the center of each. Be sure to note the position of any washers and replace them in the correct sequence.

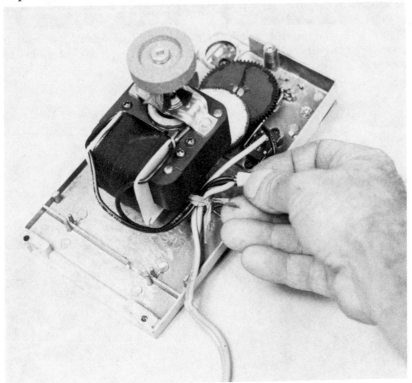

Figure 8-50 *Disconnect the wire nut terminal and disconnect the other side of the line from the switch before testing for continuity.*

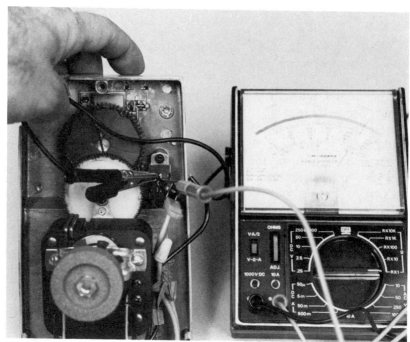

Figure 8-51 *Testing the switch for continuity. Technician's forefinger is activating the switch. You can see the linkage just off 1 o'clock from the top gear.*

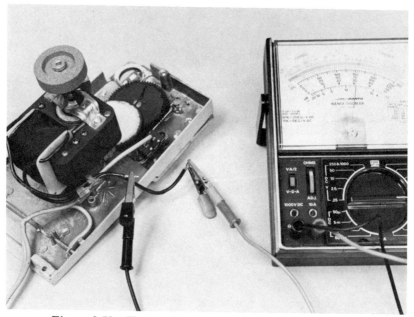

Figure 8-52 *Testing the motor windings for continuity.*

VACUUM CLEANER

A large universal motor powers both upright and canister vacuum cleaners. Many canister vacuums have power attachments driven by a small universal motor located in the beater bar head. The motor drives the beater bar assembly through a conventional V-belt. A modified squirrel cage or impeller blower fan moves a large volume of air over the motor and out the exhaust. On upright vacuum cleaners, the exhaust empties into a porous catch bag that is designed to pass air and hold the dust.

In tank-type or canister cleaners, the exhaust is sometimes located at the base of the unit and the catch bag above the motor. The fan draws air from the room through a hose, creating a vacuum that draws in dirt and debris. The term "suction" is a misnomer of sorts, but it will get the point across adequately.

Uprights such as the Hoover Convertible have a spindle protruding from the impeller blower. A large O ring running in the spindle groove is stretched over the beater bar–brush drum with a twist. The vertically mounted motor rotates clockwise and transmits its power through the twisted belt to the horizontally mounted beater bar. (See Figure 8–53.) The beater bar rotates forward. Engineers chose the O-ring drive because it works more efficiently and longer with a twist than would a conventional V-belt.

The vacuum cleaner's most common enemy is the dirt that it was designed to remove from your home. Overfull catch bags, dirty filters located between the bag cavity and the motor on canisters, clogged hoses and other air passages act individually or in concert to disable your vacuum cleaner. When any one or all of these ills attacks your vacuum, it will cause the motor to labor. The underpowered motor will leave bits of lint and other particles on your carpet that it once willingly ingested.

Carpet fibers, hairs, pieces of string, and other longish debris wind around the belt-drive spindle and the drum bearings, causing the belt to slip and the drum to bind. A toothpick, a couple of broom straws, or a hair pin may lodge sideways in the canister's pick-up hose and collect a mass of lint and clog the hose. A long broom handle works well to remove clogs from the hose. Check the canister cleaner's air filter. You should replace it at least once a year. When did you last empty the catch bag?

Open switches and line cords and broken or slipping belts are common vacuum-cleaner ills. Keep debris out of the beater bar bearings and out of the belt-to-spindle contact. Check the belt periodically for wear. Generally, the belt will crack or shed bits of rubber before it breaks.

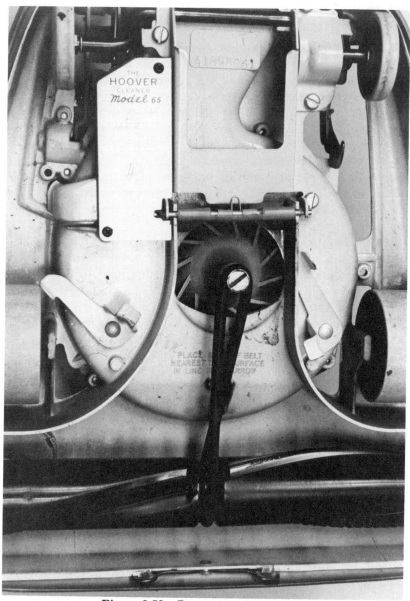

Figure 8-53   Beater bar drive belt.

How many times do we run over the line cord, trod on it, bend it around furniture, and tug on it in order to reach that last square foot of carpet? How often do we yank on the cord to remove the plug from the wall outlet? Be kind to the cord. An open line cord will keep the motor from running. If the motor dies and restarts as you push and pull the vacuum cleaner, the core is broken at some point along the cord and is opening and closing the circuit. In order to test for the latter symptom, turn the vacuum cleaner on, then move along the cord, bending and twisting it until you find the spot that stops the cleaner. If it is close to the handle or the plug, simply remove the broken section and reconnect the cord to the switch or the plug. The cords on many vacuums have molded-in strain relievers at the handle. If a break occurs just below that point, do not reuse the cord without a strain reliever.

To reach the cord terminals for replacement or testing, remove the switch plate first, as in Figure 8–54. Disconnect the cord or attach a jumper wire across its terminals and test it for continuity.

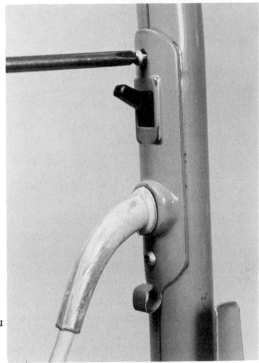

Figure 8-54 *Remove two screws and then the switch plate to expose the line cord terminals.*

On/off switches in most upright cleaners will be slide or toggle type, and they are not usually repairable. Pitted contacts, a broken actuating spring, and loose or corroded terminals will lead to an open switch. Switches are secured to the handle either by an outer plate that presses the switch body against a rubber bumper inside the handle, or by screws that tap into a switch flange. Removing the two screws

Figure 8-55 Test the switch from the line cord terminal on the left side (facing the switch) to the lower terminal on the right (two leads attached).

will allow you to remove the switch. Test the switch for continuity. (See Figure 8–55.) Replace it if it reads open. Space limitations on most cleaners demand that you replace the switch with an exact duplicate.

If your vacuum cleaner suffers from motor trouble, refer to universal motors in Chapter Six for diagnosis and repair. In order to expose the motor in your upright for inspection and testing, remove the cover that forms the second layer of the body. On the Hoover, this cover is secured to the body by two screws located on the underside of the frame. Four screws located around the perimeter of the plastic act to hold the motor and housing assembly to the chassis. Loosening these will let you lift the motor, complete with impeller, out of the chassis.

You will find one brush holder on either side of the upper, plastic motor housing. The right-side holder has an additional plastic cover protecting it. Removing a single retaining screw will let you take the

Figure 8-56 *Remove the terminal screw to release the brush.*

cover off. (See Figure 8–56.) A copper brush retaining plate transmits current to the brush pigtail through a single screw terminal. The brush receives current through a brass pick-up button and a stranded copper pigtail. The pigtail is concentric with the brush tension spring. Removing the terminal screws allows you to remove the brushes for inspection.

Hoover uses sintered, metallic, oil-impregnated motor bearings that require no maintenance In fact, the top bearing plate states "do not lubricate." If the bearings should fail, you will have to take the motor assembly to a qualified repair shop because complete disassembly requires special tools. If you discover open motor windings, the same thing applies.

A small stone, a hair pin, or a chip of firewood hidden in the carpet pile and scooped up by your upright can wedge itself between the impeller and frame and stop the motor dead. It will make an awful racket beforehand. In many cases you can retrieve the object by turning the vacuum cleaner upside down and rotating the impeller counterclockwise by hand with the drive belt disconnected and the cleaner unplugged. If this method fails, try loosening the motor mount bolts and moving the motor–impeller assembly to one side or the other.

Canister vacuums without a power beater bar attachment are very simple. You have only the motor, wiring, and air system to contend with. The motor is usually mounted to the lid or top third of the unit. Off-center mousetrap-type clamps secure it to the body. You have to remove this section in order to change or clean the catch bag.

An open cord, open switch, or open motor windings will keep the canister model from working. Switches may be located on the top (toggle) or on the bottom (foot operated). Generally, you can remove foot-operated switches by loosening a pair of screws on the side or the underside of the body. Test for continuity. You will find the line cord terminals there as well.

In order to expose top-mounted switches, you will have to remove the top-most cover. Turn the lid–motor assembly upside down and remove all visible screws from around the motor, as in Figure 8–57. Turn it upright and remove the top piece. From there, you can test both the switch (see Figure 8–58), and the line cord.

Canisters with retractable cords present another problem. Electrical contact is made through a pair of slip rings on the top of the reel. If these get dirty, they will not conduct. Dirt can work its way into the

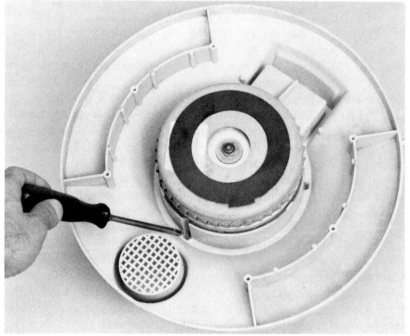

Figure 8-57   *Remove four screws from around the motor cavity to release the switch housing.*

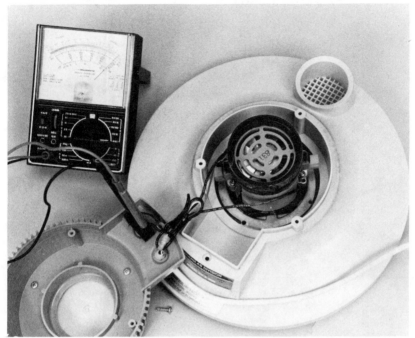

Figure 8-58 Testing the switch for continuity.

reel and make it bind. The rewind spring can break. In both cases, the cord will not retract. You can expose the reel by removing the base of the canister. Look for screws around the side or on the underside of the base section.

ELECTRIC BROOM

These are simple, light-weight upright vacuum cleaners. They do not use a beater bar or have any hose attachments. They do have a small universal motor, an impeller, and either a plastic catch tank or a reusable cloth catch bag. They are designed for quick light cleaning and do not have enough power to remove dirt from pile carpeting. These share all of the electrical problems associated with large upright vacuums—open line cords and switches (Figure 8–59), clogs and jammed impellers (Figure 8–60), worn out brushes (Figure 8–61), and shorted or open armatures (Figure 8–62). Worn-out gaskets around the motor housing can coat the windings with dirt, causing the motor to overheat and burn up its windings. Keep your electric broom clean. Empty the catch bag often.

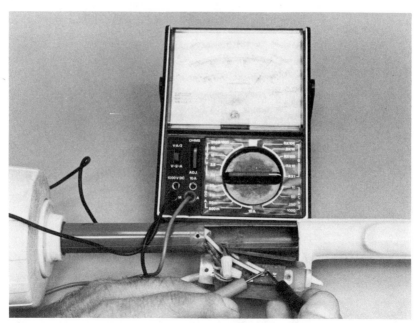

Figure 8-59   *Test the switch for continuity.*

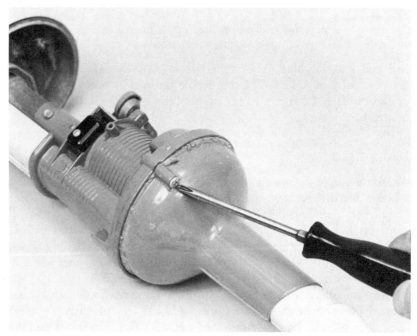

Figure 8-60   *Remove two screws and lower the bottom half of the motor housing to expose the impeller. Dust around the seam indicates a leaking gasket.*

Figure 8-61 *Checking the brushes for wear.*

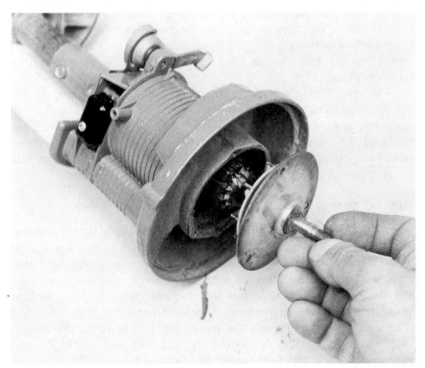

Figure 8-62 *Remove the large hex nut from the motor shaft, pry the impeller off, then remove screws around the perimeter of the bell housing to remove the armature.*

FLOOR POLISHER

Figure 8–63 shows a typical floor polisher. Home floor polishers use a universal motor with a worm gear cut into each end of the armature shaft. Each worm gear drives a large pinion gear to which a socket is attached. The sockets hold scrubbing brushes or buffing pads. The pinions are driven in opposite directions, and the gear ratio is designed to multiply the motor's torque while reducing speed at the scrubbing brushes.

The motor and drive gears are attached to the base plate of most floor polishers. In order to remove the base plate, you have to remove the handle first. You will find one or two retaining screws on the outside of the handle socket or a single nut at the base of the socket. With the handle off, turn the unit on its top and look for screws around the perimeter of the base. Removing these will free the base from the motor cover and expose all of the electrical and mechanical components. From this vantage point you will be able to service the motor brushes, commutator, bearings, terminals, and drive gears.

The drive and driven gears are similar in design to the ones found in food mixers, and they are prone to the same kinds of failures. If you use your floor polisher a lot, you should check the gear system at least once a year for signs of wear. Clean and relubricate the gear train once every couple of years.

The on/off switch is located in the handle and is similar to the one in your upright vacuum cleaner. Removing a switch plate will allow you to expose the switch terminals so that you can test the line cord and the switch for continuity. You can test the switch-to-motor connecting wiring from the switch-to-motor terminals. Refer to universal motors in Chapter Six for diagnosis and repair details.

ELECTRIC SHAVER

Some shavers, such as Norelco and Sunbeam Shave Master use a tiny dc universal motor with a diode to rectify ac to dc. Most other shavers use a vibrator motor. In these, a coil produces a magnetic field that attracts a tiny spring-loaded armature. At the height of the armature's arc, the spring load overpowers the magnetic force and returns the armature to its original position. The cycle continues and the action is extremely rapid. Although the movement is very small, it's enough to do the job. A linkage carries the finger that engages the blades and moves them back and forth under the shaving head.

These motors are not self-starting. When you plug the shaver cord into the wall outlet, you have to start it running with a thumb wheel usually located on the side of the shaver. It's a mechanical switch.

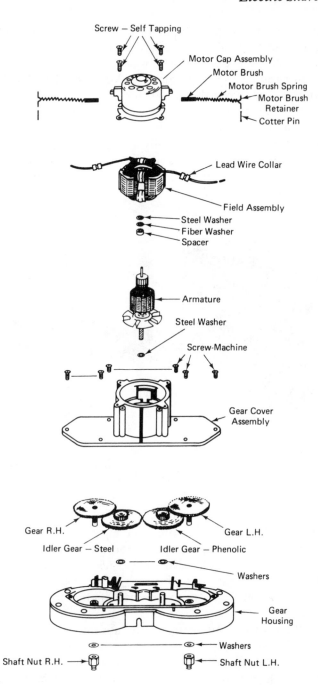

Figure 8-63 *A typical floor polisher/scrubber. This has a vertically mounted motor and two sets of gears.*

One of the most common causes of total failure or intermittent running is corrosion at the shaver's cord terminals. The socket is usually recessed and dirt and electrical corrosion build up and go unnoticed. A thorough cleaning usually restores good contact. Test the line cord for continuity when your shaver will not run.

A speed selector switch that changes connections to the field coil is used on most vibrator shavers. If it malfunctions, you will have to open the shaver by removing the tiny screws in the body. (See Figure 8–64.) Test the speed selector switch from its common terminal to the others in turn. You can test the motor windings from the switch terminals as well.

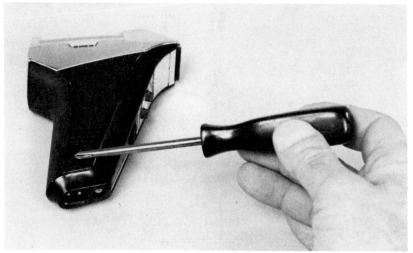

Figure 8-64 *Remove the screws from the body and separate the case halves.*

Universal-motor-powered shavers offer more home repair possibilities than vibrator types. Inspecting and replacing brushes is an easy and important job. To expose the motor, you have to separate the case halves. Refer to Figures 8–64 and 8–65. Brush tension is maintained by a single hairpin spring for each brush. Move it up and aside, then remove the brush. Refer to universal motors in Chapter Six for more details.

The motor bearings are permanently lubricated and will run longer than you will own the shaver. If the shaver fails to run on any speed, test the cord, examine the sockets (male and female) for corrosion, test the single-speed switch, brush contact, and field windings as Figure 8–66 shows. Keep the shaving head clean and check the brushes once a year.

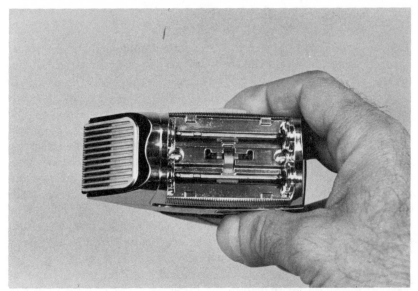

Figure 8-65 *Remove two screws from the shaving head and lift it clear of the case halves before you separate them.*

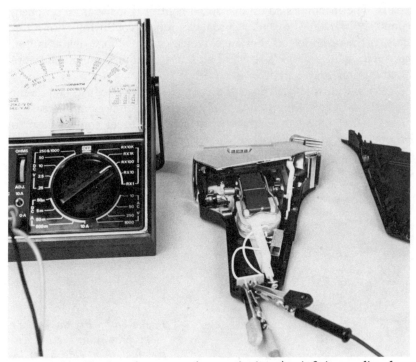

Figure 8-66 *Testing the system for continuity. An infinity reading here means further investigation.*

Cordless shavers use sealed, direct-current motors that have to be returned to the factory or taken to one of the maker's service centers for repair.

SEWING MACHINE

Sewing machines are precision tools designed to help you make or repair clothing and other cloth items. Technology has taken the sewing machine from a mere helper to a super-sophisticated and complex electronic wizard that does everything but cut the cloth. The more electronic solid-state gadgetry your machine has, the less you should consider servicing it at home. Aside from adjusting thread tension, changing a belt, or lubricating some exposed parts or any other operation covered in the owner's manual, leave it alone.

Even on simpler machines, you should not tamper with timing belts, shafts, and gears that form the mechanical bits referred to as the head. Never tamper with any part of the zig-zag mechanism. Problems with these components should be referred to a factory-trained mechanic.

We will confine our discussion to a few simple electrical tests and repairs. The machine's adjustable speed control is made from an open, wound resistance wire and a pedal-controlled conducting arm. Depressing the pedal lowers resistance, increases the voltage to the motor, and increases the motor's speed. The latest machines use a solid-state speed control that cannot be serviced at home.

Dirt and dust collected on the contact area can reduce or prevent conductivity. Open the speed-control box and brush away any dirt. (See Figure 8–67.) Clean the surface with television tuner contact cleaner. An open line from the plug to the speed control and from the speed control to the motor can keep your machine from running. Isolate the lines and test them for continuity, as Figure 8–68 shows.

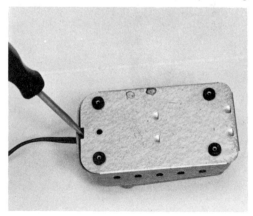

Figure 8-67 Pry the bottom plate away from the line entry side; then slide it off. A little WD-40 sprayed on the tracks will make it easier.

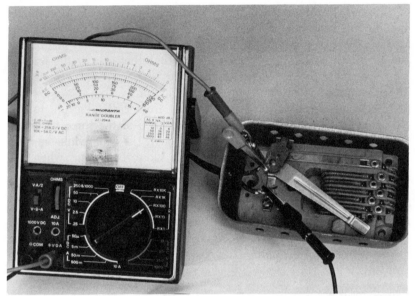

Figure 8-68   *Testing the line from the speed control to the machine.*

The easiest way to test the resistance windings in the speed control is to open the box and disconnect the lines from the terminals. Test across the terminals while you depress the pedal. Refer to Figure 8–69.

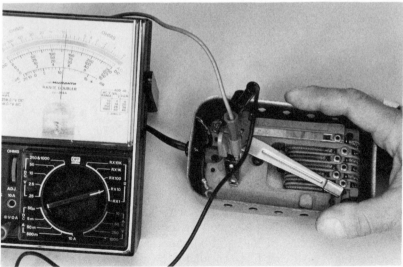

Figure 8-69   *Testing the speed control for continuity.*

To test a three-terminal speed control, set your VOM at R×1, then unplug the line from the wall outlet and the line from the machine. One of the terminals is connected directly to one side of the line all the time, another is connected to the other side of the line all the time and supplies current to the light, the third receives current from the speed control and supplies the motor.

To isolate the two line terminals, test from each plug pin to the terminal. After you have determined which two of the three terminals belong to the line, test the third one through the plug while pushing the pedal down. The control should read close to 0 ohms when the pedal is fully depressed.

To test the motor as a unit for continuity, connect your VOM leads to the common terminal and the motor terminal. You will find these terminals in a terminal box hidden either inside an access panel at the rear of the machine or beneath the machine base plate. The speed-control wire plugs into this box. Figure 8–70 shows how to perform this test.

Figure 8-70   Testing the motor windings for continuity from the terminal box.

If you find an open circuit when you test from the terminal box, open the motor and test further. (See Figure 8–71.) Refer to the universal motors section in Chapter Six for diagnosis and repair details.

When attempting to cope with any mechanical problems that your machine might give you, first consult the owner's manual for information concerning use, care, and adjustment. Most often the machine

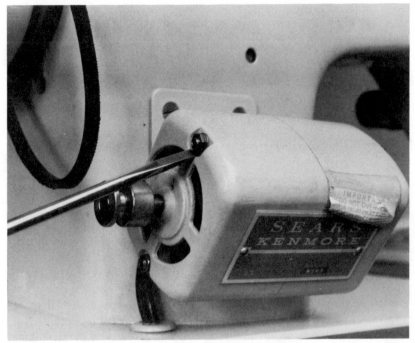

Figure 8-71 *Chisel the name plate rivet head off with a small sharp chisel. Remove two nuts and separate the motor case halves.*

just isn't sewing well, and the owner's manual will tell you how to correct the faults.

Inspect the shuttle and race assembly located under the machine below the sewing head for lint and dust. Some of these come apart by releasing two spring clips, and others are machined as a unit and do not come apart. Before reassembling the unit, lubricate the race with a number two lead pencil. Carbon acts as a lubricant and will not attract dust.

Always watch for bent needles. Keep the area around the material feed dog free from lint. Consult your owner's manual regularly for information about belt, clutch, and presser foot adjustment, and for motor lubrication. The manufacturers know best, and if you follow their instructions to the letter your sewing machine will give you years of trouble-free service.

Chapter 9

Large Appliances

Don't let large appliances confuse and frighten you. With the exception of timers in automatic clothes washers, dryers, and dishwashers, large appliances are very much like smaller ones. Many of them require more voltage than we have dealt with so far, but because you have developed safe work habits, you needn't fear the extra voltage.

More often than not the size of these appliances will prove to be less hindrance and more help than you had anticipated. For one thing, you have more working room. Those components tend to be stronger and more forgiving if you make a mistake. These appliances are, of course, a great deal more complicated than their smaller brothers, but after you have examined the belts, gears, motors, switches, timers, and so on individually, they are quite simple.

AIR CONDITIONER

Air conditioners cool, dehumidify, circulate, and filter room air. It's a marvelous device that many of us have come to depend on. With proper care, modern air conditioners perform for many years without needing attention from a refrigeration expert. Problems that can and do occur are related to, in order of frequency, air circulation, electricity, and refrigeration.

Air-circulation problems almost always result from neglect. A clogged filter or dirt buildup on the evaporator coils and fins keeps the evaporator from removing enough heat to cause the condensation necessary to keep the refrigeration system working. Once the coils and filter have been cleaned, there are two simple tests that you can perform to determine whether or not the refrigeration system is working properly.

Turn the air conditioner on and set it for maximum cool. Let it run for about 10 minutes, then hold a thermometer in the cool air flow and note the reading. Give the thermometer a minute or so to stabilize. Now, take a second reading at the inlet grill. This reading should give a temperature about 20° F warmer than the first.

Again, with the air conditioner running on maximum cool, cover the inlet grill with a blanket and leave it there for at least 2 minutes. Turn the unit off, remove the front panel and grillwork, and look at the evaporator coils. They should be evenly frosted over. If your air conditioner fails to respond to either of these tests, ask a refrigeration expert to test the system for you.

Room air conditioners are fairly complex when viewed as a unit, but the components we are dealing with are simple. The electrical system contains a three-wire polarized line cord and plug; a four-position switch with settings for off, low, medium, and high; an adjustable thermostat generally calibrated in numbers instead of degrees; a wiring harness to the motor or motors depending upon the size of the unit; and the compressor motor, which is sealed and beyond our discussion. For a lesson in basic refrigeration principles, refer to the refrigerators section later in this chapter.

When your air conditioner refuses to run on any setting, first check other electrical items on that line to see if they work or test the outlet for voltage. Your air conditioner may have blown a fuse or tripped a circuit breaker. Some room air conditioners draw as much as 15 amps and should be connected to a line of their own. In some homes, units that draw 12 amps cannot be plugged into a line shared with another appliance.

If you found voltage at the receptacle, you should next test the line cord for continuity. On most room air conditioners, you will find the cord terminals behind the switch panel. First remove all of the knobs from the panel. Look for screws around the panel edges and remove those. In some cases, you will have to remove the entire front grillwork assembly to expose the switch panel's mounting screws. Grillwork assemblies may be secured to the cabinet with screws or merely clipped into place. (See Figure 9-1.) Remove the switch panel frontispiece (Figure 9-2), then remove the panel assembly (Figure 9-3). If the panel proves stubborn, don't force it. Examine it more carefully to find what might be holding it in place.

Trace the cord from its entry into the air conditioner body until you find the correct terminals. Disconnect the cord and test it at R×1. When you buy a new cord, be sure that you tell the salesperson your

Figure 9-1 Pry the plastic grillwork assembly out from the metal cabinet and pull away.

air conditioner's make, model, cooling capacity, ampere draw, and voltage rating.

Air conditioners are wired so that the compressor won't run without the fan. Air circulation over the evaporator coils keeps them from icing, and circulation over the condenser coils keeps them from overheating. The thermostat uses a "fan only" setting to bypass the compressor and complete a circuit from the line cord through the three-speed switch to the fan motor. Used in conjunction with another switch marked "fan on" or "automatic," the system allows you to run the fan continuously with or without the compressor. When the fan selector switch is set on "automatic," the thermostat controls both the fan and compressor.

Figure 9-2 *Remove the thermostat control knob and lift the frontis-piece from the switch panel.*

In most room air conditioners, the switches are wired to allow the fan and three-speed selector switch to keep the unit from working when either fails. Test the three-speed switch across its common lead and one or all of the others in turn. (See Figure 9–4.) Refer to Figure 9–9 (p. 191) for fan mode switch test.

Figure 9-3 *Remove 2-¼-in. hex bolts from the switch panel. Pull it away from the chassis to expose the switch terminals.*

Most smaller room air conditioners rely on one motor with two fans for air circulation. A squirrel-cage blower attached to one end of the motor shaft circulates cool air into the room, and a ringed three-, four-, or six-bladed fan circulates air over the condenser coils. Large room air conditioners use a separate motor and fan for each function. The ring attached to the outside edges of the condenser fan blades picks water up from the condensate pan and sprays it over the hot condenser coils. The water helps cool the condenser and virtually eliminates the need for a separate condensate drain.

The most obvious symptom of fan motor, switch, or wiring failure is a quiet air conditioner and a warm room. Inside the air conditioner, the evaporator coils ice up and then the overload protector shuts

Figure 9-4 Testing the three-speed switch.

the compressor off. Before you open the unit up, try another switch position. If the fan runs on one or both of the remaining speeds, then you know that the switch or connecting wiring for one speed has failed. If the three-speed switch has failed, you will have to replace it. Refer to switch panel removal discussed earlier.

If the fan refuses to run on any speed setting, you should test the fan switch (look ahead to Figure 9-9, p. 191), the fan motor windings, and the run capacitor. Remove the air conditioner's cabinet. Loosening all of the ¼-in. hex head bolts from the cabinet will allow you to lift it clear of the chassis and expose the entire electrical and refrigeration system. (See Figure 9-5.)

The long, silver, oval-shaped cylinder with a forest of terminals is the run capacitor. (Refer to Figure 9-10, p. 192.) Trace the fan motor wires to the capacitor, disconnect the leads, and test across them for motor-winding continuity. If you wish to test the capacitor, discharge it as explained in Chapter Six, but only across the terminals to which the fan motor connects. Once again, refer to Chapter Six, capacitor start motors, for this test.

The air conditioner's thermostat will be either a capillary-tube or air-temperature-sensing unit. The capillary-tube thermostat's sensing

Figure 9-5 Note the location of the cabinet retaining bolts.

bulb will be mounted near the evaporator coil at the end farthest away from where the refrigerant enters the coils. Remove the bulb and warm it with your hand while testing for continuity across its two terminals. Refer to the capillary-tube thermostat discussion in Chapter Four for more details. If the trouble was with cooling, you should place the sensing bulb in ice water while testing for continuity. This test should yield a reading of infinity or open thermostat contacts.

Many smaller room air conditioners control the cooling cycle with an air-temperature-sensing bimetal thermostat. Air passing through a grill in the switch panel passes directly over the bimetal. It is not as accurate as the capillary-tube thermostat, but certainly adequate for the less-expensive air conditioners. Figure 9–6 illustrates how this type of thermostat operates.

If you want to test the thermostat throughout its working range, disconnect the three wires from the terminals, as Figure 9–7 shows, and remove the unit by loosening two ¼-in. hex bolts. Figure 9–6 shows where these are usually located. Turn the knob to maximum cool and place the unit in the cold air exiting from your freezer's fan.

Figure 9-6   *Thermostat mounting bolts. The grill at right allows air to flow over the bimetal.*

Figure 9-7   *Thermostat terminals. Test for continuity from each of the two nearest the technician's hand to the common terminal at the right corner of the unit.*

189

Figure 9-8   Testing thermostat for continuity.

You should be able to hear the contacts snap open. To be sure, test for continuity. Next, warm the unit with a hair dryer and listen for the contacts snapping closed. The first continuity test should result in a reading of infinity, the second 0 ohms.

Compressor shutdown, whether it is caused by open windings, start capacitor, run capacitor, overload protector, or thermostat will allow the fans to run, but the unit will not cool. We've discussed the thermostat, so let's look at the compressor and its related components.

Both the start capacitor and the overload switch are located on the outside of the compressor case. You can test and replace them without disturbing the compressor's internal parts. Room air conditioners built

after 1960 use an oil-filled capacitor to start the compressor. It eliminates the relay while improving power output and efficiency.

You will find the starting capacitor located on the side of the
sealed compressor housing, and it will probably be the only component
in that area. Discharge it and test it with your VOM set to R×100 or
R×1000. Defective capacitors usually have swollen or blistered cases.
Replace the capacitor with the maker's recommended part and be sure
to wire it correctly.

You will find the compressor overload protector mounted atop the
housing. It is an enclosed bimetal disc that senses the compressor
operating temperature and opens the circuit when the temperature
gets too high. A compressor will overheat when the conditioner's filter
is clogged, when the evaporator coils are covered in dust, when the fan
motor bearings begin to dry out and prevent the fan from circulating
adequate amounts of air, when the fan switch fails, or when the fan
motor windings fail. If the compressor shuts off and won't restart, you
have to investigate all of these possibilities. Refer to Figure 9–9 for
fan switch test. Test the fan motor windings from the run capacitor
terminals, as shown in Figure 9–10. Once you are satisfied that everything else is working correctly, remove the overload protector and test
across its two terminals for continuity.

*Figure 9-9   Testing the fan mode switch. Test across the middle terminal
and each side terminal in turn.*

Figure 9-10   *Testing the compressor windings from the run capacitor terminal board.*

Of course, if everything in the system but the compressor motor tests out to be good, test the compressor motor windings from the run capacitor terminals. (Figure 9–10.) If they read open, contact an air conditioner specialist to confirm your diagnosis.

Short cycling, where the compressor starts, then stops almost immediately thereafter, can, on rare occasions, have nothing to do with the overload protector switch. A shorted run or start capacitor can cause this symptom. In most cases, a shorted capacitor won't allow the compressor to run at all, but you can't really dismiss the possibility that it might cause short cycling.

The thermostat can cause short cycling as well. Rough handling could dislodge the sensing bulb from its normal position. If it settles too near the evaporator coils, the compressor will short cycle. Shorted compressor motor windings can also cause short cycling. Test for shorts to ground from both winding leads to the compressor body.

Room air conditioners should be installed in the window with a slight incline away from the sill. The incline keeps the water in the condensate pan deepest at the end where the condenser fan slinger ring can scoop it up. Units with condensate drain hoses have them located at the extreme outside corner of the cabinet. In case of leaks into the room, use a carpenter's level to check the incline. Examine the drain hole and hose for clogs.

To avoid minor, but sufficiently annoying problems, keep your filter clean, vacuum dust from the evaporator coils and fins, and oil the fan motor at least once a season. Handle your air conditioner carefully when installing and removing it from the window. Be alert for voltage drops in your neighborhood, because allowing the compressor to run at voltage less than 10 percent of that required by the manufacturer can damage it.

AUTOMATIC CLOTHES DRYER

Both electric and gas automatic clothes dryers use a combination of heat, air flow, and tumbling action to remove moisture from your clothing. A blower driven by a belt or directly off of the motor shaft circulates air over an open-coil heating element or a gas-fired heat exchanger. From there, air enters the tumbler drum cavity through a large hole or port. The entire system is sealed in a heater box.

Air circulates around and through the clothing from dozens of small holes in the drum's circumference or from a single large port cut into the stationary rear cavity panel. (See Figure 9–11.) One finds the second inlet system in dryers that use a double open-ended tumbler and a Poly-V-belt drive. Air eventually exits the tumbler through a lint filter into a duct system that opens to the atmosphere outside the house.

The tumbler drive mechanism determines whether your dryer uses a perforated or solid wall drum. Perforated tumbler drums look like large, porcelain-coated metal baskets with a bearing at the bottom center. This bearing supports the rear of the tumbler. Rollers or a Delrin bearing support the front. A motor mounted at the bottom rear section of the dryer chassis drives the tumbler through a conventional V-belt-and-pulley system. An idler pulley maintains proper belt tension.

Solid-wall tumblers are open at both ends, rotate on rubber rollers front and rear, or rollers and a Delrin bearing. They are driven by a Poly-V-belt that wraps around the outside circumference of the drum. Facing the front of the dryer and tracing the belt's path clockwise from the motor, you will see that it leaves the motor pulley, continues four-fifths of the way around the drum, cuts back to the right and around the idler pulley in a counterclockwise direction, then loops around the motor pulley in a clockwise direction. The drum is sealed at both ends by flexible seals.

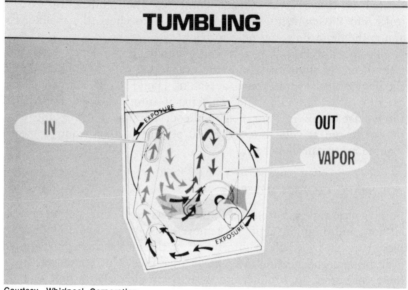

Courtesy, Whirlpool Corporation

Figure 9-11 *Note the air flow direction and the inlet and exhaust ports. The dryer's tumbling action exposes more of the clothing surface area to the heated air.*

Symptoms usually associated with slipping drive belts include slow drying because of slower than required tumbler speed, and a chirping noise. Severe slipping or a broken belt will keep the tumbler from rotating at all. Belt problems are fairly common and easy to repair. If your dryer has a solid-wall tumbler with a single large inlet port in the back panel, it is a Poly-V-belt-drive model.

To change this belt you will have to raise the top panel (see Figure 9–12), and remove the entire front panel complete with door. Look for retaining screws around the outer edges. If you find none or only a couple, you can assume that the panel is held in place with clips only or clips and screws. Raise the top. Most will be supported at the rear by a pair of hinges. You can support the top in its vertical position with a 36-in. chain that has a S hook on both ends, or place a pad over the top and rest it against the wall. (See Figure 9–13.)

The front panel will be held to the dryer cabinet with either screws or clips or both. Figure 9–14 shows how to remove the front panel. Once the front panel is free of the cabinet, you should look for the door safety switch wiring harness. You may have to remove it from retaining clips in order to move the panel out of your way. (Refer to Figure 9–15.) Now you are ready to change the belt.

Figure 9-12 Remove two screws from under the lint screen lid. Using a knife, release the front lock clips and raise the top.
Courtesy, Whirlpool Corporation

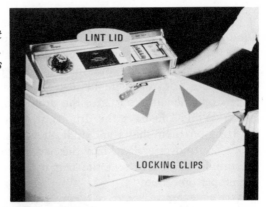

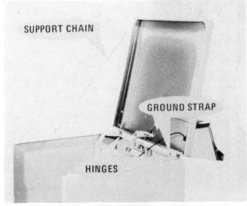

Figure 9-13 Supporting the top.
Courtesy, Whirlpool Corporation

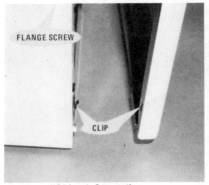

Courtesy, Whirlpool Corporation

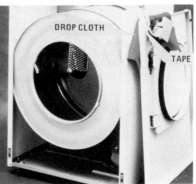

Courtesy, Whirlpool Corporation

Figure 9-14 Remove the front panel. Two screws hold the top of the panel to the side flange. Spring clips near the bottom of the panel slip into slots in the side panel flanges.

Figure 9-15 Getting the front panel out of the way. Place a pad between the dryer cabinet and front panel to protect them.

You will find the motor and idler pulley in the lower right-hand side of the cabinet. Push the idler pulley up and to the right to ease the belt tension, then slip the belt from that pulley. Remove the belt from the motor pulley, and then lift the drum out of the cabinet through the front. You might have to spread the sides a little. Some makers provide cutouts to give the drum proper clearance. (See Figure 9–16.) While you have the drum out, check to see that the pulleys are tight on their shafts and that they spin freely. Be sure the idler pulley arm moves easily. Place the new belt over the drum and install the drum. Be sure to seat the rear drum seal. Figure 9–17 illustrates the proper procedure.

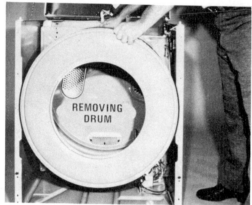

Figure 9-16 *Removing the tumbler drum for belt service.*
Courtesy, Whirlpool Corporation

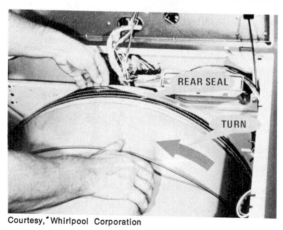

Courtesy, Whirlpool Corporation

Figure 9-17 *When replacing the drum, be sure to install the belt first with the grooves down. Rest the drum on the support rollers, connect the belt to the motor pulley, replace the front panel. Raise the drum to engage the Delrin ring and front bearings. Turn the drum counterclockwise to check that the drum seal is seated all around.*

Dryers with perforated drums usually have the motor mounted at the bottom left-hand side of the chassis in the rear of the machine. Removing the rear inspection panel will expose the drive system. Many of these units employ a third belt to drive the blower. You will find a small pulley on the motor shaft, a large idler pulley with another small one riding piggyback, and a large pulley on the tumbler. You will also find one belt running between the motor and large idler and another belt running from the small idler to the large drum pulley. The pulleys are arranged in this manner so that the idler assembly maintains tension on both belts.

To remove either belt, start the belt slipping up over the lip of the small pulley. Keep tension at that point with one hand while you rotate the large pulley associated with that belt. The belt should walk up over the small pulley and hang free after about three-fourths of a revolution. When installing the new one, place the belt over the large pulley first. Start working it over the lip of the small pulley and hold pressure there while you rotate the large pulley. The belt should walk into the pulley groove. If you have to replace worn or broken belts in your dryer, make sure that you buy the correct size and type.

Dry tumbler drum bearings will contribute to slipping and prematurely worn belts. The center sleeve or roller bearing on models with perforated drums is lubricated at the factory and permanently sealed. Rubber rollers and Delrin bearings should be kept clean.

In many cases, poor drying performance results from obstructed air passages. A clogged lint filter is the most frequent cause. Be sure to clean the lint filter before every load. It is not likely that any other part of the dryer exhaust system will clog from normal use.

A timer working with a thermostat controls the drying cycle. The simplest of timers uses one or two cams, a motor plus escapement or gear train, and two contact arms. Selecting the drying time turns the machine on while a thermostat cycles the heating element on and off. During the last ten minutes, the timer opens the heating-element circuit but keeps the tumbler going for the cool-down cycle. Figure 9–18 shows a timer in operation.

Synthetic fabrics and the simple desire to market a more sophisticated machine led engineers to develop more versatile and complicated timers. A fixed-temperature, single-pole, double-throw thermostat located in the exhaust duct is connected in series with the timer and heating element. This type of thermostat has a contact point on both sides of a bimetal disc that snaps from one position to another. The action prevents arcing at the points. When the bimetal snaps away from the heating element contact, it engages the timer motor contact. Figure 9–19 illustrates this type of thermostat.

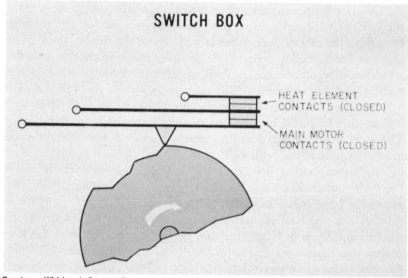

SWITCH BOX

HEAT ELEMENT
CONTACTS (CLOSED)

MAIN MOTOR
CONTACTS (CLOSED)

Courtesy, Whirlpool Corporation

Figure 9-18   *The cam has forced the cam follower up and energized circuits to the heating element and main motor.*

FIXED THERMOSTAT

Figure 9-19   *A typical fixed-temperature thermostat. You would test for continuity across the two terminals.*
Courtesy, Whirlpool Corporation

One or the other component is activated at a time; when the element is off, the timer motor runs; when the timer motor isn't running, the element heats. A short-duration timer and this thermostat establish an automatic time–temperature relationship.

Here's how it works. The thermostat, sensing the temperature of the exhaust air, turns the heating element or gas burner on when you push the start switch. At this point, the thermostat controls the dryer, and the timer motor remains idle. Clothing is dampest early in the cycle, and as the moist heated air flows through the exhaust, evaporation keeps it relatively cool. However, as the clothes dry, so does the air. Without the cooling effect evaporation provides, the exhaust air warms up. The thermostat senses the change and snaps the heating element circuit open and starts the timer motor.

The timer advances a little, and the exhaust temperature decreases. Once again, the thermostat closes the heating element circuit and opens the timer circuit. Increasingly dry and warm exhaust air shortens the heating element cycle and increases the time the timer motor runs. Finally the timer advances far enough to override the thermostat. With the thermostat out of the system, the timer runs through the cooldown stage, then shuts the machine off.

Electronic control is the latest innovation in automatic dryers. It uses the wet clothing to complete a circuit across tiny copper contacts attached to metal bands in the drum, or a single moisture sensor secured to the rear wall of the drum cavity. As the clothing drys, its resistance to electrical conductivity increases until it can no longer complete a circuit or until it is unable to stimulate the sensor. A fixed-temperature thermostat regulates the heat, and a rapid-advance timer controls the timed drying cycle.

Both conventional and rapid-advance synchronous motor timers are reasonably easy to test. Usually, when your machine shows no signs of life (no lights, no humming), you will find the timer switch contacts open. If your dryer has a dual-cycle timer, turn the knob to the other setting. If the dryer responds to this test and runs normally, you can suspect that the contacts for the first cycle are open.

To expose the timing mechanism, turn the machine off, unplug it, and remove the control panel. Four screws, two on each side, secure the panel to the end caps. On some Whirlpool models, you have to remove the tumbler speed selector knob as well. (See Figure 9–20.) There are some brands that permit access to the controls through an inspection panel on the back of the control console. Consult the wiring diagram to find which of the timer terminals you should test across. If your test confirms the open timer contacts diagnosis, you will have to replace the switch box. Service people agree that disassembling and cleaning the switch assembly is only a temporary repair at best. Figure 9–21 shows a dryer timer.

The push to start switch is one of the dryer's safety features. The operator must push it at the beginning of the cycle and at any time after the cycle has been interrupted. Pushing it closes the circuit to the motor through a set of contacts in the centrifugal switch. When the motor reaches its top speed, these contacts open, and, at the same instant, another set closes, completing a circuit from the timer to the

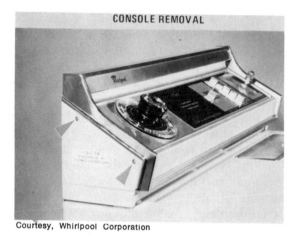

Courtesy, Whirlpool Corporation

Figure 9-20   *Removing two screws from each end cap and removing the drum speed selector knob will allow you to tilt the Whirlpool dryer's control console forward for service.*

Figure 9-21   Dryer timer. The wiring diagram will show you which terminals to test across when diagnosing a completely lifeless dryer.
Courtesy, Whirlpool Corporation

motor. The second contact set remains closed until the drying cycle ends.

When you have engaged the push to start button contacts and the dryer responds with a lighted control panel but no tumbling, you will probably find the contacts open. Unplug the machine, remove the control panel, and find the switch terminals. (See Figure 9-22.) Disconnect the wires and test across the two terminals while holding the button in.

You can't do anything to repair an electronic timer, but you can perform simple running tests. Start an empty dryer with the timer set to its shortest cycle. It should run for about 15 minutes. If it runs

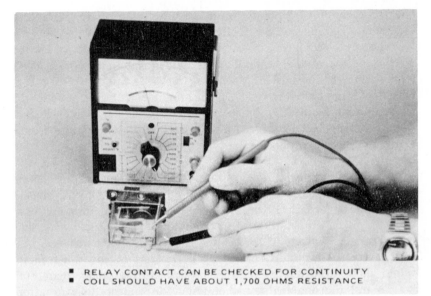

RELAY CONTACT CAN BE CHECKED FOR CONTINUITY
COIL SHOULD HAVE ABOUT 1,700 OHMS RESISTANCE

Courtesy, Whirlpool Corporation

Figure 9-22 *Testing the push to start switch. A coil holds the contacts closed when it is energized. Resistance equals about 1700 ohms.*

substantially longer, perhaps 18 or 19 minutes, unplug the machine and remove the rear panel. Find the wires that complete the circuit to the sensors or feelers. Disconnect them and tape the bare ends for insulation. Plug the dryer in and repeat the running test. If the machine shuts off within 12 to 15 minutes, there is a short somewhere in the sensing system. If your machine uses feelers in the drum, look for anything made of metal—foil from a chewing gum wrapper, paper clip, hair pin—that may have been trapped or wedged in contact with one of the feelers. If your machine uses a moisture sensor, look for shorts to ground in the circuit.

If the dryer runs longer than 15 minutes with the sensor system disconnected, the problem is in the control. Perhaps the timer motor is open or the escapement is binding. When everything else checks out to your satisfaction, call a service technician and ask him or her to test the electronic switching device. Before calling in a professional, check to see that your dryer has a good solid ground to a cold-water line. Electronically controlled dryers need this additional ground to complete circuits in the control system.

Most dryers have at least two thermostats, an operating and a safety. The operating thermostat is either an adjustable capillary-tube type (refer to Chapter 4) or a single-pole, double-throw unit described on p. 197. Whirlpool uses three fixed-temperature thermostats one for each of three temperature settings. Both thermostat types locate their sensing portions in the exhaust air flow.

The safety thermostat is a fixed-temperature bimetal device located on the outside of the heater box. It is identical to the other fixed-temperature thermostats in design and operating principles. It is connected in series with the timer and heating element and protects the element from overheating by interrupting the circuit to the element when a broken belt or clogged air passage allows temperature to rise above a safe limit. An open safety thermostat will keep the dryer from heating.

The operating thermostat controls most dryers from the beginning of the cycle to cool down when the timer takes over. An open operating thermostat of either type will keep the dryer from running. Since these are used with short-duration timers on dryers without electronic controls, open contacts to the heating element would produce no heat and a very short running cycle. Open contacts to the timer motor would allow the dryer to overheat and activate the safety thermostat.

To test the double-throw thermostat, disconnect the wires from the thermostat's terminals. Touch your VOM leads, one to each termininal, and note the reading. (See Figure 9–23). For location of thermostats your meter should read 0 ohms at room temperature. You can also test the fixed temperature thermostats by using the following procedure. Empty your dryer, clean the lint screen, and disconnect the exhaust duct from the back of the dryer at the fan housing. Disconnect all of the thermostats except the one that you want to test. Tape the leads from the disconnected thermostats to prevent a short to ground. Turn the dryer on and let it run until the thermostat that you

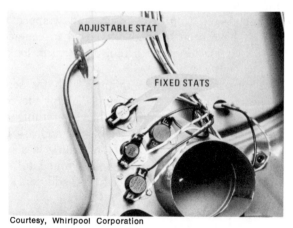

Figure **9-23** *Operating thermostats are located in the blower housing. The adjustable thermostat is shown here to illustrate its position. The dryers do not use both types of operating thermostats in the same machine.*

are testing cycles at least once. Using a thermometer that is calibrated to read temperatures accurately from 100 to 300 degrees Fahrenheit, read the exhaust temperature at the center of the exhaust outlet. You should read a figure plus or minus ten percent of the temperature stamped on the thermostat body. Figures outside these guidelines indicates a defective thermostat. The safety thermostat, tested in the same way, should yield a reading of 0 ohms at room temperature.

The capillary-tube operating thermostat locates its sensing tube in the exhaust duct, and you will find the bellows and switch-box terminals located behind the control panel. An overheating dryer might be caused by a heavy lint deposit on the thermostat's sensing bulb or stuck contacts. If you want to clean the sensing bulb, remove the blower housing, as in Figure 9–24. You can heat the sensing bulb with a hair dryer when testing the bellows and contact action. Remember that the electrical connections for this thermostat are located behind the control panel.

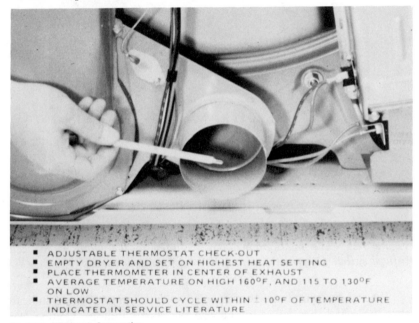

- ADJUSTABLE THERMOSTAT CHECK-OUT
- EMPTY DRYER AND SET ON HIGHEST HEAT SETTING
- PLACE THERMOMETER IN CENTER OF EXHAUST
- AVERAGE TEMPERATURE ON HIGH 160°F, AND 115 TO 130°F ON LOW
- THERMOSTAT SHOULD CYCLE WITHIN ± 10°F OF TEMPERATURE INDICATED IN SERVICE LITERATURE

Courtesy, Whirlpool Corporation

Figure 9–24 *Additional test for adjustable thermostat. Remove the thermostat sensing bulb for cleaning or test heating by loosening the two mounting screws above and to the right of the technician's hand.*

The motor's centrifugal switch serves a dual purpose in electric dryers. It opens the circuit to the start windings in the split-phase motor when it reaches 80 percent of top speed, and at the same time closes an additional set of contacts completing a circuit to the heating element. Dryers use a 5600-watt heating element (over 24 amps), and when you add the load imposed by the motor start windings, the 30-amp circuit doesn't have much chance of survival. Removing the heating element from the circuit while the motor starts protects the circuit. If the motor doesn't start, the heating element won't be energized either. The system provides a safety back-up.

When the machine lights up but won't run or make a sound, you have a symptom often associated with an open centrifugal switch. The switch is attached to the motor housing, usually on the pulley side. Depending on the working space in that area, you may or may not be able to test it while it's inside the machine. (See Figure 9–25.) Most makers provide color-coded spade terminals on the switch to prevent any wiring errors. Consult the wiring diagram to find which of the terminals you should test across. Replace the switch if it reads open.

DRIVE MOTOR ASSEMBLY

Courtesy, Whirlpool Corporation

Figure 9-25   *The multiterminal box mounted to the motor is the centrifugal switch. Consult the wiring diagram for test terminals.*

The above symptoms accompanied by a humming sound indicate that the switch has failed to energize the start windings. Contact corrosion is usually the cause of this failure, and you can test it as described earlier. Most switches will read 0 ohms or show a small amount of resistance. Midscale or near-infinity readings indicate a faulty switch.

The centrifugal switch may be responsible for a dryer whose motor runs but whose heating element produces no heat. The contacts that energize the heating element may be open. Remove the switch and hold the running contacts closed while testing it with your VOM. Buy a new switch if it reads open.

Many electric dryers use relays to complete the circuit to the heating element. The heavy-duty relay contacts can handle the element's current needs much better than the comparatively flimsy timer contacts. The relay is actually a solenoid with one movable and one stationary contact. When the solenoid receives current from the timer or thermostat, the electromagnetic action closes the contacts and completes the circuit.

An open relay means a cold dryer. You will find the relay mounted on the inside of the control console. Locate the two small leads from the relay and test across them on one of the higher VOM scales. An infinity reading indicates an open relay.

Your dryer heats through an open coil or enclosed element. The open coil is most common, and is like the ones discussed in Chapter Five. Despite the heavier gauge nichrome wire, the element will suffer the same failures associated with lighter ones. When the heating element fails, the dryer will not heat. The heater box is mounted to the back of the dryer's inside cabinet behind the inspection panel. You will be able to test the element for continuity across its terminals, which protrude from the bottom of the heater box. Refer to Figure 9–26. Test for ground from each terminal to the dryer chassis. Touch your probe to an unpainted section or scratch away paint from a small area. Grounded elements usually result from sagging or a broken insulator.

Other factors contributing to early element failure include re-

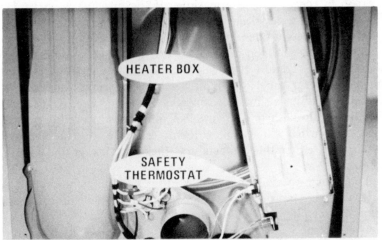

■ ELEMENT MOUNTED VERTICALLY IN HEATER BOX
■ SAFETY THERMOSTAT MOUNTED AT BOTTOM OF HEATER BOX
  ON ELECTRIC DRYERS

Courtesy, Whirlpool Corporation

Figure 9-26 Heating element terminals are located at the lower left corner of the heater box just under the safety thermostat.

stricted air flow and subsequent overheating, defective door and/or drum seals that permit air to enter directly into the drum without circulating over the element, slow turning blowers resulting from dry motor bearings, or a slipping belt. When you find heating-element failure, be sure to investigate these possible causes before you begin using the dryer on a regular basis.

If you study the wiring diagram located inside the rear inspection panel, you will discover that the motor and lights are connected from one side of the line to the neutral or ground. Only the heating element is connected across both hot sides. When the dryer runs but will not heat, check the fuse box or circuit breaker. When one of the fuses blows, the dryer is left with only its 115-volt circuit.

It is important to check the voltage supplied by your 230-volt, single-phase line. Remove the fuses that control the dryer. Set your VOM at 250 volts ac and insert the probes into the dryer's receptacle. Replace the fuses and note the reading. You should read 230 volts plus or minus 10 percent. Once again remove the fuses. Insert one of the probes into a hot slot and the other into the neutral slot. You are looking for 115 volts plus or minus 10 percent. Repeat the test for the other side of the line. Higher or lower readings outside of these guidelines indicate a problem with your power source. Low voltage will damage the motor windings if the condition persists for some time. If you discover higher than normal voltage, call the electric company. If your dryer blows fuses regularly, it might be a good idea to have an expert in to check the entire machine. If the machine is not at fault, call in a qualified electrician to examine your house wiring.

All dryers have a safety switch that shuts the unit off when anyone opens the door. An open door safety switch will keep the dryer from running at all. To test the switch for continuity, you may have to remove the front panel. On most machines, however, you can reach the switch terminals simply by opening the door. Test for continuity with the button pushed in. Figure 9–27 illustrates a door safety switch. A defective switch will also allow the dryer to run with the door open. In this case, either the contacts are stuck together or the button is binding.

Poor drying performance results from a washing machine whose spin cycle is leaving the clothes too wet, poor air circulation caused by a clogged lint filter, a slipping blower drive belt, and loose or broken drum and door seals. In these cases, with the possible exception of badly leaking door and drum seals that cause overheating, the dryer appears to be working normally.

Lint-filter assemblies are sealed against leaks into the main cabinet and exhaust ducting. It takes a massive amount of lint to clog the

Figure 9-27   Door safety switch. Test for continuity across the two terminals.
Courtesy, Whirlpool Corporation

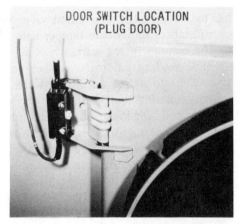

DOOR SWITCH LOCATION
(PLUG DOOR)

exhaust system, but a leak into the cabinet can cause motor failure. Lint circulating around inside the cabinet will eventually find its way to the motor where it will coat the windings. When this happens, the motor heats up and burns out. Remember to keep the thermostat sensing bulb lint free.

When you find it necessary to replace any electrical components, be sure the connections are clean and tight. Discolored terminals indicate excessive heat and/or arcing. Polish or replace them. When you replace wiring, select the same gauge and quality. To be extra safe, always run an extra ground to a cold-water pipe even if your machine doesn't require it. Always follow the maker's instructions for care and use.

AUTOMATIC CLOTHES WASHER

Your automatic clothes washer is probably the most complicated appliance in the house and it, more than any other appliance, demands that you become familiar with its variety of whirrs, clicks, thumps, and sloshes. You would be surprised at the large number of service calls that serve no purpose other than to explain that the machine is operating normally. This is especially true with first-time owners and new machines. Reading the instruction manual would have avoided unnecessary service calls.

Despite the machine's complexity, you will find many failures easy to repair. At other times, that complexity can and will render you helpless. In either case, you should understand how the washer works, so that when trouble strikes, you can deal with it yourself or explain it clearly to the service representative. Remember that time is money, and if you can save the service representative's time by directing him or her to the problem, you might save yourself a few dollars. Under no circumstances should you tamper with a machine that is still protected by the manufacturer's warranty.

The modern automatic washer uses three distinct but interacting systems to do its job, electrical, water, and mechanical. The electrical system contains a cycle-selector switch, a timer, water-temperature selector and solenoids, fill switch, lid switch, and drive motor. The water system contains a variety of hoses, inlet valves, perhaps a reuse valve, water pump, filters, dispensers, etc. Mechanical components include a gearbox to drive the drum and agitator, belts, bearings, and the tub.

When you engage your washer's timer for a normal cycle, a cam closes contacts and completes a circuit through the water-level switch to a temperature-control switch. Depending on the setting, the temperature-control switch opens hot, cold, or both inlet valves through a solenoid. During the fill stage, the water-level switch controls the machine. As the water rises to the prescribed level, air or water pressure acting through a tube forces the water-level switch diaphragm open. The series circuit to the inlet valves is interrupted and the solenoids release their plungers, stopping the water flow. Some machines use a timed fill based on average water-pressure figures.

When the water-level switch breaks the circuit to the temperature switch, it completes a circuit through the timer to the drive motor. The machine begins to run and the timer advances. A second cam engages another set of contacts that energize the agitate cam bar solenoid. This washing cycle lasts from 2 to 14 minutes, depending on the user's selection. (See Figure 9–28.) Instead of the solenoid and cam bar used by Whirlpool and Sears, some makers have chosen to reverse the motor direction to achieve the agitate or spin stages.

The water pump on Whirlpool machines runs as long as the drive motor runs. Pump direction, whether inlet or drain, is controlled by a flapper valve set into position by the agitator cam bar acting through a control lever and connecting rod. Figure 9–29 illustrates the drain cycle. The pump-out cycle begins when the number two timer cam opens the circuit to the agitator cam solenoid, which in turn disengages the agitator gears and moves the flapper valve into the drain position.

The number one timer cam opens the first circuit to keep the machine from refilling, while a third cam engages another set of contacts that keeps the circuit to the drive motor activated. The new circuit bypasses the water-level switch and the water-temperature control switch. Machines that employ motor reversal for the spin cycle generally arrive at pump flow direction through a coupler attached directly to the motor shaft; when the motor reverses for spin, the pump reverses as well.

Figure 9-28 Power from the motor runs the main drive pulley mounted on the pinion gear. When the agitator solenoid plunger and cam bar are activated, linkage in the gear case engages the agitator shaft to the oscillating sector gear.
Courtesy, Whirlpool Corporation

Figure 9-29 Drain cycle.
Courtesy, Whirlpool Corporation

A brief spin period with four spray rinses follows. The bypass circuit established by cam three remains engaged while a fourth cam closes a set of contacts and energizes the spin solenoid. This solenoid engages a second cam bar, allowing the clutch to rotate the tub at about 600 rpm. Cam one energizes the water level and temperature switches four times to allow brief spray rinses.

The cycle described above repeats for the rinse portion of the complete cycle. Agitation lasts only a couple of minutes during rinse, and the final spin lasts longer than the first. If it sounds complicated, that's because it is. You should find it easier to understand why I suggested that you spend a little time listening to and watching your machine. Once you have become familiar with your machine's cycles and accompanying sounds, you might be able to recognize a change that indicates impending failure.

The first step in repairing a complicated machine leads to isolating the system at fault. After you have done that, you can begin troubleshooting to isolate the faulty part. Despite the washer's complexity, it is merely a collection of fairly simple devices working in concert to produce a total effect.

Before discussing symptoms, causes, and repairs, I should warn you: *Do not tamper with the gearbox and drive clutch assemblies.* Clearances are critical and work on these components requires a variety of special tools. Another point—each manufacturer has its own ideas about washer design, both mechanically and cosmetically. The symptoms, causes, and repairs discussed here are general, with specific brand references inserted to alert you to the fact that your machine might be a little different. A little thought should allow you to apply this knowledge to most machines.

When the tub won't fill up, ask yourself, did someone turn off the inlet faucets? No? Then how about the filters? At each hose coupling, you will find a fine nylon screen whose job it is to remove any particles from the water before it enters the intricate inlet valve. If you live in an area where the water contains many minerals, you should remove and clean these filters frequently. Figure 9–30 shows dirty inlet-valve screens. You might find tiny particles and/or a slimy film on the filter. In many cases, the debris and slime will stop the water flow. Clean the filters with a stiff-bristled tooth brush, holding them under running water. If you can't get them completely clean, buy new filters.

WATER PROBLEMS

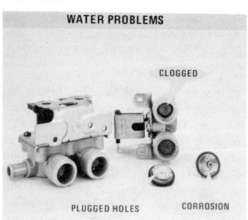

CLOGGED

PLUGGED HOLES   CORROSION

Figure 9-30 Clogged inlet-valve screens. Minute particles of sand can plug bleed holes. Corrosion and hard-water scale jam the armature in the copper guide. These problems result in water-won't-shut-off and no-water symptoms.
Courtesy, Whirlpool Corporation

If the filters are clean and your washer won't fill with water, listen for a low buzz coming from the area where the feed pipes attach. No sound indicates an electrical problem somewhere between the control console and the solenoid. The buzzing sound indicates a mechanical problem inside the inlet valve—usually a stuck solenoid plunger. In either case, you will have to open the machine's cabinet and find the inlet valve.

Unplug the machine and open the top of the cabinet. On some models, all that you have to do is pull forward and up at the front to release the top from its retaining clips. On others, you will have to remove at least two screws from the rear of the panel along the sides, lift up in back, and pull forward. Still another method is shown in Figure 9-31. You will find the inlet valve at the back of the machine under the control console.

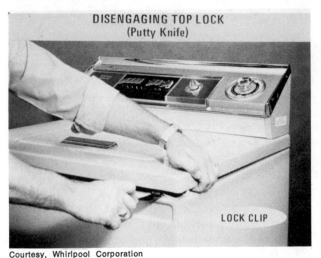

Courtesy, Whirlpool Corporation

Figure 9-31 Removing the top panel from a Whirlpool "X" model machine.

Solenoids operate the water inlet valves. Electric current flowing through a coil generates a magnetic field that raises a plunger inside the valve. Water pressure actually opens the port. When the current is interrupted, the magnetic force is also, and a spring load seats the plunger, shutting off the water supply. Depending on the number of water-temperature options your machine provides, it will have one, two, or three solenoids.

Each solenoid has two terminals and two wires attached to them with spade connectors. Remove these wires and test across the terminals, as Figure 9-32 shows. Test from each terminal to the solenoid body for ground. When either test proves the solenoid faulty, replace it with a new one from the manufacturer's parts store. If your tests show no failures, you will have to investigate further.

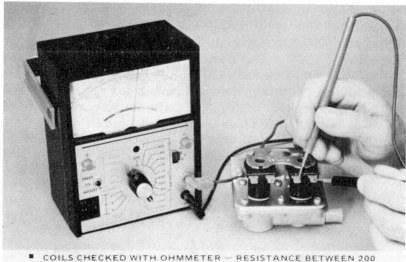

- COILS CHECKED WITH OHMMETER — RESISTANCE BETWEEN 200 & 700 OHMS
- INTERMITTENT COILS SHOULD BE OPERATED WITH TEST CORD TO ALLOW COIL TO HEAT UP AND SEPARATE BROKEN COIL WIRE

Courtesy, Whirlpool Corporation

Figure 9-32   Testing the inlet valve solenoid coil for continuity.

First, find the wiring diagram—it's glued either to the inside or the outside of the rear inspection panel. You are looking for the fill, float, or water-level switch. Remember that this little item controls the machine during the fill stage, and if it's open the machine will not fill up. Remove the control console and locate the level switch. (See Figure 9–33.) It usually has a clear plastic tube attached to it. With the wires disconnected, test for continuity, as Figure 9–34 shows.

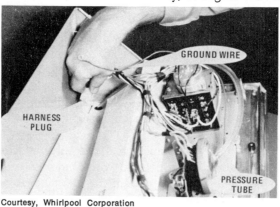

GROUND WIRE

HARNESS PLUG

PRESSURE TUBE

Courtesy, Whirlpool Corporation

Figure 9-33   The fill switch is located at the end of the plastic pressure tube. It has three terminals.

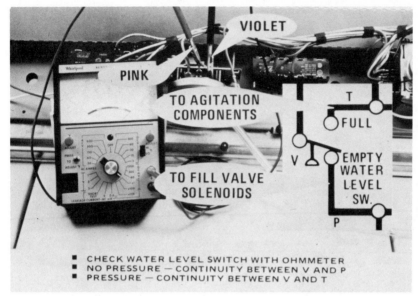

VIOLET

PINK

TO AGITATION
COMPONENTS

T

FULL

V

EMPTY
WATER
LEVEL
SW.

TO FILL VALVE
SOLENOIDS

P

- CHECK WATER LEVEL SWITCH WITH OHMMETER
- NO PRESSURE — CONTINUITY BETWEEN V AND P
- PRESSURE — CONTINUITY BETWEEN V AND T

Courtesy, Whirlpool Corporation

Figure 9-34   *Testing the pressure or fill switch.*

Should you find nothing wrong with the water-level switch, your next step is to test the water-temperature switch. Remove the control console and locate the switch. This switch uses three sets of contacts to achieve five water temperature combinations. Consult the wiring diagram to help you find the color code for the contacts involved in your selection when the tub refuses to fill. Disconnect those wires and test across the terminals. (See Figure 9–35.)

Good grief! The water won't shut off and the machine's overflowing! Turn off the inlet faucets before you do anything else, then take a moment to collect yourself. Unplug the machine before you even begin to think about what might have caused the trouble. Remember from Chapter One how dangerous it is for you to work with electricity in a wet area? What would cause the water to run long enough to overflow? It might be a corroded inlet valve plunger guide, clogged bleed holes, a grounded solenoid, a blocked water-level switch pressure tube, or a faulty switch.

Let's do the quick and easy checks first. Now that the machine is unplugged, turn the inlet faucets back on. Does the water run? If no water flows, you have a grounded inlet valve solenoid or a faulty switch. If water had continued to run with the machine off, the problem would have been within the mechanical components of the valve. Remove the top panel and test the solenoid for ground as described

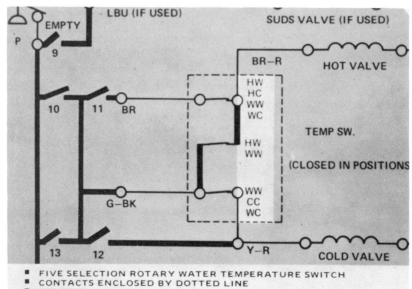

Courtesy, Whirlpool Corporation

Figure 9-35   *Schematic for a five selection rotary water temperature selector switch. You would test across terminals marked G-BK and Y-R.*

earlier. A grounded component will show 0 ohms or modest resistance when tested from a terminal to the component body. One that isn't grounded will read infinity.

You can remove the solenoid from the inlet valve assembly by loosening one or a pair of screws. As you remove the solenoid, be sure to keep track of the seals and washers and note their positions. Place them on numbered pieces of paper in their disassembly sequence. When you buy a new solenoid, ask the sales clerk to give you all of the seals and washers that go with it. Solenoids may or may not be available as parts separate from the inlet valve assembly. You might have to buy an entire unit.

Stuck switch contacts or a torn diaphragm may be keeping the switch from performing. Since the tub is full, just disconnect the wires from the fill switch and test it for continuity. You should read infinity. If the contacts are still closed with the tub full, the switch is faulty.

If you haven't found anything wrong up to this point, you should suspect a dirty inlet valve. For the inlet valve to work, it has to have equal pressure on both sides of a neoprene diaphragm. The spring-loaded solenoid plunger closes the diaphragm and water pressure opens it when the solenoid's magnetic force relieves the spring pressure. To achieve the balanced pressure, a small bleed hole is designed into one side of the diaphragm. A tiny particle of sand, rust, or other debris can easily block this hole and disable the valve. Manufacturer's service representatives and independent service people do not recommend cleaning these valves. It takes a great deal of time and you can't be sure that you will be able to remove all of the troublesome dirt. A new valve appears to be the best answer.

When removing the inlet valve, first disconnect all of the hoses, then remove the solenoid leads. Remove the two screws that secure the valve to the washer chassis. Install a new one in the reverse order.

When your washer refuses to light up and run, test the outlet for voltage first, and then test the line cord if your first test is positive. Remove the control panel and find the line cord terminals. Isolate the line and test from each side of the line to each of the plug prongs. Replace an open cord with one of the same type.

If the control console lights up but the machine refuses to run, you can make this easy test to isolate the source of your trouble. Try different combinations of cycles and water temperatures to see if the machine responds. In many cases it will. If, for example, you had selected the warm water permanent press cycle, there's some chance that the water mixing solenoid at the inlet valve is open. Perhaps your machine has an open fill switch. The last component to suspect is the motor. These $1/3$- to $1/2$-horsepower capacitor-start motors are extremely dependable and require little attention. Refer to Chapter Six for motor details.

A running visual inspection will help you locate the problem source when your machine won't run but makes a humming sound. First, unplug it, and then remove the back inspection panel. Plug the machine in, turn it on, and watch the drive mechanism carefully. After studying the cycle explanation in the beginning of this section, you should be able to discern which of the drive components isn't working as it should. You will have to let the tub fill up and begin its wash cycle before any drive problems reveal themselves.

One very important thing to remember when diagnosing drive trouble: most agitator washers keep the water pump running from the beginning of the wash cycle through the end of the last spin cycle. It is reasonable to assume that a seized water pump could stop the motor from running.

Most machines provide a means for adjusting the drive-belt tension. Loosen the lock nut and move the motor to the right. (See Figure 9–36.) Slip the belt off of the water pump pulley and try to turn the pump shaft by hand. If it doesn't turn at all or is difficult to turn, you can expect to replace the pump. Although some older

Figure 9-36 *Remove the belt from the pulleys. Turn the water pump by hand to check for a seizure.*

aluminum case pumps are rebuildable, you will benefit from replacing the unit with a newer plastic case pump. These new pumps are practically corrosion proof and should last the life of the machine. Have a professional change your water pump.

Broken belts are easy to spot, and loose belts are easy to diagnose. A properly adjusted belt should have about ½ in. of play halfway between pulleys. When you depress the belt at that point, it should move through the ½ in. without too much pressure. If you find it loose, loosen the adjuster lock nut and move the motor away from the opposing pulley. (See Figure 9–37.) Check the tension after tightening the nut. If your adjustment did not tighten the belt to the prescribed tension, check to see that the idler pulley is functioning. Some washers use a spring-loaded idler to help maintain the correct tension. If your machine doesn't have one of these and the belt won't tighten after your adjustment, you will have to install a new belt.

Changing belts is not always easy. Maytag machines have the simplest arrangement. The motor and water pump are mounted on the base of the frame with their drive shafts sticking out through the platform. The drive pulleys for the motor, water pump, and wash tub are located under the frame platform. There aren't any clutches, brakes, or pump drives to interfere with removing the belt.

General Electric mounts the pump above the motor where it is bolted to the washer tub and driven from the motor shaft by a flexible coupler. To remove the drum drive belt, you have to remove one of the very large hose clamps that secure the coupler to the pulley flange.

Whirlpool and Sears washers require a little more effort for their belt-changing procedure, but if you follow the instructions presented in Figure 9–38 you will have no difficulty. Refer to Figure 9–36 for the first step then proceed along with these illustrations.

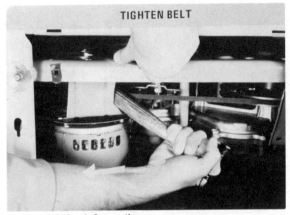

Figure 9-37 *Tightening the drive belt. Use a hammer handle for leverage and pull the motor to the left.*

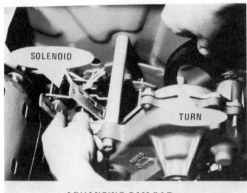

Figure 9-38a Manually lift the spin solenoid plunger and begin turning the main drive pulley. Continue turning until the spin cam bar has been completely advanced to the spin position.

Figure 9-38b Remove the brake yoke spring from the gear case cover and yoke. Remove the three support braces from the gear case. You will have to loosen the brace mounting nuts on the base plate as well.

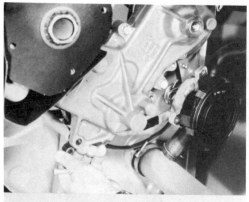

REMOVE SPACER

Figure 9-38c Remove the spacer from the short stud and the pump from the gear case. The pump hoses do not have to be disturbed.
Courtesy, Whirlpool Corporation

Figure 9-38d On the old basket drive and brake assembly it was possible to push up the clutch shaft by hand. With the shaft puller above the end of the cam bar the cam bar can be pried from the shaft slot.
Courtesy, Whirlpool Corporation

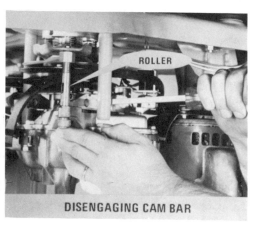

ROLLER

DISENGAGING CAM BAR

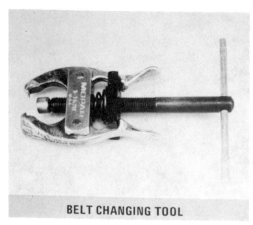

BELT CHANGING TOOL

Figure 9-38e Late model machines require this battery lug puller for raising the clutch shaft.
Courtesy, Whirlpool Corporation

Figure 9-38f Attach the puller on the gear case cover extension beneath the clutch shaft. Turn the puller screw until the shaft roller is high enough to clear the cam bar. Pry the cam bar from the shaft as shown above.
Courtesy, Whirlpool Corporation

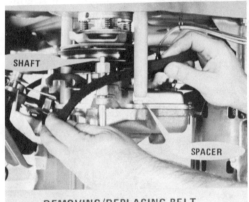

REMOVING/REPLACING BELT

Figure 9-38g The belt can be passed through the gap between the yoke and the shaft and then through the space beneath the short stud. Drop the belt from around the gear case. Reverse procedure to install new belt. Position the new belt on the pulleys and reassemble. Adjust belt tension as shown in Figure 9-37.

Courtesy, Whirlpool Corporation

Always try to discover what caused the belt to break if you feel that it happened sooner than expected. Perhaps the belt has been out of adjustment and slipping too much. Maybe the water pump bearings are binding a little, or the pump has ingested and trapped some debris that is placing too much drag on the impeller.

You can make a running inspection to discover why your machine refuses to agitate. Consult the wiring diagram to find out whether your machine uses solenoids to change gears or motor reversal. If the washer fails during a wash, turn it off, remove the inspection panel from the back of the machine, and start the cycle over again. If you can see or hear the solenoids working when the timer advances to the wash or agitate cycle, you can rule out wiring problems. In this case, examine the shift linkage for a binding, broken link pin, or a missing cotter pin. If you find nothing, get professional help. Solenoids this large usually clunk fairly loudly when they engage the shift linkage. If they remain silent, stop the machine, unplug it, and test the solenoids for continuity. In case the solenoid emits a hum, try moving the plunger by hand to check for binding.

On those machines that reverse the motor for the agitation cycle, a visual inspection will reveal slipping belts, or a motor that won't reverse. If the belt is slipping, adjust it. If the motor won't reverse, call a service technician. When you can find nothing wrong in either type of machine, but it still doesn't work properly or at all, call the expert. He or she can doublecheck your diagnosis and confirm your suspicion that the gearbox is causing the trouble.

Automatic clothes washing machine timers appear as manifestations of someone's deranged psyche at first glance, but closer inspection reveals the genius behind them. Terminals, switch contacts, and cam wheels abound. The timer is the washing machine's brain, and it completes circuits to all of those components that allow the machine to operate without human supervision. Timers, like brains, sometimes go awry. Figure 9–39 illustrates a typical washing machine timer.

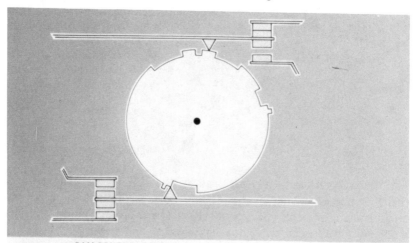

- CAM CONTROLS TWO SWITCH ARMS WITH DUAL CONTACTS
- CAM HAS CUTOUTS AND RAISED PORTIONS
- RAISED PORTIONS CLOSE OUTER CONTACTS
- CUTOUTS CLOSE INNER CONTACTS

Courtesy, Whirlpool Corporation

Figure 9-39 *A sophisticated timer cam and contact arrangement. Raised portions close outer contacts, cutouts close inner contacts.*

A small synchronous motor advances the cam wheels through a gear train, called an *escapement*, in sudden movements every minute or two. The less than fluid motion reduces contact point arcing by breaking contact quickly instead of slowly. When the timer refuses

- TYPICAL ESCAPEMENT USED PRIOR TO 1972
- SPRING LOADED AND HAS SPRAY RINSE CAM

Courtesy, Whirlpool Corporation

Figure 9-40 A *timer escapement or gear train. This one is spring loaded and has a special cam that operates the spray and rinse contacts.*

to advance, a single drop of oil on the motor shaft or on the escapement shafts often will persuade it to work normally. Figure 9–40 shows a timer escapement.

You will find the timer mounted to the inside of the control console. If you should find an open motor, burned switches, or broken escapement, you will have to replace the entire timer unit. Figure 9–41 shows how to test the timer for continuity. Lately manufacturers have made replacing the motor easy. Some unbolt and others plug into a receptacle built into the timer's switch box.

Years ago General Electric aired a television advertisement posing two socks side by side. One, arrogant and lint free, chanted scornfully, "linty sock, linty sock," while the second sock cowered in lint-covered embarrassment. The advertisement praised G.E.'s new lint filter. Lint filters are common to all machines these days, and they work very well. But if you or any of your family members insist upon washing fluffy new terry cloth in the same load that contains navy blue nylon or wool items, don't be surprised if those dark items emerge covered with lint. As good as lint filters are, they cannot work miracles. Hard water causes more linting problems than soft water. If you live in a hard-water area, add a water-softening agent to the wash water or a fabric softener to the rinse.

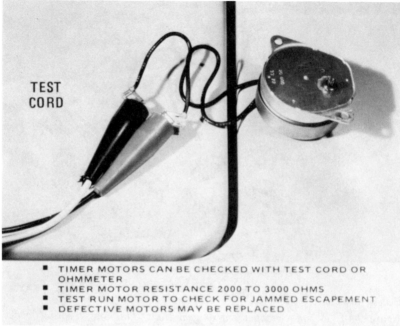

TEST
CORD

■ TIMER MOTORS CAN BE CHECKED WITH TEST CORD OR
  OHMMETER
■ TIMER MOTOR RESISTANCE 2000 TO 3000 OHMS
■ TEST RUN MOTOR TO CHECK FOR JAMMED ESCAPEMENT
■ DEFECTIVE MOTORS MAY BE REPLACED

Courtesy, Whirlpool Corporation

Figure 9-41 *You can test run a timer motor with a test cord made from
a heavy duty extension cord and two alligator clips. If the motor runs, the
trouble is in the timer cam and switch box. Timer motor resistance equals
2000 to 3000 ohms on your VOM.*

Water leaks will bring out the sleuth in you. Most leaks originate
from hose joints, but usually show up far from the source. A small leak
from a hose joint will run along the hose for some distance before it
drips off. If you open the cabinet and watch the machine during its
wash program, you stand a good chance of spotting any water leaks.
After some years, your washer may develop a leak or two in the tub
bolt holes, where it attaches to the chassis. Tubs are porcelain coated,
and the weakest part of the coating is at these bolt holes. The porcelain
might have been chipped during assembly allowing rust to grow and
a leak to develop. Most makers sell repair kits consisting of large-
headed brass bolts and neoprene washers.

Cast aluminum water pumps are susceptible to corrosion from detergent, minerals, and purification chemicals. All of these corrosives
eat tiny tracks through the pump joints and cause leaks. If you discover this problem, replace the pump with one of the plastic corrosion-
resistant units.

An open or binding gear-change solenoid, an open motor-reversal circuit, or a broken belt will keep your washing machine from spinning. Once again, a running inspection should reveal the troubled component. Remove the inspection panel from the back of the machine. You will spot a broken belt immediately.

To detect solenoid trouble, refer to the wiring diagram to find which of the solenoids engages the spinning clutch. On most machines, you can select the spin cycle without programming a complete washing cycle. Start the machine and watch to see whether or not the solenoid is working. If it is, call a service representative to come in and have a look at the gear-change mechanism and/or gearbox. If the solenoid is at fault, you may or may not be able to replace it easily. If the one in your machine is difficult to reach or requires you to remove other components before removing the solenoid, you might want to have an expert do the job.

In a machine that uses a reversing motor to engage the spin cycle, find the wiring on the diagram. Remove the control console and test the circuit for continuity, beginning with the timer switch contacts. To be sure that the timer is advancing, run the machine through a complete washing program. When it reaches the spin stage and nothing happens, try advancing the timer by hand. If the tub begins to spin, then you know that the timer is binding at this point.

On some washers, the lid safety switch works only during the spin stage. An open switch will keep the machine from spinning. To test it, remove the top panel and find the switch. (See Figure 9–42.) Isolate it from the circuit by removing the leads and test it for continuity.

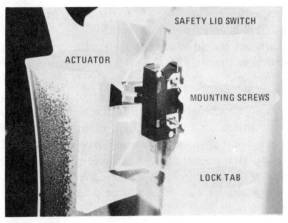

Courtesy, Whirlpool Corporation

Figure *9-42 Test the lid safety switch for continuity across its two terminals.*

Washing machines that have to drain before the spin cycle begins are subject to clogged drains. Most modern machines have a tub ring that guards against losing anything between the drum and tub. The possibility of dropping a sock or other small item into the space between the tub and drum does exist on older machines that do not have a tub ring. If your machine refuses to pump out, remove the top panel and fish around in the area between the drum and tub for any possible drain-blocking items. On those machines that use a separate belt to drive the water pump, you should check for a broken or slipping belt when the machine will not pump out.

If your machine spins slowly or hardly at all, the belt or spin clutch might be slipping. In this case, you should call an expert. Without special testing equipment, it's difficult for you to tell exactly what will cause a slow-turning drum.

Noise and vibration will come from slipping belts, glazed or wet rubber vibration dampers, rusty tub suspension springs, unbalanced load, and poorly adjusted feet. A spray lubricant such as WD-40 will work in a pinch, but you should consult your dealer for the manufacturer's recommended lubricant. Whirlpool recommends using their lubricant over all others. Noise from a slipping belt can usually be cured with an adjustment.

Be sure to load the machine according to the maker's instructions for best balance. Adjust leveling feet with the help of a carpenter's level. Check the level from side to side and front to back.

DISHWASHER

Manufacturers estimate that roughly half of all service calls on automatic dishwashers deal with problems other than equipment failures or defects. This fact should make you realize the importance of following the instruction manual. Is the water hot enough? Do you have enough line pressure? Is the detergent fresh? (Once the strong, high-alkaline detergent used in dishwashers is exposed to the air, it has a shelf life of only about two weeks.) Is the detergent suited to your area's water conditions? Is the water hard or soft? Do you need an additional wetting agent to prevent filming? Any one or combination of these factors can give poor results, causing you to blame the machine.

A dishwasher cleans with water pressure, heat, and chemical action. An impeller spinning in a water sump or a high-speed pump forcing water through holes in a spray arm supplies the water pressure. A heating element located in the sump helps keep the water at the correct temperature. The water, aided by the detergent, serves as the scrubber. After the final rinse and drain, air heated by the element that keeps the water hot circulates through the machine. Some makers use a small squirrel-cage blower to circulate air, whereas others rely on a thermal-siphon effect, where warm air rises, escapes and is replaced by cooler air entering through vents low in the machine. The washing cycle is physically simple, electrically complex, and almost as delicately balanced as nature's ecological system.

Whether you have owned a dishwasher for years or are new to one, you might not be getting the most from your investment. Probably every 50 out of 100 dishwashers in a given area could be doing a better job. If you are less than satisfied with your unit's performance, try these checks.

1. Water temperature: With the machine empty, close the door and start the washing cycle. When the first wash cycle ends, advance the timer slowly and let the machine drain. Let the machine refill for the second wash, but stop the timer before it has a chance to energize the pump. Open the door and take the water temperature with a candy thermometer. Ideally, the reading should be between 150° and 160° F. Anything below 140° F is too low to melt grease.

The most obvious cause of water temperature problems is a water heater that is set too low. Turn it up and test the results after the heater has had an hour or so to stabilize the water temperature in the tank. The distance between the water heater and the dishwasher influences the temperature. Copper pipe absorbs about 1° F of heat for every foot the water has to travel. If distance is a problem in your house, wrap the hot-water pipes with closed-cell foam insulation. A greasy film at the lower front corners of front-loading machines indicates inadequate water temperature.

2. Most washers use a timed fill cycle calculated on an average line pressure. The water should reach the sump heating element during the preset time. A machine that leaves food particles on the dishes is probably suffering from insufficient water supply. If your dishwasher shares the line running to the kitchen sink, you can perform this simple test. Fill a gallon container from a fully open hot-water tap and note how long the line takes to complete the task. Adequate pressure should have filled the container in 30 seconds or less.

Dishwashers control inlet flow with a valve much like the ones used in automatic clothes washers. The dishwasher valve has only one hose attachment for hot water and one solenoid. These are subject to the same problems that plague the valves in clothes washers. If you discover inadequate line pressure in the machine and adequate pressure at the faucet, perhaps the inlet valve filter is dirty.

In many dishwasher inlet valves, you will find a small flow-regulating device called a flow washer. This neoprene disc's chamfered opening constricts to reduce flow. When the neoprene tears or becomes brittle, the flow washer cannot perform its job; too much or too little flow results. If your machine suffers from inconsistent or inadequate water level, do not try to compensate by adjusting the water-level switch. Preventing overflow is the switch's only function.

3. You can check for detergent oxidation with this simple test. Put 2 teaspoons of detergent into a glass of water whose temperature is at least 140° F and stir for 2 minutes. If a gritty residue settles after you have finished stirring, the detergent is not good enough for efficient cleaning. Lumpy or caked detergent indicates oxidation as well. Don't be afraid to experiment with different brands. Try all of them if you have to and settle for the one that gives you the best results.

4. Filming, which usually shows up as dull glassware or "those awful drops that spot," is caused by extremely hard water, poor quality detergent, or inadequate amounts of detergent. You can remove the film by adding ½ cup of citric acid (no detergent) to the machine's wash cycle and a cup of vinegar to the rinse. A wetting agent such as Jet-Dri will help break the surface tension of hard water and prevent or reduce filming. If all else fails, install a water softener in your home water system.

5. Etching is damage caused to dishes and glassware by extreme heat and strong chemicals used in dishwashers. There is really nothing that you can do about it except stop using the machine. Most modern dish and glassware is tough enough to resist etching. If you plan to buy fine china or crystal, ask the salesperson if the items are dishwasher safe. To be safe, avoid washing antique or other valuable dish and glassware in your dishwasher.

6. Be sure you are loading the machine according to the maker's recommendations. A badly loaded machine will return badly washed dishes.

On many machines, virtually every diagnostic procedure demands that you remove the panels from your portable dishwasher or pull your built-in dishwasher from under the counter. You will find the inlet valves, pump, and motor in the bottom of the chassis with the best access from the back. Whirlpool machines, however, are serviceable from the front, a feature that makes home repair easier and professional repair less expensive. Some units even locate the timer switch assembly close to the other components. Some washers may have many of their operating controls located in the door. You can expose these by removing the screws and molding from the door sides and pulling the panel free. Refer to Figure 9–43 for removing the panels from Whirlpool models.

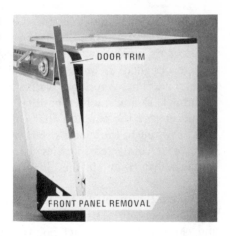

You may or may not have to remove your dishwasher from under the counter to service it. If you do, first open the door, then find the retaining clips or tabs that hold the top of the machine to the underside of the counter. Remove the screws. Next, remove the toe or bottom panel so that you can gain access to the lower compartment. Turn the leveling feet up and into the chassis to lower the machine. Pull the washer out slowly. Unplug the line cord and disconnect the water hose and drain hose. Now you are ready to work on the machine.

In place of the impeller used to sling water over the dishes, modern spray arm washers use a stainless steel or plastic arm perforated with water jet nozzles. A high-speed, high-efficiency pump supplies water to the spray arm. The nozzles are angled so that the water pressure forces the arm to revolve at a fairly high speed. The action directs hot scrubbing water to every square inch of the machine. Some units have a spray arm at the top as well. The pump motor rotates in one direction for spray and reverses for drain. The reversible motor will have four leads and most likely a start relay.

The dishwasher fulfills its task through three distinct stages. First is *wash–rinse*, where the dishwasher sump fills with water and a pump circulates it under high pressure through one or more spray arms; detergent is added automatically during the second wash in this cycle, and a wetting agent is injected into the rinse portion of this stage. Second is *drain*, where the pump motor stops, reverses its direction, and pumps water out of the machine. Third is *dry*, where a heating element, sometimes aided by a small fan, provides drying heat. The element may be energized during the entire period or cycled on and off for lower heat drying. A timer containing a subinterval switch, a push-button selector switch, the motor start relay, and the thermostat control these functions.

Let's examine a typical wash cycle. You push a button and select a cycle designed to wash a mixed load, then turn the timer dial to correspond. The Whirlpool washer's timer has one position for cycles A through D and another position for cycles E and F. Push the dial in and engage the contacts that complete a circuit through the push-button switch to the motor's start relay. The current-draw relay's armature coil is connected in series with the motor run windings, and the contacts that complete the circuit to the start windings are normally open.

When the circuit to the relay is complete, the current draw in the relay coil sets up a strong magnetic field that pulls the armature up and closes a set of contact points. This action completes a circuit to the motor start windings. When the motor reaches about 80 percent of its running speed, the current draw decreases and reduces the relay coil's magnetic field strength until it is too weak to hold the armature up. When it drops, contact to the start windings is broken, and the motor continues on its run windings.

At the same time, the machine has completed circuits through the door safety switch, push/pull switch, timer motor, fill valve, and over-fill safety switch. At the instant all of these circuits are completed, the machine sump fills with water. The subinterval switch in the timer divides the timer's first 60 seconds into intervals so that everything doesn't happen at once. After the timed fill period, the motor begins pumping water through the spray arms. During the first wash, about 4 minutes, detergent is introduced into the machine from an open cup in the door. The first wash is designed to remove loose, heavy soil.

A complete drain follows the first wash and lasts about a minute. After the wash, the timer interrupts the circuit to the motor. During drain, the timer engages a set of contacts that start the motor through the relay, but through a second circuit that causes the motor to run in a direction opposite to the wash cycle. Circuits to the fill valve, over-fill switch, and thermostat are inactive.

Two rinses with a drain period separating them follow, and all of the circuits outlined in the first wash are active. The two rinses last about 3 minutes, each with a minute for drain. The first of these rinses flushes loose food particles and most of the detergent away. The second one removes the remaining detergent.

The second wash, 6 to 8 minutes, follows. It is designed to remove the more stubborn soil left on the dishes from the first wash. All of the circuits active during the first wash participate in the second with the addition of the detergent dispenser.

The detergent dispenser lid is held closed by two magnetized metal strips in the dispenser's body. They act on a metal washer that is attached to a spring-loaded button on the lid. When the circuit to the dispenser is completed, the current flows through a coil attached to the metal strips, interrupts the magnetic field, and allows the lid to open. This occurs during the fill portion.

The second wash is followed by a complete drain, a short rinse, another drain, and the final rinse. Active circuits are the same as those responsible for the first pair of rinses. During the last rinse, the thermostat interrupts the timer to hold the water in the sump until the temperature rises to or above 140° F. The wetting agent dispenser circuit is introduced into the last rinse cycle. A bimetal heater is connected in series with the main heater to provide the voltage drop necessary for this component. The bimetal warps away from a steel check ball and releases the wetting agent. The main heating element remains energized during all wash, rinse, and dry cycles.

During the final cycle increments, the timer shaft pulls the timer knob in toward the console face, eventually causing the push/pull switch contacts to open. The last timer contact completes a circuit that bypasses the push/pull switch and allows the timer motor to continue running. At the end of the drying increment, the last timer contact set opens, and the machine is ready to be used again. Understanding the cycle and knowing which components and circuits are active during each stage will allow you to arrive at the cause of a breakdown more quickly and easily.

When the washer's sump won't fill, the first component to examine is the inlet valve filter screen, especially if you live in a hard water area. You will find the water inlet valve located under the tub. On Whirlpool machines, it is bolted to the chassis just behind the front access panel. Remove four screws, two from either side, and remove the panel. Other machines may have a lift-up, pull-out panel with no screws, or a panel secured with screws along the bottom and tabs at the top corners. On the second type, you must remove the screws, then lift up and out at the top. To find the filter screen, disconnect the screw-on inlet-hose fitting. Most portable washers rely on the faucet filter screen.

An open inlet valve solenoid will prevent the fill stage of the cycle from beginning. Test the solenoid, wires disconnected, across its two terminals and replace if open. Generally, two screws or ¼-in. hex bolts hold the solenoid to the bracket. (See Figure 9–44.) The solenoid may not be available as a separate unit, in which case you will have to buy a new inlet valve assembly.

An open door interlock safety switch will keep the machine from running. To find this switch you will have to remove the control con-

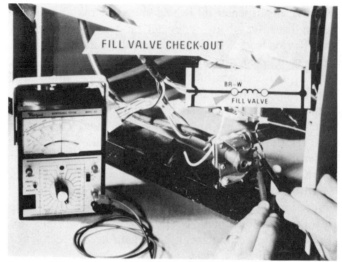

Figure 9-44 *Check the solenoid coil for continuity across its two termi-nals. Resistance equals 850 to 900 ohms.*

sole. On many machines the door latch handle and timer knob have to come off first. The latch handle on Whirlpool machines is held in place by one Phillips head screw. Screw the knob counterclockwise to remove it, then simply pull the dial off. On other brands you may be able to pull the entire assembly off. Open the control console. Figure 9–45 illustrates this procedure. Look for screws in similar locations when working with other brands. Generally, you can tilt the console down from the top. Test the switch for continuity, as shown in Figure 9–46. If you find that the switch is good, perhaps the latch strike is not completely engaging the switch. Many of these are adjustable through elongated mounting screw slots. Loosen the screws and move the strike out just a hair at a time until the switch works as it should.

Figure 9-45 *Remove the door latch handle (four screws, two at each end of the console, and one from each door bumper). Rotate the console forward.*

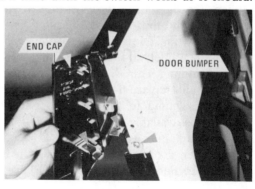

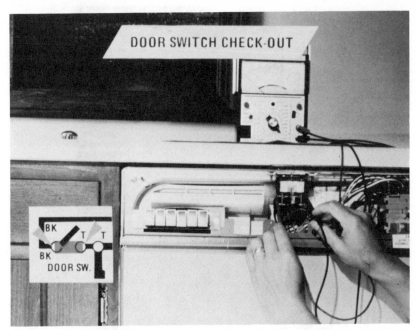

Courtesy, Whirlpool Corporation

Figure 9-46 *The door switch should show continuity with the door and latch closed. Meter shows an open switch in this picture.*

A jammed or open overfill switch will keep the sump from filling. During the fill stage, the circuit to the inlet valve passes through the overfill switch. The float and plunger and pressure-sensitive diaphragm overfill switches are common to most machines. You will find these in the right front corner of the tub.

The float type uses a hollow plastic dome-shaped float with a plunger attached or molded to its underside. (See Figure 9–47.) The plunger rides in a standpipe or tube, at the bottom of which you will find a microswitch and control arm. Figure 9–48 shows how to test this switch for continuity. The float and plunger hold the contacts closed. Rising water lifts the float, thus breaking the circuit to the inlet valve and shutting off the water.

Pressure-sensitive diaphragm overfill switches are bolted to the bottom of the tub and sealed against leaks with a gasket. The weight of the water flowing over the diaphragm forces the contacts open. See Figure 9–49 for an illustration of this switch. Both types should indicate 0 ohms in their normal positions. Check to see that each type opens and closes when you activate them by hand.

On rare occasions, you will find that the water won't shut off.

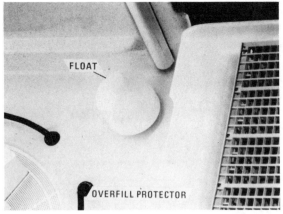

Figure 9-47   *Overfill protector float located at the right hand front corner of the machine.*

Figure 9-48   *Test the switch for continuity across its two terminals. The pal nut keeps the plunger in the stand pipe during shipping and service.*

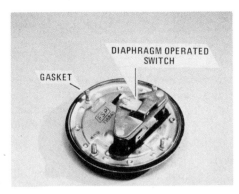

Figure 9-49   *Pressure sensitive diaphragm operated overfill switch.*

Corrosion in the inlet valve can prevent the solenoid plunger from seating, and no matter what the overfill switch does the water just keeps running. This trouble is outside electrical intervention. Although you may wish to disassemble and clean the inlet valve, the safest and most long-lived cure is replacement.

A grounded solenoid will not respond to the overfill switch command to shut off the water. Test for a short to ground from each of the solenoid terminals to its body. Refer to Figure 7–8. When the solenoid checks out good, you can assume a dirty valve or a deteriorated plunger diaphragm. Figure 9–50 shows a typical inlet valve.

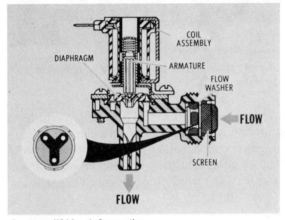

Figure 9-50   Typical inlet valve. Service technicians recommend replacing corroded or broken inlet valves.

When the machine fills with water but the motor won't run, you can suspect open timer contacts. You know that the push/pull switch is working because the sump filled with water. Consult the wiring diagram to see which timer contacts are responsible for completing the circuit to the motor. Whirlpool timer switches marked "BU" and "TM-W" combine to complete the motor circuit. Remove the leads from these terminals and test across them for continuity. (See Figure 9–51.)

If you don't have a wiring diagram for your machine, you will have to trace the circuit backward from the motor and relay to the timer. One motor lead is common to all windings and is usually white. Next, trace the wire from the start relay to the timer. Disconnect the two leads and test the timer switches. If the timer is open, replace it with a new one.

An open motor start relay will keep the motor from running. Most

Courtesy, Whirlpool Corporation

Figure 9-51 *Timer assembly on this* Whirlpool *model may be electrically tested without removing it from the console.*

relays will have terminals marked "M" and "S." Whirlpool relays use larger spades for the M terminals than for the S terminals to reduce the chance of wiring errors. Test the relay across the two M terminals. Some relays are position sensitive and will be marked with an arrow indicating up or with the word "top." Figure 9–52 shows a start relay.

START RELAY

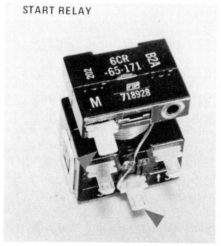

Figure 9-52 *Start relay. Note the different size spade terminals.*
Courtesy, Whirlpool Corporation

Open motor windings may be responsible for keeping the motor idle. Test across the blue and white terminal prongs for the run windings. You should get a reading of about 6 ohms at R×1. (See Figure 9–53.) If you find open run or start windings, replace the motor.

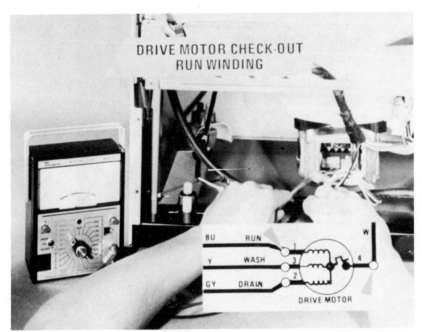

DRIVE MOTOR CHECK-OUT
RUN WINDING

Courtesy, Whirlpool Corporation

Figure 9-53 *Test the start winding for continuity across the yellow and white wires. Resistance should equal 6 ohms or slightly higher.*

Before you can remove the pump motor, you will have to remove the spray arm, filter screen, and drain filter. Refer to your owner's manual for instructions. On most machines simply unscrewing a hubcap will allow you to remove the spray arm. Remove all hoses from the pump. Next, look for mounting screws or bolts around the pump. Figure 9-54 shows one of three pump assembly mounts used by Whirlpool. Disconnect all wiring and pull the pump out from inside the washer tub. Replace the pump motor with a manufacturer-made part. If, through process of elimination, you have discovered that the pump impeller is jammed, take it to a qualified service representative for repair.

When the motor will not pump out your machine, suspect an open circuit to the motor reversal leads. Refer to the wiring diagram for color coding. No voltage to the motor? Test the timer-to-motor switch terminals for continuity.

If the timer won't advance, perhaps the escapement is binding or the motor windings are open. (See Figure 9-55.) A pinion gear on the timer motor shaft drives the timer switching cam gear. These two gears require proper alignment to work as designed. If they mesh too tightly, the motor won't have enough power to operate all of the timer

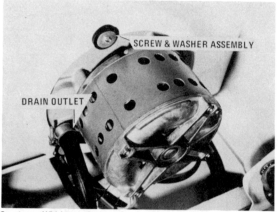

Figure 9-54   One of three different pump assembly mounts used on Whirl-pool machines.

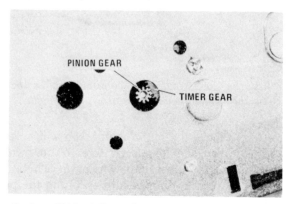

Figure 9-55   Pinion and timer gears mesh as seen through the inspection hole on the back of the timer.

cams during the cycle. A too loose mesh will cause binding. To adjust, loosen the motor mounting screws and retighten when the pinion and cam gear rotate easily. A drop of oil may help. To test for open timer motor windings, disconnect the motor leads from their terminals and test across them.

In case of leaks, try to determine their origin by examining the machine during its cycle. You have to do this with the panels removed, so be careful. Keep your fingers out of the works and away from all electrical connections. Often the amount of water leaking and whether it is clear or sudsy will give you some clue to the source. Clear water leaks originate in the inlet system; sudsy leaks come from the drain system. Check all hose connections, the pump housing, the siphon break, inlet valve, and door seal. When stumped, call an expert.

DISPOSAL

Americans create more waste than any other society in the world. Solid-waste disposal is a continuing and almost insurmountable problem. We burn it, feed it to the sea, and bury it in the ground. What does all that have to do with the garbage disposal? As small as it is, the disposal helps alleviate the solid-waste problem. In some parts of the country, city building codes require builders to install garbage disposals in all new residential developments. Not only does the garbage disposal relieve the solid-waste burden, it helps control rats, a problem that has plagued societies throughout the world for centuries.

There are two types of garbage disposals currently available—the continuous feed disposal, with the on/off switch on the wall, and the batch feed disposal, with the on/off switch built into the sink stopper. The batch feed model requires the user to position the stopper a certain way, then turn it to engage the switching mechanism. Batch feed models tend to be more expensive to buy, but are less expensive to install and are safer.

Modern disposals look pretty much the same as they did twenty years ago, but design and material improvements place them light years ahead of their ancestors. (Figure 9–56 shows a modern garbage disposal.) The newer models last longer, perform more efficiently, run more quietly, and are easier to service. Proper use and care is extremely important to the life of your disposal, so get out the instruction manual and get acquainted with this helpful appliance.

Here's how it works. Food scraps placed into the disposer land on a spinning impeller that is attached directly to the motor shaft. Centrifugal force drives the scraps out against the grinding ring, where cutting elements pulverize the scraps into tiny bits. The flow of cold water necessary for efficient operation carries the debris into the sewage system. Modern disposals are so good that you can even use them with a septic tank. Most builders recommend a larger than normal tank to deal with the extra sewage, but a smaller tank pumped out more frequently works just fine.

Garbage disposals can be dangerous. A hand caught in a whirling disposal means certain mutilation. Before you attempt any kind of diagnosis or service on your unit, disconnect it from its power source. Merely turning the switch off isn't good enough. Trip the circuit breaker to the line or remove the fuse.

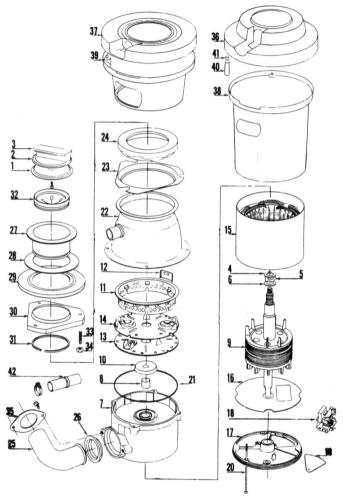

Courtesy, Tappan Company

Figure 9-56   *A typical garbage disposal broken down into its many components. Follow the lines and note how the parts relate to one another in assembly.*

Jamming is the most common disposal problem. It's easy for a person using either a continuous feed or batch feed to overstuff the hopper. Large bones or a fork or knife can stop the machine in its tracks. You can break most food jams by reversing the motor either electrically or with the special tool often supplied with a new unit. Most modern disposals have a reversing switch on the case.

Before you engage the reversing switch, you should try to discover what exactly caused the jammed impeller. Anything other than food scraps should be removed before you attempt to reverse the motor. A hopeless jam means that you will have to remove the unit from the sink and take it to a service center for repairs. Do not disassemble the disposal beyond the motor housing and hopper.

In order to remove the unit from the sink, first disconnect the discharge pipe by removing two screws from the flange. Many units dismount by twisting counterclockwise to free them from the three-eared mounting ring. Others dismount by loosening three lock nuts and three slotted screws. (See Figure 9–57.) To remove the hopper, loosen the tension screw in the retaining ring or loosen four screws around the hopper mounting flange, as in Figure 9–58. Once the hopper is free from the unit, you will be able to see what has caused the jam.

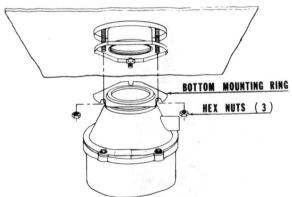

Courtesy, Tappan Company

Figure 9-57 *Motor and grinding unit mounts to the sink with three slotted screws and three lock nuts.*

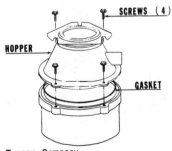

Courtesy, Tappan Company

Figure 9-58 *Hopper bolts to the motor/grinding unit with four bolts. Always replace the gasket with a new one after disassembly.*

You can service the motor components such as the start relay, overload protector, reversing switch, or start capacitor (if your disposal has one), from outside the unit. (See Figure 9–59.) Disposals use split-phase motors producing up to ¾ horsepower. Refer to Chapter Six for details on split-phase motors.

In many homes, especially new ones, the garbage disposal is hooked into a separate 115-volt line with its own fuse or circuit breaker.

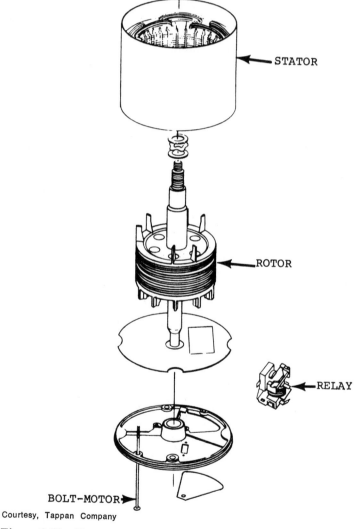

STATOR

ROTOR

RELAY

BOLT–MOTOR

Figure 9-59   *You can test, remove, and replace the start relay by removing the bottom motor bell housing. Four long bolts hold the motor together.*

If your disposal ever refuses to run and makes no sound, check the fuse or circuit breaker first. If the fuse is blown, install a new one. If your disposal continues to trip the circuit breaker or blow the fuse, call in an expert.

A tripped overload protector will keep the disposal from running. Push the reset button located on the outside of the disposal shell. If your unit uses an automatic reset, wait at least 30 minutes and try the disposal again. Examine the hopper for the overload cause. Packing the hopper before turning the unit on is the most common reason for a tripped overload protector.

Perhaps a defective wall or stopper switch is keeping the disposal from working. Remove the fuse or trip the circuit breaker on that line and investigate. Refer to Chapter Ten for the wall switch test. You will find the stopper switch under the sink on the outside of the hopper. Remove at least one of the leads and test the switch for continuity.

A motor that hums, won't run, or trips the overload protector probably has something jammed in the impeller. Disconnect the power source and try to find the cause. If you find nothing in the hopper, restore power and push the reset button. If that doesn't work, try reversing the motor. Many modern disposals provide a switch on the shell that allows you to reverse the motor to free a jammed impeller. If the symptom occurs in the reverse direction, try the unjamming wrench. If your search reveals nothing, you can suspect a seized motor bearing. Take the unit to a professional for further diagnosis and repair.

Open motor windings, an open start capacitor or relay, or a defective centrifugal switch will produce the humming symptom, but without tripping the overload protector. Your disposal's motor will use either a start capacitor and centrifugal switch to remove the start windings while running, or it will use a start relay that both starts the motor and removes the start windings from the circuit. All of the motors use an overload protector. You may find these components on the outside of the disposal or just inside the lower motor bell housing. (See Figure 9–59.) Refer to Chapter Six for testing details about the split-phase and capacitor-start motors.

Removing the bottom motor housing cover will expose the motor winding terminals or leads. You can test the windings for continuity across these leads. If you find open windings, take the unit to a qualified repair person for motor replacement.

Water leaks from around the outside of the disposal usually originate from loose or poorly sealed sink flanges. Study the mounting system from under the sink to determine the source. Try tightening any nuts, screws, or bolts associated with the mount. Figure 9–60 shows the relationship among these parts. If it continues to leak, remove the

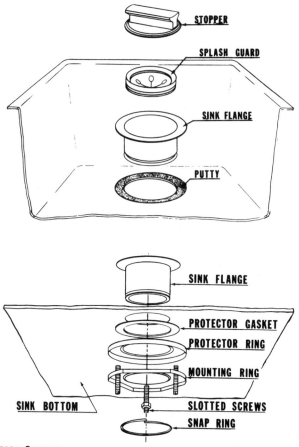

STOPPER

SPLASH GUARD

SINK FLANGE

PUTTY

SINK FLANGE

PROTECTOR GASKET

PROTECTOR RING

MOUNTING RING

SINK BOTTOM

SLOTTED SCREWS

SNAP RING

Courtesy, Tappan Company

Figure 9-60 *Upper mount parts and their relationship to the sink and to one another.*

disposal and remount it using plumber's putty to seal the sink flange.

Water leaking from inside the disposal housing usually comes from a worn impeller seal. Although these should last the life of the unit, failure is not impossible. A poorly manufactured or poorly installed seal will fail early. Remove the unit and take it to your dealer for service.

Unusual noise or vibration may be caused by a loose mount, loose impeller, or an indigestible object bouncing around inside the hopper. First check for stray indigestibles, then look for other possibilities.

Disposal-related drain clogs usually result from insufficient water supply during operation. Turn the cold water tap on all the way before you turn the disposal on. If you have an old unit, perhaps the grinding ring is worn and leaving large scraps to flush into the sewage system. You might wish to get a professional opinion about your old unit's efficiency.

Many newer disposals provide an automatic reversing switch that changes the motor's direction in case of jamming. If your disposal won't reverse, test the switch with your VOM. The automatic switch is located near the motor shaft and is part of the centrifugal switch. Manual reversing switches are located on the outside of the unit.

To take full advantage of the disposal's helping hand, you have to follow the maker's instructions for use and care. Use plenty of cold water during operation, don't pack the hopper before turning the unit on, and keep silverware, glass, plastic, and so on, out of the hopper. Always grind stringy waste such as corn husks in small quantities and with other scraps such as small bones.

TRASH COMPACTOR

The trash compactor, working in concert with your garbage disposal, provide an excellent combination in the fight against solid-waste disposal. The compactor keeps your kitchen neat, eliminates the bevy of trash cans usually found in the garage or at the side of the house, and helps the community sanitation department cope with solid-waste-disposal problems. The compactor jams a week's worth of trash from an average four-person household into a single 18×18×10 inch bag.

Here's how it works. After you have placed the bag into its container and dumped a load of trash in, close the drawer, which also closes a safety switch. Turn the key switch to on, then press the rocker switch to on. The compactor will not work with any other sequence. All of these switches are designed to protect the user from injury. Figure 9–61 illustrates a typical compactor.

A powerful split-phase motor drives a pair of screw shafts through two gears, three sprockets, and a chain. The screw shafts turn in threaded power nuts, which are either bolted or welded to the compactor's ram foot. The ram foot is the same shape as the bag compartment, but slightly smaller.

As the motor turns the screw shafts, the ram moves down toward the bottom of the bag until it reaches a level about 5 in. from the bottom. If you have enough trash in the bag, the ram foot will stop at a higher level. Rubber bumpers attached to flanges on the compactor frame stop the ram at the correct level when the bag isn't full enough for the contents to do the job. At a predetermined pressure, the motor stalls.

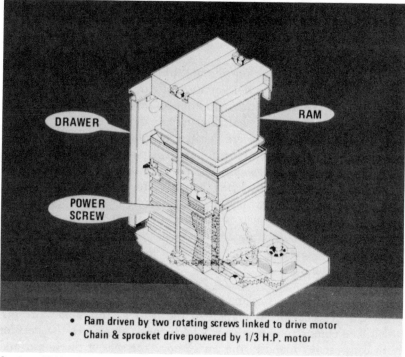

- Ram driven by two rotating screws linked to drive motor
- Chain & sprocket drive powered by 1/3 H.P. motor

Courtesy, Whirlpool Corporation

Figure 9-61 *Ghost view of a typical trash compactor.*

Split-phase motors can be reversed by reversing the relationship between the start and run windings. A switch located near the top of the frame has a feeler arm that rests against the ram when it is at its highest position. When the ram depresses the switch arm, the switch sets the motor for forward rotation. Once the ram releases the feeler arm, a linkage changes the position of the contacts.

A relay or centrifugal switch has already disengaged the start windings from the circuit, so the change in switch contact position has no effect on the motor. As soon as the motor stalls and restarts, the motor turns in the reverse direction because the directional switch has changed the start and run windings relationship by completing a second circuit. When the motor reverses, the ram rises. If the ram stops for any reason, such as a power failure, someone trying to open the drawer, or if you shut it off, it will return to its top-most position after power is restored. At the top of its travel, the ram engages both the directional switch and the top limit switch, which shuts off the unit.

Compactors require very little attention. Wash the ram head and wiper once a week or so. Check the chain tension once every 6 to 8 weeks depending on use. The chain should have about ¼ in. of play at the midpoint between sprockets. Belt-driven models should have about ⅛ in. of play at the same point. Make sure that the screw shafts are adequately lubricated. The motor is sealed and needs no attention.

You can service your trash compactor either through the back, bottom, or top. You can expose those components located at the top by removing the top panel. Removing all visible screws around the cabinet edges will allow you to expose the entire frame and all of the compactor's mechanical and electrical components. Whirlpool compactors allow you to perform electrical checks on the start/stop switch, top limit switch, directional switch, drawer safety switch, motor centrifugal switch, motor start and run windings, and the overload protector by merely removing the control console. You can service all of the switches either through the console or the bottom pan assembly.

When your compactor won't run and makes no sound, check to see that you have closed the drawer all the way and turned the key switch through its full arc before you begin to search for malfunctioning components.

Improper loading can cause the drawer to tilt and jam. When it tilts, a safety switch shuts the unit off. If this happens to your compactor, call in a qualified repair person to free the jammed ram foot and drawer. Always follow the maker's loading instructions. Some of the latest compactors, including Whirlpool, mount a stop block on the right rear corner of the ram. When an improperly loaded compartment tilts the ram, the block allows enough tilt to open the circuit through the safety switch, but it keeps the ram from jamming in the drawer.

When your compactor refuses to run, you have six switches as well as the motor's windings to investigate. There is no easy way to determine which it might be without testing each in turn. Remove the control console and test the key and rocker switches. Some compactor models combine the key and rocker into one unit. Next test the top limit switch. If these test out good, go on to the other switches. Follow the directions in Figures 9–62, 9–63, and 9–64. Replace any defective switches with new ones.

You will find the motor mounted to the chassis toward the rear of the unit. You can test the motor windings as indicated in Figure 9–65. Open motor windings will keep the compactor from running or making any telltale hums. If you find open windings, you will have to replace the motor.

CHECKING THE DRAWER SAFETY SWITCH

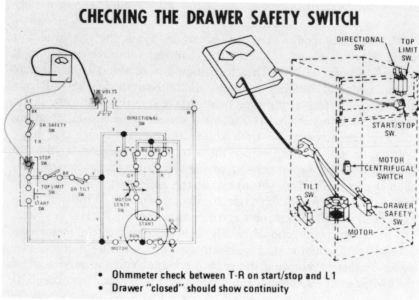

- Ohmmeter check between T-R on start/stop and L1
- Drawer "closed" should show continuity

yCourtesy, Whirlpool Corporation

Figure 9-62 *Drawer switch continuity test. Disconnect the tan and red wire from the start/stop switch. Connect your VOM between the tan and red wire and the L1 side of the power cord. The switch should show continuity with the drawer closed.*

CHECKING THE DIRECTIONAL SWITCH

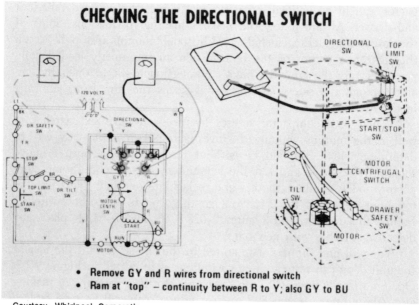

- Remove GY and R wires from directional switch
- Ram at "top" – continuity between R to Y; also GY to BU

Courtesy, Whirlpool Corporation

Figure 9-63 *Directional switch test. Remove the gray wire from the start/ stop switch. With the ram at the top, you should read continuity between the R and Y and GY and BU terminals.*

246

CHECKING THE DRAWER TILT SWITCH

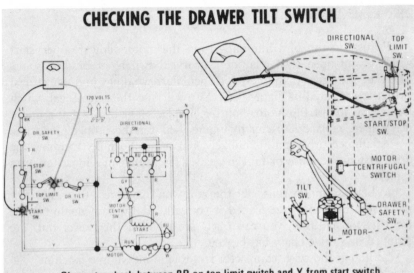

- Ohmmeter check between BR on top limit switch and Y from start switch
- Drawer "closed" should show continuity

Figure 9-64 Drawer tilt switch test. Remove the brown wire from the top limit switch and the yellow wire from the start switch. Attach your VOM to these leads. You should read continuity with the drawer closed.

CHECKING MOTOR RUN WINDING

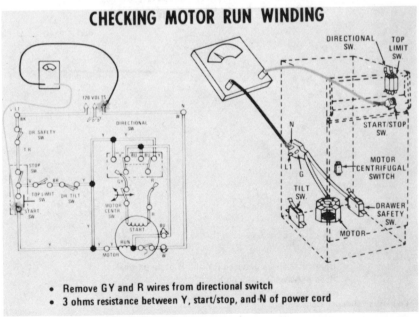

- Remove GY and R wires from directional switch
- 3 ohms resistance between Y, start/stop, and N of power cord

Figure 9-65 Testing the motor run windings. Disconnect the red and the gray wires from the directional switch. Connect your VOM leads to the yellow wire from the start switch and the neutral side of the line cord. Windings will indicate about 3 ohms.

Refusal to run plus humming from the motor indicate open start windings, an open start relay or centrifugal switch, or binding somewhere in the drive train. Test for open start windings and centrifugal switch as indicated in Figure 9–66. You will find the centrifugal switch located on top of the motor housing. Replace it if open. If the motor reads open, replace it. Refer to Figure 9–67 for the proper procedure.

A jammed drive train is unlikely, but not impossible. Examine the drive system for loose or broken gears. Has the chain slipped off of a sprocket?

When the motor runs, but the ram won't compress the trash, first make sure that you have loaded it correctly. If the ram doesn't move from its top position, you can easily see whether the power nuts are stripped or a drive chain has broken.

Although the trash compactor is a tough and simple machine, you should not neglect it. Keep it clean and lubricated where necessary. Follow the manufacturer's instructions for use and care.

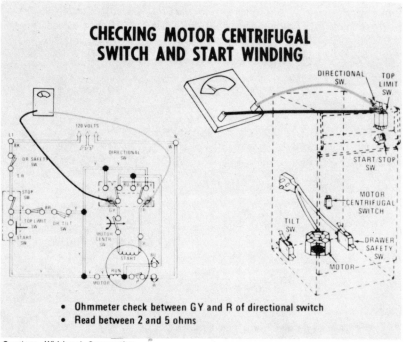

CHECKING MOTOR CENTRIFUGAL SWITCH AND START WINDING

- Ohmmeter check between GY and R of directional switch
- Read between 2 and 5 ohms

Courtesy, Whirlpool Corporation

Figure 9-66   Testing the centrifugal switch and start windings. Remove the gray and red wires from the directional switch. Connect your VOM to these leads. You should read 3 to 5 ohms on the meter. An infinity reading means that you will have to test the components at the motor.

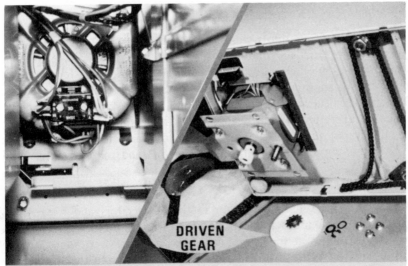

- Motor centrifugal switch can be replaced from top
- Motor replaced from bottom only

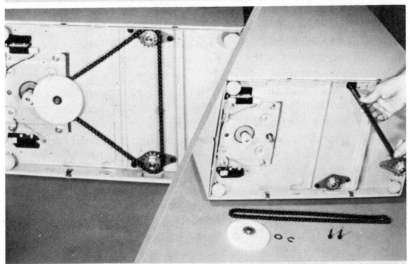

- Power screws removed from bottom
- Turn drive gear by hand to the right

Courtesy, Whirlpool Corporation

Figure 9-67 *You can replace the centrifugal switch from the top of the compactor. To remove the motor and bracket assembly (from the bottom only) you must remove the drive-gear assembly, which is held on by a ring clip.*

REFRIGERATOR AND FREEZER

Mechanical refrigeration systems, like the ones found in most refrigerators, freezers, and air conditioners, remove heat from one place and transfer it to another. Any time two surfaces of different temperatures are near one another, the warmer one will always lose heat to the cooler one. When heat transfer is complete, the objects stabilize at a roughly equal temperature. When dealing with liquids and gases of different temperatures, pressure is a factor in heat transfer. These principles play an important part in the operation of modern refrigerators and freezers.

Compressor: The compressor in the refrigerators and freezers designed for home use is an electric motor-driven pump. A rotor mounted off-center rotates at high-speed within a cylinder. Two vanes on the rotor wipe the cylinder walls and form a seal similar to that formed by a car's piston rings and cylinder wall. Centrifugal force provides some assistance in creating an effective vane–cylinder wall seal.

As a vane passes the inlet port it creates a vacuum that opens a reed valve and allows refrigerant vapor from the evaporator coils to enter the cylinder under low pressure. At the same time, the off-center position of the rotor enlarges the space between the rotor and cylinder wall, creating a vacuum that further induces vapor flow. Figure 9–68 illustrates this operation.

Oil pumped into the cylinder through a passage in the center of the rotor shaft helps form the vane–cylinder wall seal and forms a seal between the rotor and cylinder wall at their point of closest contact. The second seal is very important, because it prevents refrigerant blow-by. Without the oil seal between the rotor and cylinder, refrigerant would escape out the discharge port located 90° clockwise of the inlet port. (See Figure 9–69.)

The second vane, positioned 180° opposite the first, passes the inlet port and triggers another surge. Meanwhile, the rotor's eccentric rotation begins to compress the refrigerant already captured between the vanes. (See Figure 9–70.) The first vane passes the discharge port, and high pressure, heated refrigerant flows into the condenser coils. Figure 9–71 shows this part of the cycle. The cycle continues in this fashion until interrupted.

The compressor motor and pump assembly are hermetically sealed and extremely dependable. The entire refrigerator will probably fall apart before the compressor fails. The terminals, start capacitor, and overload protector are the only accessible compressor components. Motor or pump failure requires replacing the entire unit.

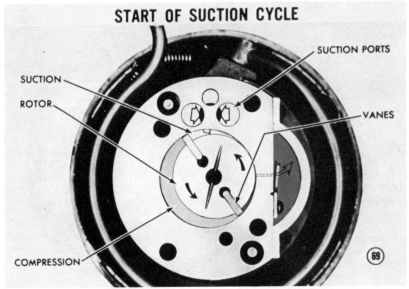

Courtesy, Whirlpool Corporation

Figure 9-68 *The upper vane passes the inlet or suction port. A vacuum forms behind it and draws refrigerant vapor into the cylinder.*

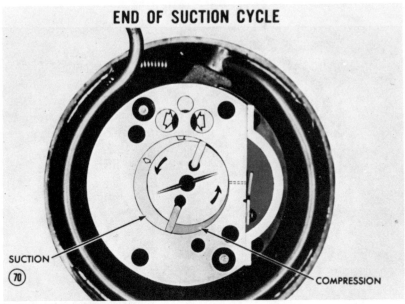

Courtesy, Whirlpool Corporation

Figure 9-69 *As the vane turns almost halfway around, it has drawn in its capacity of vapor.*

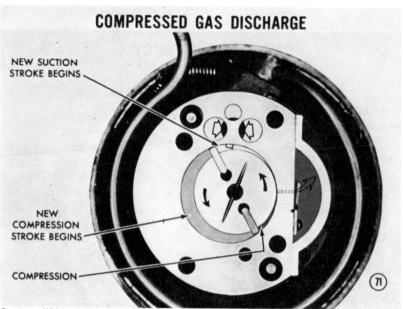

Figure 9-70 *The second vane passes the inlet port, starts another cycle, and pushes the vapor already in the cylinder ahead of it.*

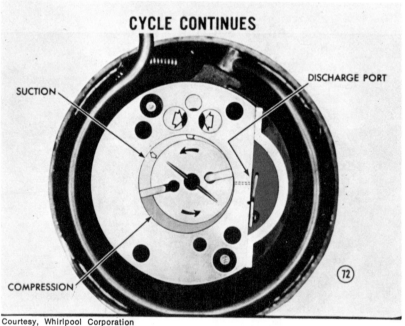

Figure 9-71 *The first vane has already discharged its vapor; the second vane begins compression and discharge.*

Condenser: The condenser coil assembly is the second component of the refrigeration system. Hot pressurized refrigerant vapor enters the condenser from the discharge port. Small, inexpensive refrigerators use a static condenser. These are mounted on the back of the cabinet and need more surface area for cooling than forced-air condensers because they rely on normal room air circulation.

Forced-air condensers, normally found on larger, more expensive and sophisticated refrigerators, are located under the cabinet where a fan circulates air over them. The toe boards on these models are slotted to allow air to pass through. Both static and forced-air condensers cool the refrigerant and convert it to a liquid.

Cool liquid refrigerant leaves the condenser under high pressure and enters a capillary tube that reduces the pressure of the refrigerant to an acceptable level before it enters the evaporator. Without the pressure differential, the system would not cool.

Evaporator: The evaporator on the simplest refrigerators serves as the freezer compartment and is located in the top portion of the cabinet. The drip pan beneath it serves as a baffle and keeps the coldest air in the freezer. It also acts as a condensate pan during defrosting. Most modern units locate their evaporators under the partition that separates the freezer from the refrigerator or behind the liner panels. Some refrigerators use a separate evaporator for the freezer and refrigerator. In these units, the freezer evaporator receives refrigerant first.

Refrigerant enters the evaporator as a liquid under low pressure and exits as vapor under low pressure. The refrigerant removes heat from the compartments. This heat converts the liquid refrigerant to a gas, and the gas enters the compressor to continue the cycle.

In the split-evaporation system, the freezer evaporator is separate and, in most cases, insulated from the refrigerant compartment and its evaporator. The system is designed so that the freezer evaporator receives refrigerant before the refrigerator evaporator. The freezer must become sufficiently cold before any refrigerant enters the second evaporator. Separators allow the engineer to provide for refrigerator evaporator defrosting without disturbing the freezer unit.

The cycle defrost unit's thermostat sensing bulb is located near the end of the evaporator. This is the last part to cool. The thermostat control knob allows the user to raise or lower the compartment temperature. Each time the compressor cycles off, it will not start again until the evaporator temperature reaches 36° to 38° F. This temperature increase is enough to melt the accumulated frost from the refrigerator evaporator.

Enclosed evaporators rarely ice up unless a system component failure causes them to. Ones located just under the freezer compartment will ice, because they are exposed to a variety of contaminants such as oil from the skin on your hands, milk carton wax, and whatever else may touch the surface. The residue allows water drops to stay on the coils during the defrost cycle. When the compressor cycles on again, the water drops freeze and act as collection areas for frost. During the next defrost cycle, some frost remains on the evaporator because more than the normal amount has accumulated. To eliminate this problem, turn the refrigerator off during the next defrost cycle and clean the evaporator with a dishwashing detergent that will not harm aluminum. Do not use regular detergents, because they will leave a film of their own that makes the frosting continue.

Most modern refrigerators are either automatic cycle defrost or frost free. Early cycle defrost models used a single evaporator with a defrost heating element clamped to it. Later models use the split-evaporation system with a heater attached to the freezer evaporator only. A timer connected in series with the element and compressor interrupts the compressor circuit at predetermined intervals. The heater raises evaporator temperature to about 38° F. The frost melts, and the condensate runs into a trough. From there it drains into a pan located at the bottom of the refrigerator. Condenser heat or heat from a low wattage element helps evaporate the water into the room air.

Twenty-four and twelve-hour timers are commonly used to initiate the defrost cycle. The twenty-four hour timer is marked day and night and is usually set to defrost the unit during the early morning hours between 2 and 4 a.m. when no one is using the refrigerator. How many of us have forgotten to reset the timer after a power failure, witnessed the defrost cycle, and called a service man because we thought the refrigerator had broken down? Twelve-hour timers defrost at midafternoon and early morning.

Some manufacturers connect the timer motor to the thermostat so that the timer runs every time the compressor cycles on. In this case, the defrost cycle relies on the compressor's running time. Frequent refrigerator use or long periods of time with the door held open makes the compressor run more often and causes more frequent defrosting. In other units, the timer motor is connected to the door switch. Every time someone opens the door, the timer runs. The defrost cycle begins after the door has been open for a predetermined period of time.

These early automatic-defrost refrigerators use a heavily insulated enclosed heating element to assist with the defrost. All terminals and connecting wiring are waterproof. Many have a fusible link between the element and the wiring harness to protect the element from overheating. The link is located near the heater and should be tested for continuity when inadequate defrosting causes you to suspect a faulty heater. You will find the heater clamped to the evaporator coils either in the back wall or freezer–refrigerator separator. Removing the lower separator panel or a rear panel will expose the heater.

Instead of a resistance heater, some refrigerators use a solenoid-operated valve at the condenser that allows hot refrigerant gas to enter the evaporator coil before the condenser has had a chance to change it to a cooler liquid. The wiring diagram will tell you which of the two methods your unit uses. A timer energizes the solenoid and a thermostat controls the timer.

Frost-free refrigerators use a single evaporator located behind the rear wall of the freezer or between the freezer and refrigerator compartments. A thermostatically controlled baffle or damper allows cold air from the freezer to enter the refrigerator. A single air-temperature-sensing thermostat located in the refrigerator compartment controls the unit. Many newer models use two thermostats to monitor both compartment temperatures. With help from forced air circulation, frost-free refrigerators provide more consistent and even temperatures than any other system.

Storage Freezer: Large frostless freezers operate on the same principles as refrigerator–freezers. They have only one compartment, and the evaporator is huge by comparison. One evaporator plate might cover the entire back wall, or the freezer might have a double-bank, fin-and-tube evaporator around the bottom of the compartment. The refrigeration system and controls are designed to provide temperatures of 0° F and below. Air passages are larger than those of the refrigerator, and the thermostat is calibrated to maintain the extremely low temperatures.

Home freezers are storage freezers. Ideally, all of the food placed in them should already be frozen. You should place warm food in the freezer in small quantities of roughly 10 percent of the compartment's volume. Placing large amounts of warm food in the freezer will raise the interior temperature above freezing. Some later models provide the user with a slightly colder fast-freeze section located either next to a cold-air outlet or surrounded by additional evaporator coils.

Faults, Diagnosis, Repair: Most problems associated with refrigerators and freezers are electrical or related to air circulation. Despite the speed at which these appliances are manufactured, they are remarkably dependable. Refrigeration system failure is rare and is something that should be left to experts.

The compressor unit on the simplest refrigerators contains all of the major moving parts. The unit is sealed, but you can diagnose trouble from outside. All refrigerators and freezers, regardless of price, size, or number of features, share compressors that are essentially the same. Many operating components are similar, as are the symptoms caused by failure.

Many new refrigerators and upright freezers are installed on large plastic or nylon rollers that permit the owner to slide the unit out from the wall. It is possible that when your refrigerator stops running the plug may have been pulled out of the wall socket. Have you moved the appliance today?

Line cord failures are rare, because the cord suffers little or no abuse. Shipping, crating, or installation damage may cause an open cord. When your refrigerator stops working, test the line cord for continuity. You will find the terminals at the bottom rear of the appliance.

Standard and cycle defrost refrigerators use evaporator temperature-sensing thermostats. These are capillary-tube units, and the sensing bulb is clamped directly to the evaporator coil. The thermostat body with control knob is mounted to the inside refrigerator wall with one or two screws. Removing these and carefully pulling the thermostat away from the wall will expose the terminals. Figure 9–72 shows how to perform the test.

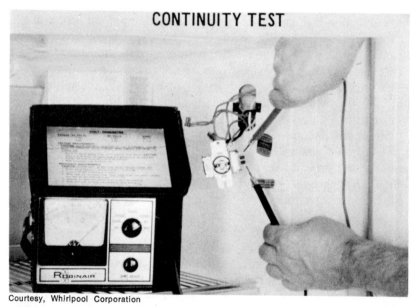

Courtesy, Whirlpool Corporation

Figure 9-72 Capillary-tube thermostat continuity test. Remove one lead, warm the sensing bulb with your hand to make sure it's above cut-in temperature, and note your VOM reading.

An open thermostat will keep your refrigerator from running. Disconnect at least one lead and test across the terminals for continuity at R×1. To be sure the sensing bulb is warm enough to close the contacts, hold it in your hand. To reach the sensing bulb on cycle defrost models, you will have to remove the evaporator cover panel; most are held in place with screws. When you replace the thermostat, be sure to mount the sensing bulb in the same position that you found the old one. (See Figure 9–73.)

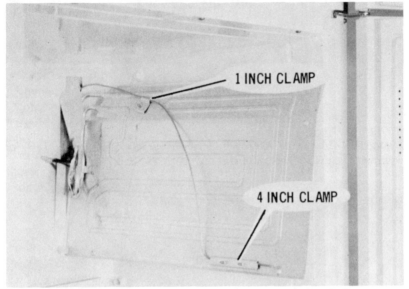

Figure 9-73 *Sensing bulb mounting system and location.*

Air-sensing thermostats mount the sensing tube inside the plastic housing. A plastic sheath protects and insulates it from the inside wall. Terminals are spade type. (See Figure 9–74.) The thermostat assembly either screws or clips into place on the compartment wall. (See Figure 9–75.) You can warm these units for testing with a small hair dryer. When replacing one of these units, make sure that you position the sensing tube correctly, with the sheath in place.

Open compressor overload protector, open relay coil, and open motor windings will keep your refrigerator from running. Generally, you will find the overload protector and relay mounted atop the compressor housing, as in Figure 9–76. The protector is the smaller of the two, and it's cylindrical. Test for continuity across its terminals. Figure 9–77 shows how. Test the relay at the gray and white terminals. (Refer to Figure 9–78.) If either one is open, replace it.

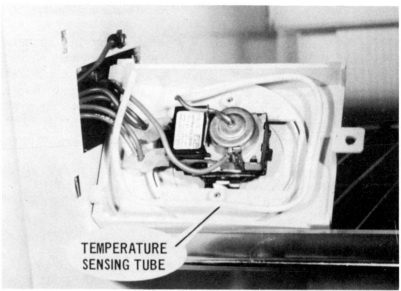

TEMPERATURE
SENSING TUBE

Courtesy, Whirlpool Corporation

Figure 9-74 *Air-Temperature-sensing, capillary-tube thermostat. Test for continuity across its two terminals.*

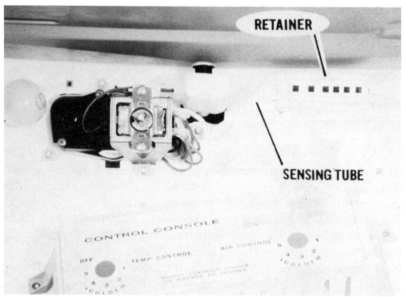

RETAINER

SENSING TUBE

Courtesy, Whirlpool Corporation

Figure 9-75 *To reach the thermostat and sensing tube, snap off the light lens and remove two screws that hold the cover to the liner. The sensing tube must be snapped securely into each retainer, because continuous contact is necessary for proper operation.*

258

Figure 9-76 *The overload protector is located in the relay case on this model. It senses compressor temperature and amperage draw. To expose the overload protector, unsnap the wire bail.*
Courtesy, Whirlpool Corporation

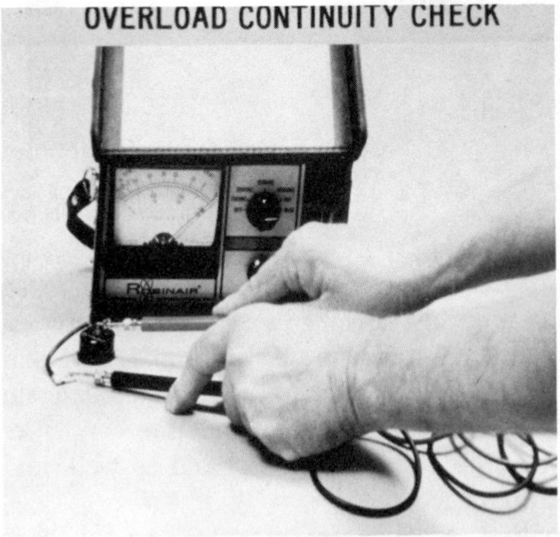

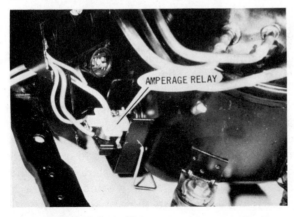

Figure 9-77 *Overload protector continuity test.*
Courtesy, Whirlpool Corporation

Courtesy, Whirlpool Corporation

Figure 9-78 *Test the relay coil for continuity across M and L1 or the terminal whose lead runs to the overload switch.*

Test for open motor run windings across terminals marked "C" for common and "R" for run. Some motor run terminals will be labeled "M." Figure 9–79 shows the compressor terminals. Test for start winding continuity across terminals labeled "C" and "S." Open motor windings mean that you have to replace the compressor unit.

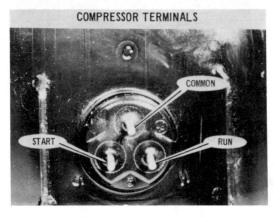

Figure 9-79   Compressor terminals.
Courtesy, Whirlpool Corporation

When your refrigerator or freezer refuses to run, it will often make a clicking sound at fairly long intervals—as long as 30 minutes between clicks. The most common cause for this sort of symptom is dirt and dust blocking air passages. So much dust and lint can accumulate on the slotted toe board of a forced-air condenser unit that the condenser overheats. When this happens the compressor overheats as well, and the overload protector shuts it off.

Standard refrigerators with the condenser mounted on the back of the cabinet are less prone to the dirt and lint problem because of their massive cooling surface area. Keep air passages and condenser coils dust and lint free.

A malfunctioning forced-air fan motor will cause the condenser and compressor to overheat. Some makers connect the fan and compressor in series so that the compressor will not run without benefit of cooling air. Open windings in the fan motor will keep the refrigerator from running. A binding fan motor, however, will cause symptoms identical to the ones described for blocked air passages. If you discover a slow-turning fan, the entire motor will have to be replaced. The units are sealed and not field serviceable. Open start or run windings in the compressor can also cause the clicking symptom. Test as discussed earlier. If all of your electrical tests show positive results, call an expert.

The position and location of the thermostat sensing bulb in cycle defrost and standard refrigerators is critical. If the sensing bulb has come loose from its mount for any reason, the compressor will run too long, and the temperature inside the refrigerator will be too low relative to the thermostat setting. A defective thermostat will cause the compressor to run constantly or not at all. A visual inspection will reveal a loose sensing bulb. Remount it. If the compressor won't run, test the thermostat for continuity while cooling the sensing bulb with an ice pack. When the compressor runs constantly, try heating the sensing bulb with a hair dryer. A warm bulb should produce an infinity reading on your VOM. Be sure that the control knob is set at a normal temperature.

The tray located directly beneath the evaporator–freezer on standard refrigerators acts as a baffle and helps keep the coldest air in the freezer compartment. Do not run your refrigerator without the tray in place because the entire compartment will become too cold.

A leak in the door seal will keep your refrigerator's compressor working overtime. You should be able to spot any defect in the door seal large enough to produce this symptom. Most modern refrigerators, regardless of size and price, use magnetic door seals to keep the door closed as well as keep warm air out. If you pinch the sealing edge, you can feel the magnetic strip.

You can buy replacement gaskets, and they are easy to install. On late-model standard and most varieties of older-model refrigerators, the door's inner liner holds the sealing gasket in place. Lift up the inside edge of the gasket and expose the retaining screws. Loosen these all around the liner and pull the old gasket out. Tuck the new gasket in place and tighten the screws. It's best to start remounting at one point then move along the gasket tucking and tightening until you have completed the job.

Most newer and more deluxe models use a retaining strip to secure the gasket to the door. When removing the old gasket, loosen the screws just enough to easily remove the old gasket without removing the retaining strip. Tuck the new gasket in, tightening screws as you go along.

If your new gasket has a kink in it, heat it with a hair dryer to straighten it out. New door seals take about two weeks to seat. During that time, you may want to hold the door closed with a piece of masking tape. A well-seated gasket on a properly adjusted door will compress only slightly when the door is closed. If your door continues to leak, have a professional come in and adjust it for you.

If you use your refrigerator a great deal and have a habit of holding the door open while you decide whether it's an apple or a peach that you want, the compressor will cycle on more often. On really hot days, the compressor may run almost continuously. Curing these bad habits will prolong the appliance's life and save energy.

Insufficient cooling in a refrigerator that appears to be working normally can be caused by dirty condenser coils and partially blocked air passages. In this case the resultant overheating isn't enough to trip the overload protector. Vacuum the toe board and condenser coils.

Dust buildup on static condensers will cause the same poor-cooling symptom. Pull the refrigerator out from the wall and vacuum the coils. Insufficient clearance around the refrigerator causes poor performance as well. This rule applies to both static and forced-air condenser models. Consult your instruction manual for correct clearance figures.

If you've just returned from a shopping trip and have loaded a nearly empty refrigerator with warm food, the compartment will warm up and stay that way for some time. The compressor will cycle on and run until the interior temperature returns to normal.

A warm compartment accompanied by what appears to be a normally operating refrigerator is often the result of evaporator icing. If you have a cycle defrost model, remove the evaporator cover panel and look at the frost pattern. An even pattern indicates that the refrigeration system is working properly. A defective thermostat might be cycling the compressor on before the defrost cycle has had a chance to completely melt the frost away. A defective thermostat might also be keeping the compressor running longer than necessary for the setting. The second failure lowers the compartment temperature and freezes food in the lower sections. As the evaporator icing becomes more severe, the compartment warms up. The only way for you to test the thermostat under these conditions, is to replace it with a new one and wait for the refrigerator's response. If it works normally, you've solved the problem.

A partially frosted evaporator accompanied by a constantly running compressor indicates a leak in the refrigeration system. Frost will accumulate only at the point where the refrigerant enters the evaporator. The thermostat sensing bulb is at the other end of the evaporator. Inadequate refrigerant supply will make the thermostat act as if the refrigerator is warm. That's why the compressor keeps running. This problem requires an expert.

Rising temperatures in one or both compartments of a frost-free refrigerator usually indicate evaporator icing. Remove the evaporator cover plate and look at the pattern. Is the ice clear or frosty looking? Clear ice indicates a clogged defrost drain system. Food particles or algae growth may have blocked the drain. Turn the refrigerator off and clean the drain. Let the evaporator ice melt away, then flush the drain with about a quarter cup of household ammonia to prevent algae growth.

Some models use a drain trough heater to keep that section above freezing. If the heater is open, water draining from the evaporator coil will freeze and eventually back up to the coils. At this point, call in an expert. Water on the refrigerator floor indicates a clogged drain.

Frost-free models will suffer evaporator icing from a grounded or open defrost heating element. Most of these are mounted directly to the evaporator and should be serviced only by qualified personnel.

A defective defrost timer will cause evaporator icing. The accumulated ice will be white and snowy looking, but hard as rock. Most defrost systems use a timer to shunt the thermostat out of the circuit and close a circuit to the defrost heater. A bimetal limit switch turns the heater off when the evaporator plate temperature reaches 60° F or more. Some models use a timer-activated solenoid that releases hot condenser refrigerant into the evaporator.

For a preliminary test, turn the defrost timer knob until you hear the defrost system click into action. If the heater is working, you should be able to hear it crackle and pop as it expands. If you can hear the heater working, leave the timer set to defrost. If the timer is working correctly, the compressor will cycle on again in about 25 minutes. If it doesn't, test the timer motor for continuity at R×100 and the switch contacts at R×1.

You will find the timer either behind the toe board (Figure 9–80) or in the compartment control panel (Figure 9–81.) The single-pole, double-throw switch in the timer is designed to prevent the defrost heater and compressor from running at the same time. A defective switch can let this happen, and when it does the condenser will be hot and the evaporator either cool or warm but not cold. Eventually, the overload protector shuts the compressor off.

Courtesy, Whirlpool Corporation

Figure 9-80 Defrost timer located behind the toe board. It is sealed cannot be repaired.

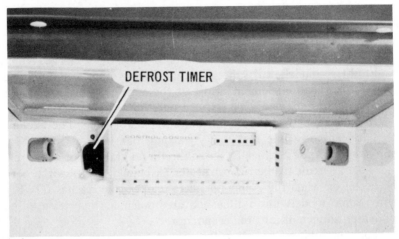

Figure 9-81   *Defrost timer in the control console. It is sealed and cannot be repaired.*

If the compressor continues to run under these conditions, but the system refuses to cool, refrigeration experts can be pretty certain that the refrigeration system is okay and that the bimetal limit switch is at fault. If the condenser is cool and the evaporator warm, then there is a leak in the system.

An open defrost limit switch will cause evaporator icing. Refer to the wiring diagram for location. Usually you will find it clamped to the evaporator coils. (See Figure 9-81.) Test the switch across its two terminals. Heating it should open the contacts and cooling close them. There is, however, no way to tell if it's operating within its designed temperature ranges or if it's working only intermittently. Many refrigeration experts feel that if a problem exists within the defrost system, and the timer and heater are working normally, the limit switch has to be the cause.

Exterior cabinet perspiration is caused by insulation voids and wet insulation. Make sure that all joints between the liner and cabinet are thoroughly sealed. Late-model, thin-wall refrigerators and freezers use heaters to help prevent cabinet sweating. These heaters are located around the door gasket contact area and in the mullion or partition between freezer and refrigerator compartments. If your unit perspires, feel the areas near the heaters. If they don't feel warm, call an expert for further investigation.

Use your refrigerator wisely. Don't overload it with warm food. Decide what you want from it before you open the door, and keep the toe board and condenser coils clean.

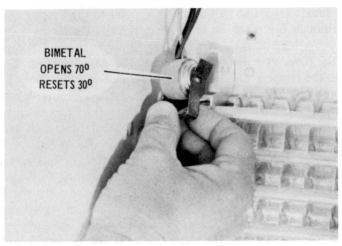

BIMETAL
OPENS 70°
RESETS 30°

Courtesy, Whirlpool Corporation

Figure *9-82 Defrost heater bimetal thermostat.*

ELECTRIC RANGES AND WALL OVENS

Natural gas is a clean and efficient cooking fuel, but it is just too dangerous for part-time repair persons. Under no circumstances should you attempt to diagnose or repair any fault with your gas range.

Electric ranges and wall ovens use a three-wire, 115–230-volt circuit. The middle wire is the ground, and on some units acts as part of the 115-volt circuit. The 115-volt circuit powers the lights, timer, and low-heat settings for surface elements that are controlled by five- or seven-position switches. Infinite-heat switches use only the 230-volt circuit. Refer to switches in Chapter Seven for more details. Five- and seven-position switches control two-coil, three-pronged terminal heating elements. Infinite-heat switches control single-coil, two-pronged terminal or double-coil, four-prong heating elements.

When your electric range or wall oven refuses to work at all, including lights and timer, check for a tripped circuit breaker or a blown fuse. Check the line cord terminals at the back of the range behind the rear panel. Generally, wall ovens have to be pulled out to service the terminal board. Since removing and replacing the unit can be tricky, I recommend leaving that to a professional.

The 230-volt circuit uses two 115-volt fuses. If one blows out, the lights and timer will work, but the oven and surface elements will not heat. Ranges that use a five- or seven-position switch will show heat from the 115-volt section of the elements. Remove the cartridge fuse and test for continuity.

On most ranges and wall ovens, the circuit to the heating elements passes through the timer contacts. Most timers have an on or manual setting that disconnects the timer motor from the circuit but continues to use the timer switch contacts. If your oven refuses to heat after you have set the temperature control knob, be sure that the timer knob is set on manual. You might have moved it during cleaning. Some oven timers have a timed bake setting that removes the timer from the circuit at all other settings. Failure in this type of timer will keep the oven from heating only when it is set to timed bake.

When your oven won't heat on manual, the timer contacts are probably at fault. Unplug the range before attempting to diagnose or repair it. Remove the control console. There are so many different ranges on the market and an almost equal number of ways to remove the control console or range top for servicing, that the best advice I can give you is to search the appliance carefully for screws and clips that hold things together. The timer switch box is small and rectangular with two or more spade terminals and is located adjacent to the timer motor. Consult the wiring diagram that is glued to the back panel to find which of the terminals you have to isolate for a continuity test. You should be able to replace a faulty switch box without purchasing an entire timer assembly.

Many electric range accessory circuits are fused within the appliance, and in some cases the timer is part of that circuit. A blown internal fuse or a tripped minicircuit breaker will remove the timer from the circuit and keep the oven from heating. This does not apply to ovens whose timer contacts carry oven current only when the timer is set. You will find the fuse receptacle located under one of the rear surface elements or inside the storage drawer. Use only the correct fuse.

An open oven temperature control thermostat will keep the oven from heating. This is an adjustable, capillary-tube device with the sensing bulb mounted to, but insulated from, the oven wall. If the tube touches the wall at any point, you will get erratic oven temperatures. (See Figure 9–83.) The switch contact terminals are located behind the control panel with the rest of the wiring and switches; test across them at R×1. They should read continuity at room temperature. If your oven overheats and won't shut off, test the thermostat's contact operation by heating it with a hot hair dryer while maintaining VOM contact.

Open heating elements will, of course, keep your oven from heating or broiling. Most modern ovens allow you to test for continuity without removing the back panel from the range. Inside the oven, you will find a retaining plate where the element enters the oven wall. Remove the screws, then pull the element forward to gain access to the terminals.

Courtesy, Whirlpool Corporation

Figure 9-83 *The oven thermostat sensor must have clearance between itself and the oven liner so that air can circulate around it. The liner generally is much hotter than the thermostat dial setting.*

Disconnect at least one lead and test for continuity across the terminals, as in Figure 9–84. Test for ground from one terminal to the oven wall. Some ranges use a relay to control both oven elements. If the relay fails, the oven won't heat or broil. You must test the relay for voltage. Figure 9–85 shows how to perform this test.

Courtesy, Whirlpool Corporation

Figure 9-84 *Both oven elements may be removed from inside the oven of this Whirlpool range by removing a screw from each mounting plate. Pull out carefully so that you won't disconnect the spade terminals.*

BROIL RELAY   BAKE RELAY

Courtesy, Whirlpool Corporation

Figure *9-85   Relay voltage test. Turn the oven on and attach your alligator clip VOM leads to H2 and L2. Set the meter to 250 or 300 volts ac. The meter should read 240 volts. After 15 to 30 seconds, the meter should indicate no voltage, because the relay contacts have closed.*

All ovens are ventilated for the best cooking results. Air enters through gaps in the door seal and exits through vents in the rear of the oven. Air leaks from any other source, however, will upset oven performance. Leaks usually originate from ill-fitting doors. Oven doors weren't designed to hold any weight to speak of. You shouldn't, for example, use the door for a step. If your oven door doesn't close tightly, remove the inside panel and look for adjusting features designed into the closing mechanism. Many brands provide an adjusting screw at each closing spring. If you remove the inside door panel for service, do not disturb the insulation. Those empty spaces are designed to provide cooling air circulation.

Cooking utensils play an important part in the results. Consult your instruction manual for the maker's suggestions on which utensil is best for what type of cooking.

If you suspect that the temperature control knob settings bear little or no relation to actual oven temperatures, have a professional test them for you. Most, if not all, home testing methods will yield inaccurate results. Most often you will have to be satisfied with oven temperature that is plus or minus 25° F. Adjustments inside that range are unlikely, because the calibrators aren't accurate enough. If it tests way off, have a qualified technician adjust it for you.

If all of the surface elements refuse to heat and the oven works normally, test both line leads from the terminal box to the switches for continuity. If only one of the units won't heat, check the terminals for good clean connections. Boil-overs and excessive grease buildup may have insulated them. Make sure the connection is clean and tight. Figure 9–86 shows where the terminal blocks are located.

Figure 9-86   Surface element terminal blocks and infinite-heat switch terminals are located on the underside of the range top. You can perform all wiring and switch continuity tests from there.

An open element may be the reason your surface elements aren't working. Those elements used with an infinite-heat switch are made from a single length of heating element that ends in two prongs. A break or short anywhere along the element will keep it from heating. Elements used with five- or seven-position switches are made from two lengths of element and will heat on high or low, depending on the location of the element failure.

An open infinite-heat switch will keep the element from heating at all, whereas a five- or seven-position switch can operate on one or more of its settings and still be open on others. Refer to switches in Chapter Seven for more details.

Here are some more operating suggestions. If you place aluminum foil in the surface element tray, be sure to leave vent holes corresponding to those already in the tray. Surface elements need a certain amount of ventilation to perform as designed. Lack of ventilation causes overheating and early element failure. Don't heat large pots on small elements or leave a surface element on with nothing cooking atop it. Never completely cover the wire oven racks with foil. Be sure to use the correct cooking utensil for the job.

Chapter 10

Lighting, Basic Home Wiring, and Devices

Lighting is another electrical phenomenon that we take for granted. We walk into a room and immediately reach for the light switch. Many of us fear darkness; we have learned that it holds many terrors, both real and imagined. We are also sight dependent, and become disoriented without the usual visual references light provides. How many of us, once we find the light switch in a dark room, sigh with relief?

Electric light allows us to go about the day's activities independent of the rising and setting of the sun. Electric light cheers our homes on wet and gloomy days. It helps us to celebrate holidays and advertise products. Electric light is the greatest of all inventions until a bulb burns out and we can't find a replacement, or until a power failure sends us floundering about the house in search of a candle and flashlight. Only then do we recognize our dependence on electric light.

Some of us love light so much that we leave bulbs glowing all through the house despite, or perhaps because of, its emptiness. We have learned to curb this extravagance somewhat since the oil embargo and subsequent government pleading made energy waste a moral issue.

INCANDESCENT LIGHTING

Leaving lights burning in unoccupied rooms not only wastes energy, it shortens the bulb's life span as well. Rough handling, using a higher wattage bulb than recommended for a fixture, and deteriorating fixtures will also shorten the bulb's useful life. Fortunately, replacing a burned-out bulb is the simplest household repair that you can perform. Bulbs usually announce failure with a distinct "tink" or "poof."

270

Ceiling Fixture: Lamp or ceiling-fixture failure is not always the result of a blown bulb. In many cases, the lamp or fixture socket is at fault. Sockets use copper strips to conduct electricity to the bulb. Years of use can corrode and loosen the contact so that it no longer makes a good connection. Figure 10-1 shows good and bad sockets. When you screw a new bulb into the socket and it doesn't light until you jiggle the bulb or screw it in a little more, the socket is probably worn out.

Figure 10-1 Bent and corroded from arcing, the lamp socket at the right would light the bulb only occasionally. Compare it with the new one on the left.

To replace a ceiling fixture, first disconnect it from the power source by removing the fuse or tripping the circuit breaker that controls the line. Ceiling fixtures mount to light boxes by a center stud or hanger strap and two screws threaded through ears on the light box. (See Figure 10-2.) The hanger strap mount uses a pair of studs and nuts to hold the fixture in place.

After you remove the glass dome, remove the nuts or screws and lower the fixture enough to allow access to the wire-nut connections. Remove them and untwist the wires. The fixture is free to take down. (See Figure 10-3.) Install the new fixture by reversing the procedure. Be sure to connect white wires to white and black to black.

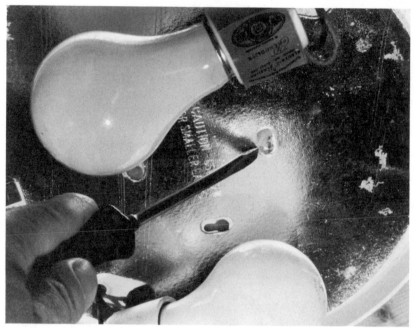

Figure 10-2 *Remove two screws from this light fixture to lower it from the ceiling.*

Figure 10-3 *Disconnect the wire-nut terminals and remove the fixture.*

Single, center-stud mount fixtures are often characterized by a large ornamental dome nut used to hold the glass cover in place. Remove the glass cover. In the center of the fixture, you will see the hollow stud that secures the fixture to the light box by a single, large-diameter nut and lock washer. Remove the nut and washer and lower the fixture to gain access to the wire-nut connections. Install the new fixture by reversing the procedure. Make sure that all of your connections are tight and that you have left no bare wire. You can test a socket for a short to ground by touching one VOM lead to a socket contact and the other to the light box.

Lamp Switch–Socket: Lamp sockets contain the switch and cannot be repaired beyond a shot of contact cleaner inside the rotary switch or a thorough socket contact polishing. Crackling noises and intermittent operation indicate a faulty switch, socket, or a combination of both.

To replace the socket, first unplug the cord, then remove the shade, halo, and bulb. Now, carefully pull the top section of the socket out of its mounting cup, as in Figure 10-4. Loosen the terminal screws and remove the wires. If the bare wire ends are a little ragged, cut them off, remove a half inch of insulation, then twist the fresh bare strands together tightly. (See Figure 10–5.) You may want to solder them. Attach the wires to the terminals, as in Figure 10-6.

Figure 10-4 ☛*Removing the socket-switch from the mounting cup.*

Figure 10-5 Wire ends prepared for soldering and terminal connection.

Figure 10-6 Attaching wiring to the terminals.

If the lamp refuses to light, first try another bulb. If that doesn't work, suspect an open line cord or an open switch. Remove the lamp socket and switch assembly, disconnect the cord, and test it for continuity. Lamp cords usually fail at the plug end, where they are subjected to the most punishment. With the VOM leads still attached, bend and twist the cord along its length until you find the break. Usually, this will cause some resistance to show on the VOM. If you can isolate the break in this manner, and it is close to the plug, simply remove the short end and install a new plug.

To install a complete new cord, disconnect the wires from the lamp socket terminal and pull the cord out of the lamp. Pushing the new cord through the lamp may be a little difficult. Some lamps are assembled in sections and held together by a long stud. You will find a single nut on the bottom of the lamp under the felt pad. Remove it and disassemble the structure.

Feed the new cord through, a section at a time, while restacking the sections. When you insert a new cord through a one-piece lamp, lubricate the cord with a little silicon rubber lubricant. After you have fed the cord through the lamp to the base of the socket, split the cord apart for about 3 in. Strip the insulation, solder the core, and connect the cord to the switch terminals.

If the cord tests out good, test the switch for continuity across its two terminals. Be sure to turn the switch on.

FLUORESCENT LIGHTING

For a given wattage, fluorescent lights burn about six times brighter and last about five times longer than incandescent lights. Fluorescent bulbs are more expensive than incandescent bulbs, and in order to produce light, they need a starter and a ballast. Fluorescent lighting tends to distort our color perception as well.

Most home fluorescent light fixtures and lamps are either rapid-start or preheat types. Rapid-start fixtures incorporate the starter within the ballast. The ballast is a transformer that acts to build voltage within the light tube. Preheat fixtures use a separate starter. Is is the small, cylindrical, aluminum cartridge located under the tube. Instant-start fixtures are found in most commercial installations and are characterized by tubes with a single contact pin on either side. The other fixtures use tubes with two contact pins on either side.

Healthy fluorescent tubes have a darkened band at both ends that extends about 2 in. toward the center of the tube. When the band begins to grow toward the tube center, it indicates that the tube is wearing out. Generally, a burned-out tube will have a blackened area extending beyond 6 in. from the ends. The darkened band gives you a quick visual check of the tube's condition.

When your fluorescent light won't work, check for those darkened ends. Installing a new tube is another quick check. If the new one lights, your're in business. If the new tube doesn't light, install a new starter. Remove the tube, turn the starter a quarter turn counterclockwise, and pull it out. Install a new starter, replace the tube, and try again. A new tube that has been stored at temperatures below 50° F will not light until it warms up to room temperature.

Oxide film buildup on the tube contact pins will keep it from lighting. In most cases, simply rotating the tube in its holder will clean away the oxide and restore the tube to good working order. If that fails, clean the pins and the tube holder contacts with a piece of fine sandpaper and contact cleaner. When all else fails, examine the tube holders for cracks.

When you are changing a damaged tube holder, first disconnect the lamp or fixture from its power source. Disconnect the wires from the tube holder. In many cases, you will have to remove the fixture end cap to expose the holder terminals. Some end caps merely press on, whereas others are held in place with one or more sheet-metal screws. Generally, a single screw secures the tube holder to the fixture. (See Figure 10–7.)

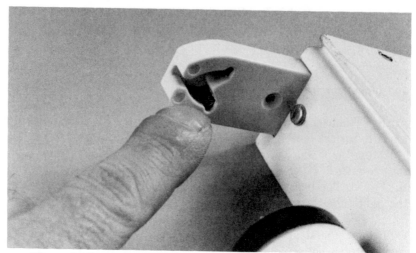

Figure 10-7 Removing one screw will release the tube holder.

Finally, excessive dirt and dust buildup can keep a rapid-start fluorescent tube from lighting. Remove the tube from the fixture, wash it in warm soapy water, rinse, dry, and replace it. It should light.

In most cases, flickering indicates a worn out tube. Are the ends blackened beyond the usual 2 in. band? Poor contact between the tube holder and pins caused by oxide buildup, an improperly installed tube, or out-of-line holders will make the tube flicker. It's fairly easy to install a double-pin tube the wrong way. Usually one of the pins will ride on the outside of the holder because you have not pushed the tube up into the holder far enough.

Rotating the tube several times will remove the oxide buildup. Check to see that the holders are tight and meet the tube ends squarely. Loosen the set screw and adjust as necessary. A fixture operating in temperatures below 50° F will cause flickering tubes as well.

A defective starter as well as an aging tube will cause the ends to darken beyond the normal 2 in. Trying a new tube in the fixture will tell which of the two possibilities is causing the trouble. Replace the starter with a new one if that proves to be the culprit. Discoloration at one end only can sometimes be cured by turning the tube end for end and reinstalling it.

A humming fluorescent light unit indicates ballast failure. It may have been incorrectly installed, be the wrong wattage, or simply be defective. Overhead fixtures have ballasts mounted behind the cover plate just under the tubes. Remove the tubes, disconnect the fixture from its power source, then remove the cover plate.

Some cover plates are secured to the frame with screws, whereas others clip into place. Figure 10–8 shows a cover plate attached with screws. Compare the wiring connections with the diagram on the ballast to make sure that it has been correctly installed, then check the wattage. If everything is okay there, you need a new ballast.

Figure 10-8   Remove the screws from the cover plate and lower it from the fixture.

Cut the ballast leads at a point about 5 in. from the ballast. The new one will come with 5 in. leads attached to it. Unbolt the old ballast from the fixture. Figure 10–9 shows a ballast and connections. Strip the appropriate amount of insulation from the new ballast leads, then bolt the unit into place. Connect the wires with medium-size wire nuts. Be sure to match wire colors when you connect the wires.

Most fluorescent desk lamps have the ballast mounted inside the base, and you can expose it by removing the base cover plate. Most table lamps are rapid-start units with the starter in the ballast.

When the tube ends glow, but the tube will not light, either the starter or the ballast is at fault. You will have to replace the ballast–

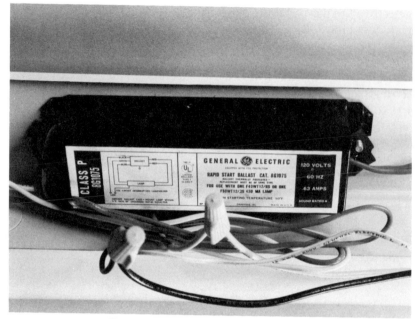

Figure 10-9   Ballast and connection.

starter assembly in the table lamp. Replace the preheat ceiling fixture's starter first. They burn out about as often as the bulbs. The ballast usually outlasts both components. If the starter doesn't allow the bulb to light, try a new ballast.

LIGHT SWITCHES

Most household switches are simple toggle units rated at 10 amps, 115 volts, or 5 amps, 230 volts. The ampere rating holds true only when the voltage is at the recommended amount or less. When you buy a new switch, take the old one with you for comparison.

Modern switches are silent. A simple L-shaped armature contacts the terminals to complete the circuit. In mercury switches, a small bead of mercury flows back and forth in a cylinder with wire leads connected to both ends. The mercury completes the circuit between the leads. Push-button switches work through a ratchet to move contacts and complete a circuit. Many of these have a small light in the button that glows when the switch is off. Rheostat switches push on and off like the push-button switch, and they vary the switch resistance to vary the bulb brightness. Household switches are sealed and cannot be repaired.

Toggle switches are either single-pole, characterized by on/off printed on the toggle and two terminals; three-way, with no toggle markings and three terminals; or four-way, with no toggle markings and four terminals. Single-pole switches control a light or outlet from one location. Three-way switches control a light or outlet from two locations when used in pairs. Four-way switches control a light or outlet from more than two locations when used with a pair of three-way switches.

Both terminals of a single-pole switch connect to hot wires, and the neutral wire runs directly to the light box or the outlet box. This provides a ground at the switch. Black or red wires are hot; green or gray wires are neutral.

Worn out switches will work either intermittently or not at all. After you've checked for blown fuses, tripped circuit breaker, and burned out bulbs, have a look at the switch. To test or replace a wall switch, first remove the fuse or disengage the circuit breaker to that line. Loosen the cover plate screws and remove the plate. Figure 10–10 shows how to remove the cover plate.

Figure 10-10 *Remove the cover plate.*

The switch will be secured to the switch box by two screws through two flanges, as shown in Figure 10–11. Remove these and pull the switch out far enough to allow yourself access to the terminals. Refer to Figure 10–12 for how to disconnect the wires from the terminals, and then test the switch for continuity, as in Figure 10–13. Use the same testing procedure for three- and four-way switches. Test push-button switches as you would a single-pole toggle switch. Test the rheostat's on/off contacts as you would a single-pole switch. If a rheostat fails to dim or brighten your lights, replace it with a new one.

Figure 10-11 *Remove the switch mounting screws.*

Figure 10-12 *Disconnect wiring from the terminals (one on either side).*

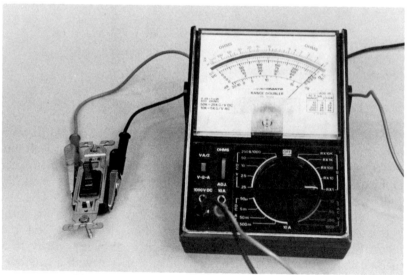

Figure 10-13 *Testing the switch for continuity.*

PLUGS

Plugs are categorized in three ways, two-prong, three-prong, and appliance. The amount of variation within each category is staggering. Sales personnel in electric supply stores are usually knowledgeable enough to interpret your needs if you present them with a reasonable explanation.

For the most part, plugs of all types are tough. The cord usually gives up long before the plug. Plugs, however, do suffer bent and broken prongs. Simply straighten a bent prong with a pliers.

In many cases, prongs are riveted to the plug body and have a flange with a small hole drilled and tapped into it to accept a terminal screw. Occasionally, mistreatment will pull the prong and rivet out of the plug, in which case you will have to replace the plug. Most plugs cannot be repaired.

Appliance plugs, because they are the female half of the connection, often suffer from some form of contact corrosion. Cleaning the contacts with a tiny brass bristle brush and contact cleaner usually restores conductivity. Refer to the section on attaching plugs in Chapter Three for more details.

FUSES

Fuses are used at the service entrance panel of your home to protect the electrical system from overload damage. Without fuses or circuit breakers in the system, overloaded wires would become very hot. Eventually, the insulation would melt and cause a fire. The most frightening thing about an electrical fire of this sort is that it usually breaks out behind a wall and smolders undetected for some time. *Never*, under any circumstances, place a penny or other metal object in the fuse socket as a substitute. Always keep a supply of the correct amperage fuses near the entrance panel. Figure 10–14 illustrates the various types of fuses.

Once screwed into its socket, the Edison base fuse completes a circuit through a metal alloy strip. The alloy is rated at 10, 15, 20, or 30 amps and has a low melting point. In the event of an overload or a short to ground, the extra current flows through the fuse, melts the metal strip, and breaks the circuit.

The fuse will always be rated at the same amp load as the line it protects. You can see the metal strip in the Edison base fuse through a tiny window in the top center. Blown fuses will have a gap in the strip. The National Electrical Code states that Edison base fuses can be used only as replacements in existing fuse boxes using that type. Any new installations using fuses have to use the S-type fuse.

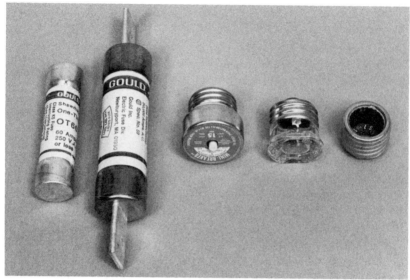

Figure 10-14 *From left to right: ferrule cartridge fuse, knife-blade cartridge fuse, mini circuit breaker fuse, Edison base fuse, and an S type fuse adapter.*

S-type fuses were developed to further protect the home owner from careless emergency measures. S-type fuses use a rated adapter that screws into an Edison base socket. Once the adapter has been installed, you cannot remove it. Only fuses of the same rating as the adapter will fit. It is impossible to install a 30-amp S-type fuse into a 20-amp adapter. S-type fuses use the same type of metal strip and window at the Edison base fuse.

Ferrule-type cartridge fuses clip into the socket and use their metal ends as pick-ups. They are available in ratings from 10 to 60 amps and are employed to protect individual 115–230-volt appliance circuits such as those of your electric dryer and range. You can't see the internal conductor. When you suspect a failure, you have to test the fuse for continuity. Removing these fuses can be a little dangerous. They fit tightly in their holders, and you can grasp them only near the center. To be safe, buy a fuse-removing tool from your local electric supply store. Test for continuity by touching a VOM probe to each end of the fuse.

Knife-blade cartridge fuses use a solid copper conductor with a blade extension at both ends to engage the holder. These are rated at 70 amps and higher and are used to protect the service entrance line. Removing these fuses will break the circuit between the source and the entire house. Test for continuity as you would the ferrule fuse.

DOOR BELL

Your door bell works at somewhere between 6 and 24 volts depending on the transformer and chime assembly. This little step-down transformer works on the same principle as the large ones you see on utility poles. Both of them reduce high voltage to a level acceptable for the application.

When your door bell refuses to work, check the fuse or circuit breaker that protects the line. If everything checks out there, have someone push the door bell button while you listen to the bell or chime box. A humming sound indicates that the transformer is working and that your problem lies on the low-voltage side of the transformer. No humming indicates a faulty transformer.

Depending on the type of bell or chime assembly that you have, you will find the transformer either in the assembly or located in some convenient spot between the entrance panel and the chime assembly. Remote transformers are usually located in the basement directly beneath the wall to which the chime assembly is attached. After you have found the transformer, disconnect the high-voltage leads (be sure to disengage the circuit breaker in that line) and test for continuity across them, as Figure 10–15 illustrates. On the low-voltage side, disconnect the wires from the middle or common terminal and one of the others

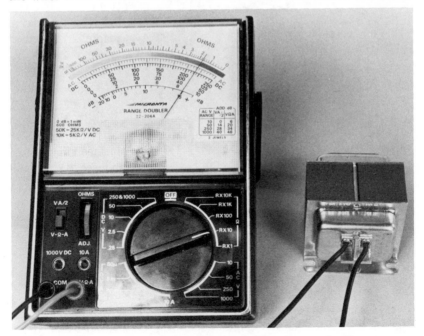

Figure 10-15 Testing the transformer for continuity.

and test across these for voltage. Most transformers are labeled at these terminals, and you should expect a reading of plus or minus 10 percent of the indicated voltage.

If the problem is on the low-voltage side, remove the chime assembly cover and look for loose or broken connections. Move the chime striker bars by hand to make sure they are not binding. Many chimes use a tiny 16-volt synchronous motor to produce the chime sequence. Three sets of contacts attached to an arm assembly on the motor shaft open and close circuits on a printed-circuit board. As each circuit is completed, a striker bar hits the designated chime. Figure 10–16 shows the contact arm and striker contacts. An open motor will keep the chimes from working. Test the windings for continuity as in Figure 10–17.

Figure 10-16   Motor-driven contact arm and printed-circuit chime striker contacts.

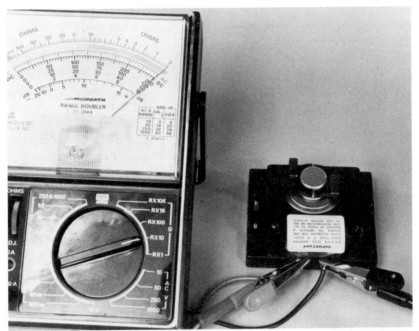

Figure 10-17   *Testing the motor windings for continuity.*

An open door bell switch will keep the chimes from working. Disconnect the chimes at the service entrance panel and remove the switch for testing. Test across its terminals with the button pushed in, as Figure 10–18 shows. You can clean the button contacts with #600 sandpaper and contact cleaner.

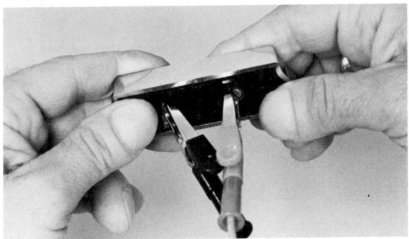

Figure 10-18   *Testing the switch for continuity.*

Index